Faith in a[...]
Quaker social [...]imony

writings from Friends in Britain Yearly Meeting
including an essay by Jonathan Dale

Edited by Elizabeth Cave & Ros Morley

Quaker Home Service

First published in April 2000 by Quaker Home Service
Friends House, Euston Road, London NW1 2BJ

ISBN 0 85245 320 5

Editors: Elizabeth Cave and Ros Morley
Design and layout: Jonathan Sargent
Printed by Headley Brothers Ltd

Contents

Foreword

The exercise of Rediscovering our Social Testimony has been an invitation to renewal in Britain Yearly Meeting. During the last few years of the twentieth century, members and attenders of the Society of Friends have been praying, studying and sharing together, to explore and clarify the meaning of our social testimony.

This book draws on material from recent times, and makes up the ground for us to stand on at the beginning of the new century. Testimony is lived witness, and here Friends give examples, and share their understanding. Different sections of the book may be used in different ways – for study, meditation or discussion, by individuals or by groups.

A single book cannot contain descriptions of all the discernment and all the ways in which Quakers are living our faith. But we hope that both Friends in their meetings and those new to Friends will find fresh insights and much cause for celebration in these writings.

Rachel Carmichael
Clerk
Britain Yearly Meeting Rediscovering our Social
Testimony Group,
January 2000

Acknowledgements

We warmly thank Jonathan Dale for his inspirational and challenging writing, Elizabeth Cave and Ros Morley, our editors, for their effective ordering and organising of much diverse material, and Rachel Carmichael for her buoyancy in keeping this project moving forward. We also thank everyone who contributed the many thoughts and words from which, with difficulty, we had to select, and without which this book could not have been produced.

The Britain Yearly Meeting Rediscovering our Social Testimony Editorial Group

Part I – Introduction

The Rediscovering our Social Testimony (ROST) process, 1994-2000

In the autumn of 1994 a new group met at Friends House. During the whole of this first meeting, the Monteverdi Choir rehearsed Haydn's *Creation* in the Large Meeting House, conducted by John Eliot Gardiner. What a start! The group was considering how to help Britain Yearly Meeting clarify and rediscover the Quaker vision of social responsibility, and its spiritual basis in testimony.

We had been formed following a Quaker Social Responsibility & Education (QSRE) Central Committee meeting at Damascus House in June that year – the omens were good! The Central Committee, having had to make cuts in our work, realised that our task was now to focus for yearly meeting on the key elements of Quaker social testimony. But we could not do this alone. So we invited Friends from other central committees of Britain Yearly Meeting (BYM) – Quaker Peace & Service (QPS) and Quaker Home Service (QHS) – to join us in this search. Was this going to be a new creation, or a re-creation?

This was not the first time the concern had been raised. In the inter-war years, soon after the corporate unity achieved around the Eight Foundations of a True Social Order in 1918 (*Quaker faith & practice* 23.16), there had been calls for a reassertion of Quaker social testimony. These calls became more insistent after the Second World War. Although many Friends felt that the welfare state would prove an adequate incarnation of our Quaker social testimonies, Quaker radicals still felt that we should be renewing them. The Quaker Socialist Society, in 1982 at Warwick

Yearly Meeting, recommended Friends 'to seek urgently for a new basis for a corporate social testimony'. This was never lost sight of, and Grace Crookall-Greening wrote 'Still missing – a social testimony for today' in the *Quaker socialist* of February/March 1994. This was only a few months before the ROST process was born.

What perhaps was different about the ROST process was that it quickly became focused on the process rather than the form of words. It also managed to involve representatives from both QPS and QHS, and thus avoid the danger of appearing just a sectional interest.

By the next spring the ROST group had compiled a pack, including a selection of personal testimonies, a 'developing statement', and discussion questions. QSRE Representative Council was introduced to the pack in April 1995, and members were encouraged to work with their monthly and preparative meetings by discussing and shaping the concern. Meetings and individual Friends were invited to send responses by the following March. *Quaker news* highlighted the work, as did the October QSRE Representative Council. Representatives did not always find it easy to involve their meetings, but persisted.

Thirty Harrogate Friends met during November 1995 to discuss the QSRE Central Committee initiative, 'Rediscovering our Social Testimony'. The initiative was warmly welcomed as a challenge to us as individuals and as a meeting.

Our discussions, while addressing realistically the difficulties we face... did reveal a unity in discerning what is distinctive in a Quaker social testimony. We saw that its basis is identical with that of our peace testimony, which we agreed is best expressed as a testimony to non-violence. Both stem from our fundamental belief in that of God in every person.
Steve Londesborough/Harrogate PM

Friends met in small groups, and in large groups. We wrote our own stories, and shared them with each other. We inspired each other, and we struggled together to search for our social testimonies. Some of us found the work hard, but often were inspired by what we shared. We found strength, clarity and energy.

I had attended just four or five meetings for worship at Rugby Meeting when I heard of the project 'Rediscovering our Social Testimony' and was surprised and pleased when I was invited to take part. Surprised, because from my very first meeting I knew I had discovered an extraordinary privilege in the Quaker worship. I try to respond like a person soon to reach his sixtieth birthday, but am not successful and resort to using words like joy and presence, not words predominant in my vocabulary before. Imagine my relief when I read what Thomas Kelly wrote about his difficulty in containing 'this burning experience of a Living Presence' within 'traditional Quaker decorum'.

What struck me was the Power, Presence, the Overawing feeling in that first meeting to discuss personal testimonies. Quakers carry this ability/capability about with them! They don't need to be gathered in the meeting house. Why was I so surprised? I'd learned that Quakerism was not a 'Sunday thing', and having bathed in the warmth of special ministry, had it not already affected my life? Nevertheless it was a revelation. There were about fifteen people and for some of us it was a case of discovering rather than rediscovering our social testimony. We were all invited to make a statement if we wished to do so, and listening to Quakers illustrated to me the term 'faith and practice'. It became obvious that 'seeking' had been a great ingredient in the personal testimonies expressed. Imagine how I felt to be told that 'Seekers' was an early name for Quakers.

Further meetings were held; we relished the testimony of Friends in *Quaker faith & practice*. This book, together with the earlier *Christian faith & practice*, continues to speak to me more directly than any words I have read. Time and again they lift me to stand where I have never stood before nor ever thought I was worthy to stand.
Gren Gaskell, *Quaker monthly*, October 1996

By April 1996 over one hundred responses had been sent in to the ROST Group. There were individual stories, group responses, and minutes from preparative and monthly meetings. Some representatives calculated the number of hours spent on this discernment by their meetings, and in a random sixteen reports, more than 1,775 'Quaker hours' were committed. QHS Representative Council was now working on ROST, and QSRE Central Committee was examining race equality as part of social testimony, and more recently, crime and community justice, education, housing, employment and voluntary action. Understanding of the links between peace and social testimony was growing.

At Yearly Meeting a month later a highlight was the Swarthmore

Lecture given by Jonathan Dale, entitled *Beyond the Spirit of the Age*. Jonathan had been the Clerk of QSRE Central Committee until the end of 1995, and was a member of the ROST Group throughout its life. A new essay from him forms a substantial part of this book. He challenged us to renew our social testimony by moving back from accommodation with the world to dissent. Sessions of Yearly Meeting also focused on Faith in Action and Seeds of Hope.

In the autumn of 1996 a selection of the responses and ideas sent in by Friends and meetings was published as *ROST – Responses and challenges*. This included suggestions for study and discussion, and sold 750 copies in the first month. Friends were getting involved in local groups of the Real World Coalition, and the *Quaker guide to general election issues* was produced. We were becoming more aware of how our Quaker faith was working in our lives.

At Yearly Meeting in Aberystwyth in 1997 two further sessions were devoted to consideration of the spiritual basis of our social testimony, and *An expression in words of Britain Yearly Meeting's corporate social testimony drawn from its experience and understanding at this time* was agreed, with a sense of joy and some achievement. Later that year, following a day conference at Woodbrooke on the Swarthmore Lecture, the informal Social Testimony Network was formed, to link local Friends and give us an opportunity to support, challenge and inform each other. Friends gathered in Birmingham again in July 1998 to celebrate social testimony activity, and to learn from and inspire each other.

1999 saw a conference at Woodbrooke for representatives of monthly meetings and central committees to consider together ways in which social testimony can continue to be at the heart of all our local and central life. The conference urged that testimonies should be reflected on by all central committees at regular intervals, that work should be monitored in relation to testimony development, and that a report should be made at least triennially to Meeting for Sufferings. The conference also urged that there should be frequent consideration of testimonies by yearly meeting. This book, bringing together the experiences and discernment of the last few years, is published to enable Friends to pray, learn and increasingly grow in confidence to discern how we should be living and working as a faithful and inspired community.

Rachel Carmichael, Clerk, ROST Group

An expression in words of Britain Yearly Meeting's corporate social testimony
drawn from its experience and understanding at this time

This paper was prepared in draft by the BYM Co-ordinating Group on Rediscovering our Social Testimony (ROST) at the request of Yearly Meeting Agenda Committee. It was distributed at the rise of a session at Yearly Meeting 1997 in Aberystwyth, and was considered and approved in general terms at a later session. It was then amended by the ROST Group, as requested by YM, drawing on written comments and spoken contributions in the sessions. It has been sent to preparative and monthly meeting clerks.

September 1997

1. OUR BELIEFS

1.1. Quakers believe that every aspect of life can be lived in ways which lead us closer to or further from our true, deeply human, spiritual nature and from God. This applies equally to our face-to-face relationships and to the social, economic and political structures in which they take place: these strongly influence how we relate to others as well as to the whole of the natural world. Our understanding of faith is that true human fulfilment comes from an attempt to live life in the spirit of love and truth and peace, answering that of God in everyone.

1.2. We need to turn again and again to the Light of God's Spirit to show us both the present reality of our lives and new possibilities of living that are more in harmony with God's ways. The life of Jesus speaks to many about these, with his astonishing refusals of the temptations of wealth and power. In his identification with the poor and the excluded, in his warnings against wealth and possessions he shows us that faith is not separable from how we live.

1.3. From the earliest days of Quakerism, Friends have sought to respond to the leadings of God, both individually and corporately. Often these leadings urged Friends to stand against common social practices which, they were convinced, led people away from God. So, for example, early Quakers were led to refuse to take off their hats to the rich and powerful because it negated the fundamental spiritual reality of the equality of all in the sight of God. This refusal of hat honour was rooted in faith, corporately discerned as a true leading, was practised by individual Friends and was intended to be a sign of the equality of all to the whole world. Such principled personal acts are examples of what we call Quaker testimony.

1.4.   We need now to relate our testimonies to the realities of late twentieth century Britain and the wider world. What do we see?

2.   THE CONTEMPORARY WORLD

2.1.   Scientific progress has created amazing new technologies which have changed the possibilities of human life. The development of means of communication, from aeroplane to computer, brings almost every part of the world within our reach. Biological and medical sciences have developed remarkable new powers, for example in the fields of reproductive technology, organ transplants and genetic engineering. Agriculture and industry have been so mechanised and automated that, in wealthy countries like the United Kingdom, only a fraction of available material resources is needed for keeping most of us fed, clothed, housed and warm.

2.2.   Sadly our social wisdom has not kept pace with the development of these new capacities. For all its immense success in utilising the world's resources to expand human opportunity, the modern industrial economy has not brought universal fulfilment. It provides the material rewards – very unequally – but leaves the individual defenceless against its remorseless development. Often, technological change is made to happen regardless of its ultimate effects. Both economic and technological progress appear at the present time to be beyond our control.

2.3.   Nowhere is this truer than of the global economy. We are ceaselessly persuaded that it is part of the natural order that we should be able to buy cheaply from, and sell dearly to, the two thirds world; that there is little we can do about the dramatically widening gap between the richest and poorest countries. But it is our spiritual conviction that God's will is for us to work towards right relationship with all our neighbours and that we must not accept such inequality, either in our pockets or our hearts.

2.4. Family, social and community relations are also weakened by this tidal wave of market and, therefore, money relationships. In so far as lives become founded on material rewards, when these vanish or fail to fulfil, the individual is left isolated and lost. A belief in happiness and fulfilment through wealth, success, security and power produces damaged/damaging individuals – and this is true both of those with the power and those without who may long for it.

2.5. We are all responsible for the society in which we live. We cannot dismiss the casualties of the system by saying they have brought it all on themselves. It is our belief that there is that of God in everyone. In those who create the hurt and those who are hurt. In different ways and degrees we are all both. This may be denied by society and, indeed, by the individual. But we cannot join in the widespread 'writing off' of people, without denying our central testimony to and experience of the potential of love to transform violence and hatred.

2.6. It is, therefore, our spiritual responsibility to examine the nature of society: how far does it encourage the great Christian virtues of selfless love, simplicity, peacefulness, truth and a sense of the equality of all as children of God which is the foundation of true community? And does it recognise in the natural world something which is inherently precious? 'All too little' is the answer. Hence our need to renew our social testimonies.

3. OUR TESTIMONIES

3a. Equality and Community

3a.1. Our testimony to equality stems from our underpinning conviction that we are all equally children of God. It sets us against the prevailing inegalitarian temper of the times. The prevailing belief is that the individual should keep more and more of what they are given through employment or investment, to spend as they wish. This has led to massively increased inequality in British society. It has also meant that there is less available for decent standards in our common life – for instance, in education, housing, health provision and the maintenance of our public spaces. There is more public squalor than there should be, and more private affluence too, and these are two sides of the same coin.

3a.2. If the economic system is based on giving individuals free reign and the political consensus is that the resulting inequalities should not be markedly reduced by taxation, then we believe society will remain deeply divided and crime will be widespread; there will be too little sense of community. Indeed, in such conditions of gross inequality of wealth and power, it will be impossible to create the equality of esteem which we believe is central to any faith which sees all human beings as equally children of God. We are, therefore, clear that taxation is a fit instrument for a fairer sharing of the community's resources and the provision of good services for all.

3a.3. The very fact that such inequality is now known to increase death rates amongst those at the bottom end of the income scale suggests that it is sensed as a form of neglect, even contempt. It speaks of a fragmented society in which the importance of our common humanity is lost from sight. Where the sense of mutual obligation is weakened and the model of the self-interested consumer is promoted we witness the results both in the many forms of individual despair and in the widespread vandalism and crime which take root in the soil of disintegrating communities.

3a.4. If that is true within British society, how much more so does it apply to the deepening of global inequalities. The gap between the richest 20% of the world's population and the poorest 20% has more than doubled in the last thirty years. In so far as we value our luxuries more than the basic needs of others we acquiesce in this appalling inequality, which condemns millions of people to malnutrition, disease and preventable death. Yet our testimony is to the equal worth of all as children of God.

3b. Simplicity

3b.1. The testimony to simplicity is integral to our faith: in its practice we know that our closeness to God, our spiritual responsiveness, depends on our being as free as possible from dependence on the securities that seem to be offered in possessions and the power of money to acquire them. In so far as we are led towards true simplicity we will increasingly be called to dissent from a central thrust of the world we live in.

3b.2. The market economy functions by fuelling our wants; it manufactures new desires, passing them off as needs. Ceaselessly, advertising implores us to consume. Such a system works constantly against sufficiency and simplicity. It is our experience that true human fulfilment is not to be reached through the worship of money and all that it can buy. Friends seek to resist the temptations to define our value by acquiring possessions. All the same, we are drawn almost inexorably into spending more on some types of luxuries. It is, therefore, our conviction that developing resistance to consumerism is an essential spiritual practice today.

3c. Stewardship

3c.1. We are born into a world which is a wonderfully rich resource for our material and our spiritual needs. We should treasure it and preserve its capacity to delight and sustain.

3c.2. However, in the process of the relentless search for new profit by creating new desires the resources of the natural world are despoiled and exhausted. Habitats and species are sacrificed to products and services which often are very far from essential. The future is constantly sacrificed to the present and the needs of others to the wants of the self. It cannot be right to leave the world poorer than we found it in beauty or in the rich diversity of life forms. Nor to consume recklessly in the knowledge that our actions carry the likelihood, many would say the certainty, of future tragedies.

3d. Integrity and Truth

3d.1. Friends have long witnessed to the importance of truth, both in private life and business and public affairs. We sense once again the essential nature of this witness. Our complex social, political and economic system gives a great deal of cover for deceit and half truth. The recognition that parliament and people have been repeatedly deceived by the executive has done much to weaken public confidence in democracy.

3d.2. We are clear that the practice or otherwise of truth cannot be a matter of pragmatic judgement: without truth there is no relationship to God; without truth there is no real community. Our culture needs to prize truthfulness and integrity, not just in scientific work but in every aspect of our social life.

3e. Peace

3e.1. Our peace testimony derives from our conviction that God is love and that in every human being there is that of love, of God.

3e.2. We do not assume that we can escape from the realities of a world in which violence looms large. The existence of weapons of mass destruction and their threatened use, the multitude of violent conflicts mostly between ethnic and religious groups within nations, and the day-to-day violence that destroys peace of mind in many of our deprived communities are our constant challenge. However, it is our experience over the centuries that 'to live in the life and power which takes away the occasion of all wars', when we can, is to be closer to God.

4.   LIVING OUR TESTIMONIES

4.1. We recognise that our testimonies stand against many of the current strands of economic, social and political change. We are, therefore, clear that we have to dissent from fundamental aspects of the contemporary social order.

4.2. This will mean developing our experience of living out our testimonies against the ways of the world, while holding up an alternative vision of human fulfilment. One way of doing so is to share with one another our practice of living in accordance with testimony much more openly and adventurously, in the expectation of being led into more faithful discipleship.

4.3. We are also clear that we have to seek, both individually and corporately, locally and nationally, to express our alternative vision in ways which contribute positively to political decision making. Such political expressions of our faith will not stem from a party spirit but will express our understanding of God's leadings. We acknowledge that we do not have all the answers. We aim not for a facile dissent but to encourage a return to fundamental values despite the difficult realities of day-to-day politics.

4.4. We welcome the fact that our voices are amongst many which share such fundamental values. Together we need to dedicate ourselves to keeping alive an alternative vision of a society centred on meeting real human needs rather than ever changing desires; a society where inequalities of wealth and power are small enough for there to be real equality of esteem; a society which, mindful of the quality of life and the needs of future generations, limits its use of natural resources to what is sustainable; a society which is content with sufficiency rather than hankering after excess; a society in which justice is an active basis for social peace and community.

4.5. In all that we say and do we intend to hold firm to our core testimony to the sacramental nature of each aspect of our lives in so far as we sense in it God's loving purpose. So, in the crucial economic and political areas of our common life we must practise spiritual discernment. And then act.

Yearly Meeting Minutes
on reaffirming the spiritual basis of our testimony

Our Quakerism is shown first by what we do, rather than by what we say. Yet, while we express our testimonies in action, we do the job only in part if we do not engage with people at a deeper level, the level of their need and our need, and try to express our faith to people as we act.

We affirm that we in Britain Yearly Meeting are moving into a new place of unity in our understanding of the inter-relatedness of spirituality and action. This is not a stopping point for us but a milestone on our journey.

Steadfastness and prayer and love and risk are asked of us as we go through the painful process of feeling the call but only partially discerning it; then full discernment, perhaps followed by terror at what is being asked of us.

We welcome this document and affirm the work it represents. It calls us to a style of living and a generosity of giving that perhaps we cannot all yet attain, but we feel called to recognise the principles expressed in this document. Small steps, taken in faith, make a joyful journey.

Minute 24 and part of minute 37 of Britain Yearly Meeting 1997

Concerns in which Friends in Britain Yearly Meeting are involved

The concerns listed below are the main ones which Friends within Britain Yearly Meeting are upholding, whether they are working at local, regional or national level. The many projects and groups are not listed here; neither are specific areas of the world for which Friends have concern.

Corporate concerns

Prejudice reduction and working towards equal treatment of people whatever their:
- ethnic origin
- gender
- sexuality
- ability/disability
- age
- national identity

Care of and supporting the rights of people with specific disadvantages:
- prisoners
- homeless people
- frail elderly people
- HIV positive people
- unemployed people
- refugees and asylum seekers
- victims of crime
- mentally-ill people
- people in areas of violent conflict

Working to provide directly, and to ensure society provides for all, good quality:
- housing
- work
- access to legal advice
- health services
- community care
- education (throughout life)

Campaigning for:
- integrity in public affairs
- civil rights
- freedom of information
- better prison conditions and more use of alternatives to prison
- economic justice
- preservation of the natural environment/sustainability
- animal welfare
- international reconciliation
- human rights

Campaigning against:
- gambling/ National Lottery
- capital punishment
- over-use of prisons
- weapons' manufacture, export and use
- taxation for military purposes
- poverty and marginalisation

Developing and promoting new models of social relationship:
- mediation
- creative conflict resolution
- achieving social change by non-violent means
- economic structures which serve people and planet

Other ways in which many Friends uphold the testimonies and follow individual leadings

- affirming rather than swearing oaths
- not using titles
- being honest and as open as possible in all dealings
- living as simply as possible/resisting consumerism
- not using corporal punishment
- nurturing relationships in the family, the meeting and the wider community
- learning/using conflict resolution skills and alternatives to violence
- abstaining from, or using in moderation, all non-medical drugs including alcohol
- not eating meat
- getting involved in democratic politics
- recycling/ reusing/ reducing use of manufactured products
- respecting and valuing all individuals
- refusing to contribute to war or preparation for war
- using inclusive language

Part II – Quaker understanding of testimony

An essay by Jonathan Dale

1. Why do we need to rediscover the social testimonies?

'Zeal for the testimonies is one of the characteristics of the Quaker way.'

(John Punshon, *Testimony and tradition*, p.68)

Let me answer that question by showing how social testimony came alive for me, because it reveals how the tradition had almost stopped renewing itself and because testimony is always about our stories of how we respond to what Friends have come to understand as the great truths of the spiritual life.

My own experience of the social testimonies as I grew up as a birthright Friend may reflect that of many Friends. I was born in 1940 and vividly recall my parents' involvement in peace activities in opposition to the deepening Cold War in the late 1940s and early 1950s. It was later as natural as breathing to take part in the Aldermaston Marches. And to feel that this was a part of Quaker corporate witness. The peace testimony was clearly quite central to our Quaker faith.

It is true that my parents were also deeply committed to social justice and equality within British society, being active in the Labour Party. There was also a very fierce commitment to truthfulness – including 'not defrauding the public revenue' – in the upbringing we received. These values were, I'm sure, integral to their Quaker faith too – but somehow they did not come across as *testimonies* in the way that the peace testimony did. The fact that the more specific named testimonies in *Christian faith and practice* were mostly no longer of immediate relevance also must have played a part in the very uncertain sense that testimonies (other than the peace testimony) left in my mind – the refusal of hat honour, the refusal to swear oaths, the rejection of gambling and alcohol, all came over as issues of the past more than fundamental outcomes from current Quaker conviction. And yet, the values of simplicity, truth and equality were breathed in and lived out in day-to-day faithful practice.

My own commitments, like those of many Friends, were in the fields of peace and east-west relations, throughout the 1950s and 60s. It was not until the mid 1970s that I was led to turn my attention to conditions closer to home, becoming involved in issues around poverty, housing and gender equality. For the first time, at about the age of forty, I encountered the *Journal of John Woolman*. Even then, although I was active in a wide range of Quaker contexts, I was never involved in any concentrated reflection on the nature of Quaker testimony or on social testimonies in particular. That had to wait until 1993, when I was invited to run a workshop on the theme by Hebden Bridge Meeting. So I had to start thinking about it – at last, after over thirty years as an adult Friend!

The discovery that testimony was not an explicit working dimension in my Quaker faith came as a shock, and was, indeed, shocking. What made it all the more shocking was that it came at a time when the Thatcherite revolution had destroyed the consensus around the welfare state. I felt an acute spiritual need to connect my Quakerism and my political horror at the aggressively materialist and individualist philosophy and policies of the new right.

And, as I reflected, I came to see that I had been neglecting a precious and fundamental part of our heritage. The invitation to deliver the 1996 Swarthmore Lecture provided a further opportunity to continue that reflection. Shortly afterwards, the Central Committee of Quaker Social Responsibility and Education, in an acute state of frustration at a constant agenda of managing the cuts – and at a time when the social and political agenda nationally was still one aimed at destroying much that Friends had struggled to create – felt strongly led to initiate what quickly became the Rediscovering our Social Testimony process, which has brought social testimony into the lifeblood of Britain Yearly Meeting once again. The clarity of the Committee's response was the mark, I believe, of an authentic leading.

Ralph Hetherington was one of those who responded to the Rediscovering our Social Testimony exercise. This is what he wrote:

> The first and abiding impact the Society of Friends had upon me when I first came across Quakers was not the beliefs held by Friends, nor their place in the religious spectrum, but rather their social testimonies – how they lived their lives and what they thought was important. It was only later that I came across such phrases as 'the Inward Light' or 'That of God in everyone' or 'What canst thou say?'
>
> What was immediately apparent to me was the integrity and dependability of Quakers themselves. One could depend on being told the truth, or at least not to be told a falsehood. One could rely on confidences not being broken – a sense of mutual trust that made one feel safe in Quaker company.
>
> There was an insistence that every individual was of equal worth and importance, however insignificant or ill-equipped they seemed to be, and that whatever opinion expressed was worthy of careful and serious consideration.
>
> I was intrigued and much attracted by the complete absence of the use of titles of any description, whether social, academic, medical, ecclesiastical, political or military, and by the use of both first name and surname in addressing a Friend one was meeting for the first time.
>
> Being already a pacifist, I knew of the Quaker peace testimony, but I quickly learned that this was part of a much wider testimony of compassion for the vulnerable and disadvantaged members of society, stressing the importance of doing nothing to add to the world's misery and of doing what one could to alleviate it.
>
> It also quickly became apparent that Quakers were studiedly unostentatious in their life styles. Although some were clearly affluent, they seemed to be careful not to spend money on those things that they thought were unnecessary. Thrift, temperance and opposition to gambling and financial speculation seemed a natural part of the Quaker life-style. (A submission to the ROST process, September 1995)

Ralph Hetherington's response shows us something vital. There is little point merely listing the testimonies. What we most need is to come to know what the Quaker testimonies mean for us today. We have neglected this reflection until lately and we now need to renew the tradition, to see our practice of testimony as a process of faith. As John Southern put it, 'To exercise our trusteeship of this inheritance we must work out our own practicalities for our own time, not to copy those who came before, but to find our own expression of that God-experience.' ('God is community', *Quaker monthly,* October 1996)

What do we mean by testimony?

So, the question, 'what is testimony?' is a necessary question for Friends at this time. But it is a hard one, because we have not used the language of testimony enough to know easily how to answer it. The religious thought world which created it has disappeared from the cultural mainstream to be replaced by a more secular discourse which has little or no place for it. If that analysis is true, it will clearly take deep reflection and much spiritual struggle for most of us to gain an inward sense of what testimony is. So, how can we begin to find that inner understanding?

What is testimony?

We need to start with testimony in general, rather than social testimony in particular. John Punshon characterises Quaker testimony as a trunk with several branches. He sees its trunk as the Christian faith in its Quaker understanding. It can also be seen as our understanding of the truth at the heart of the Christian faith. This is, of course, very broad as the term has to cover issues of doctrine as well as the ethics of Quaker social practice. Issues such as the refusal to ordain ministers or to baptise in water are matters of testimony as much as is the refusal to honour any but God by removing one's hat. So, testimony in general is the Quaker understanding of how we witness to the truth in our doctrine and in our social practice. We would be wise not to expect to make too neat a distinction between testimonies which relate to doctrine, church order and social practice. They are interwoven. The testimony to the priesthood of all believers is closely linked to the testimony to equality, for example.

Harvey Gillman offers us a more concrete understanding of what is involved:

The word 'testimony' is used by Quakers to describe a witness to the living truth within the human heart as it is acted out in everyday life. It is not a form of words, but a mode of life based on the realisation that there is that of God in everybody, that all human beings are equal, that all life is interconnected. It is affirmative but may lead to action that runs counter to certain practices currently accepted in society at large ... These testimonies reflect the corporate beliefs of the Society, however much individual Quakers may interpret them differently according to their own light. They are not optional extras, but fruits that grow from the very tree of faith. (1988, *QFP* 23.12)

Contained within Harvey Gillman's quotation there are a number of quite central responses to the question, 'what is testimony'. I propose to highlight and expand on a number of them, before adding some additional ones at the end.

What Pam Lunn writes of the peace testimony is equally true of all our testimonies: 'The peace testimony is not a form of words but a way of living, not a creed but an active witness, not an ideology but an always imperfect and faltering attempt to live out a fundamental spiritual perception.' *Deeds not creeds,* QPS, 1993

Testimony is different from a secular form of value

The word 'testimony' is used by Quakers to describe a witness to the living truth within the human heart as it is acted out in everyday life.

The prevailing view of action as the *result* of faith fails totally to catch the distinctive power of the Quaker understanding of testimony. Faith, spirituality, God, our sense of the ultimate – however we refer to it – is not a separate place or activity, some secret garden apart from our everyday world. It is experienced in every context of our lives. The 'living truth' longs to be embodied in all that we are and say and do. That is what our testimonies are: our experience of the living truth, expressed in the world of time and mortality. Therefore, the testimonies, whether to truth, simplicity, peace, equality or anything else, are not abstractions, notions or ideologies. Rather they distil our corporate spiritual experience over time. As John Punshon puts it: 'We adopt them because we come to discern the truth they are showing us. They are revealed to us by the Light.' (*Testimony and tradition*, p.70)

Testimony is about bearing witness *to the truth*. It is not a question of opinion or reason or hearsay – what I think, what someone else has told me. It is about affirming our own experience of something as true, as fact, as surely known.
'Testimonies in the Quaker tradition' in *The Quaker peace testimony*, p.13

This cannot be too often re-emphasised precisely because the weakness of our spiritual language renders us liable to interpret the testimonies as largely secularised abstractions. We have to be able to show those who join with us that 'the testimonies are not pragmatic responses to the spirit of the age... but the outcome of the Quaker religious tradition'. (*Testimony and tradition*, p.19) This is by no means easy, for Liberal Quakerism overlooks the sense of testimony both as a religious truth claim and as a means of evangelism. Instead it tends to see the testimonies as values which relate to particular social and political questions. When that happens the testimonies can come to seem pallid and indistinct; such broad and abstract values, divorced from their original illuminating power as leadings from God, come to appear indistinguishable from the general currency of liberal attitudes. Then their power to guide our lives is sorely weakened.

Somehow we must recover, against the spirit of the times, something of the original sense of testimony and the testimonies. The especial importance of the testimonies in the practice of Quaker faith is that they form unbreakable bonds between spiritual insight and social action. This unbreakable bond preserves us from the dualisms which oppose faith and action, personal salvation and the building of the kingdom of God. But this can only be maintained if the spiritual basis of our understanding of testimony is clear.

I know that some Friends say we don't need to dress our actions up as testimony; we should just get on and do what we should. I'm not without sympathy for that impatience. Yet I do believe that our actions may feel deeper and more sustainable when they are integral to our spiritual understanding. I wrote in my Manchester Conference centenary address about the way in which my litter picking round is enriched as I find in it the great themes of our testimonies, in terms of equality, community and the sacredness of creation. The passage continues: 'Seeing a particular action as testimony is important to me: it reminds me that I am doing something more: I am testifying to the values of faith which lie so much deeper than self-interest, but which can so easily be obscured by it. In that way everything that we do becomes part of a whole faith and not just a series of separate actions on separate issues. And so faith becomes much more continuously real.'

Testimony, then, is both difficult for contemporary Friends and absolutely crucial. It is difficult in that modern culture is far from fostering 'a feeling sense' of what testimony really is. It is crucial in that it can enable us to transcend a purely secular, humanist or political approach to the action we undertake. If it is true, as some have alleged, that Friends are too dogmatically political, too breathlessly activist and, in ministry, too shallowly rationalist, is it not because too many of us have failed to show how our enthusiasms grow deeper and are better nourished when rooted in our testimonies? And so we have not been able to convey their spiritual vibrancy to others. Testimony is a different and deeper way of responding to the needs of the world, in that it relates our current human concern to the ultimate source of all concern.

This different way is bound up with what early Friends saw as the Lamb's War. We can be too impatient with such terms; they repay a little wrestling with. It suggests that we live in a world of struggle between that which is of God and that which is not, which is surely just as true as it ever was. And, if it is true, it means that the invitation we face is to live in ways which embody God's spirit in the here and now even as we look forward to a world transformed into the kingdom of God. That is how testimony is always an invitation to both a personal and social transformation. The challenge is to live here and now within the spirit of the 'new creation', even as we struggle in the service of the Lamb towards its realisation in wider social forms. That is why testimony, rooted in the conviction that the ultimate values in God are open to us individually in some measure, retains an ultimate faith in the realisation of God's spirit in the wider world, however humanly impossible this may seem.

That was implicit in the development of the testimonies in the early years of Friends. For example, R. Melvin Keiser quotes George Fox's opposition to war-making: 'But I told them that I lived in the virtue of that life and power that took away the occasion of all wars ... Still they courted me to accept of their offer ... But I told them I was come into the covenant of peace which was before wars and strifes were' (R. Melvin Keiser, *Inward Light and the New Creation,* p.17). This points to early Friends' experience of

a life that is joined to the Kingdom of God; they were convinced – just like
Bob Johnson today – that those who are involved in conflict and violence
can yet come to 'dwell in unity with creation in the depths of the world
which the Light opens us to'. (p.18)

We Quakers are ... in danger of being utopian because we tend to play
down the evil in the world. But we falsify our belief if we suppose that
human beings are fundamentally good and are led to do wrong only
unintentionally. The present abuse of the earth from blatant self-interest
and greed is enough to bear witness to the power of evil in human life.
But we do have confidence in the God-given capacity of human beings to
respond to the Light when it is shown to them, and fundamentally to
change their ways. It is a confidence precisely in God's working in them
based on the experience of God's working in us, and often against the
grain of self-will. We need not therefore be devastated by the evidence
of human destructiveness. We can still believe that human hearts are
vulnerable, *and we can believe this of everyone without exception since*
the God we believe in is precisely the God within creation.
Rex Ambler, 'Befriending the earth', *Friends quarterly*, January 1990 (The
emphases are mine.)

Testimony is a way of living not a creed

It is not a form of words, but a mode of life based on the realisation
that there is that of God in everybody, that all human beings
are equal, that all life is interconnected.

For many years the yearning for a renewal of Quaker social testimony
was centred on finding a formula to match one or other of the historical
formulations of the peace testimony. It was a mistaken point of departure.
The words may come, but they must come from the lived witness. That is
what we need constantly to rediscover. If the will to truth, to simplicity, to
peace, to equality, to the nurturing of creation's glory are illuminations
shed by 'the living truth within the human heart as it is acted out in
everyday life', all that we do will be under that guiding light. We will know
our separation from the testimonies through the Light which convicts us of
the truth when we do not act out that living truth in our lives. And, when
we do so act, we will come into the sustaining Light of faithfulness. Our
lives preach our faith – and, of course, our fear.

If our testimonies are what unite us as Quakers, then they should go beyond mere words and become ... a way of life. They are public statements of our commitment. This may have drastic implications: if the world appears less good than it might be in the light of our testimonies, then we must act to change it. It is not just through agreement with the testimonies that we identify ourselves as Quakers, but also through our commitment to upholding them.

P6 in *Who do we think we are?*

Testimony must not be seen as an oppressive body of regulations to which we have to conform. It is nothing of the sort. It is of the utmost importance that we understand that, although testimony derives from corporate discernment, each individual Friend has to interpret it and find ways of making it true for her or himself. What we then need is to know how our individual path sets off from the corporate highway and constantly rejoins it; to know how our path relates to the path taken by the Friends in my community and how, together, our paths relate to the common highway of our testimonies. 'Testimonies show us the route to follow if we want to reach a particular destination. They may offer a choice of destination or of routes (some more scenic than others!)'. (P6 in *Who do we think we are?*)

That's why we need to find ways of sharing our journeys with each other. Through this, in a spirit of support and challenge combined, we invite each other to sense the joys and tribulations, the advantages and the disadvantages of the slightly different routes we are taking towards a common destination. This is surely the way to enrich our understanding of the relationship of our multiple individual paths and that common highway.

This theme is well caught in a section of *Who do we think we are?*:

'How far is enough? Should we feel virtuous for being vegetarian or guilty for not being vegan? Is it good to trade in a BMW for a mini, or should we be cycling to the station? Such questions arise continuously, yet there can be no straightforward answer. A testimony must be a way of behaving, not a set of rules.' (N2 in *Who do we think we are?*)

Testimony is both individual and corporate

These testimonies reflect the corporate beliefs of the Society, however much individual Quakers may interpret them differently according to their own light. They are not optional extras, but fruits that grow from the very tree of faith.

Testimony is a synthesis of the individual and the corporate, not in the sense of being a bit of each but of being fully both. And, once more, this is because truth cannot be merely accepted from a tradition but has to be made our own; yet our truth, to be more than mere personal preference, also has to connect with that core of significance in the universe which is beyond the merely subjective.

The relationship of the corporate and the individual is one of John Punshon's preoccupations too. When he shows how the testimonies are 'religious, ethical, collective, demanding, developing – and vague' he argues that this fluidity is their greatest strength. However, he is careful to add: 'It would be a mistake to interpret them as granting licence, however, for they have a strongly corporate dimension.' (*Testimony and tradition*, p.19)

I suspect that this is one of our problems: many of us find it difficult to accept the deep spiritual challenge of the testimonies because we see them through the individualistic eyes of contemporary culture. Seen that way, it is easy to feel that there is no gauge of our actions other than our own subjective opinion. This is what John Punshon categorises as 'Supermarket Quakerism', where we each load our trolleys with our own spiritual, moral and political preferences. He continues: 'Supermarket Quakerism can dispense with the ideas that the testimonies are part of a greater whole from which they derive their cogency, and that there is a basis for them which is not necessarily sympathetic to the presuppositions of rationalism and humanism.' (*Testimony and tradition*, p.23) Such a position would indeed make us prey to equating the testimonies with whatever we, as individual Friends, feel like doing. That is not the Quaker way.

Testimony is necessarily corporately discerned

This is one of the hardest aspects of testimony for present day Friends to fully grasp. The individualistic approach to matters of truth, faith and practice in almost every institution of society has percolated down into the depths of many a Friend's heart and mind. This historical evolution cannot simply be wished away. Nor is it to be condemned out of hand. Indeed much of the authoritarian and hierarchical mindset which individualism undermined would itself run sharply counter to our testimonies.

However, our testimonies can only develop as testimonies from a shared conviction that there are some things which, together, we are led to affirm about the nature of God, or, if that is a difficult word for you, perhaps the nature of the divine. And that necessarily will have repercussions for our understanding of how we human beings should live together.

It is clear that some Friends are sceptical as to whether we can corporately discern leadings into testimony. It can quickly be assumed that we are so individual and so different that 'no two Friends have the same view on anything', as the well-known but false Quaker commonplace goes. Fortunately that view, however widespread, is shallow and fails to make several important distinctions.

Firstly we need to distinguish between the general direction and the precise path. Testimony is mostly in the realm of the general direction rather than the precise path. And it's here, in terms of general direction, that we can realistically hope for a substantial measure of unity. For example, we may not agree on the exact taxation regime that would accord best with our testimonies, but we would be in unity on the need to curb growing inequalities, to encourage careful energy and other resource use, etc.

Secondly it is too often assumed that, if there is one Friend who supports the Western armed intervention in Kosovo, there is no longer a peace testimony. Unity is not the same as uniformity. Whenever there is a real testing of the peace testimony, locally or nationally, Friends recognise that that testimony is still, for all the complexities, a continuing spiritual leading.

Thirdly, when we look at the sort of people we Friends in BYM form and what it is that holds us together, we find that unity on the broad thrusts of the social testimonies is one of the crucial ingredients of our sense of Quaker identity. Ben Pink Dandelion has shown how crucial a cohesive factor, in the absence of unity of belief, is Friends' shared sense of social values. (*A sociological analysis of the theology of Quakers*) If we were not only very different in our theological formulations but also in our understanding of testimony, we would simply not hold together. For example, if we had ministry in praise of capital punishment, conspicuous consumption, governmental secrecy and white superiority, a number of Friends would find their practice of Quakerism a good deal less satisfying. Moreover, just imagine if we could not speak out of a united conviction? If we were unable to assume a common commitment to peace, to truth, to simplicity, to equality broadly understood? If there were as many Friends who were hangers and floggers as penal reformers, what would meetings for worship or yearly meetings feel like then? Do you see what I mean? No! Quaker social testimony is absolutely central to Quaker unity. Without it the Society would certainly not hold. We are still a long way from properly valuing the very real unity that we find in our social testimonies. Indeed it is something we should actively celebrate as another 'amazing fact'.

This theme was caught in the 1998 Swarthmore Lecture: 'In a religious society that respects the individual spiritual paths taken by its members and attenders, testimonies are what unite us. They provide some unity of value and belief, in the way in which silence provides a unity of method.' (P6 in *Who do we think we are?*)

The difficulty contemporary Friends have in understanding testimony as simultaneously relating to our corporate and our individual search for truth, and our constant tipping of the balance towards the personal and the subjective can be seen in a different context. Here again is R. Melvin Keiser writing about two of the early positions of Friends – the Inner Light and the New Creation: 'While opening to the Inward Light explains Friends' radical individualism, dwelling in the New Creation explains our radical communalism.' (p.17) However, he shows that contemporary Friends do not by any means have that balance between the two. The 'inner light', with a generally individualist interpretation, is a commonplace; whereas neither the 'new creation' nor the associated 'gospel order', with their implications for corporate discipline and social action, is at all familiar. We have to overcome these distortions in our worldview if we are to be at home in the world in which the testimonies were first discerned.

Testimony is lived out individually as well as corporately

In striving to counterbalance a contemporary minimising of the corporate, care is needed not to suggest that testimony is all about corporate discernment and practice. Quaker faith is built on the ever-present need for the truth to become absolutely real for oneself – indeed truth requires nothing less. Our testimonies all need to be owned afresh by each individual Friend as we grow in faith and practice. Testimony cannot be second hand. No element of faith can.

What Quakers believe is not dictated by the majority view. If ninety-nine out of a hundred Quakers hold to a particular belief or course of action, the hundredth is not bound to agree with them; rather the hundredth is bound to follow the Light that illuminates his/her understanding. The one Friend

who disagrees is not obliged to disregard personal conviction and fall into line, nor should the majority compromise in order to achieve a false unity. Both are, however, forced to a more careful examination of their own attitudes. This may involve a pressure towards conformity, but it also offers a protection against wild enthusiasms and personal whims masquerading as the will of God. It becomes part of one's attitude of mind to stop short and think again when one finds a marked difference between one's own belief and the corporate testimony of Friends. The obligation then rests on all to reconsider their positions, to ask themselves whether they are indeed following the Light, or whether from pride or laziness they are not allowing themselves to stand in the way of the Light. From such an examination it is then possible to move on towards a true unity of testimony.
Mary Lou Leavitt, 'Testimonies in the Quaker tradition', p.15

Testimony is affirmative; therefore, it often leads us to dissent

It is affirmative but may lead to action that runs counter to certain practices currently accepted in society at large.

Testimony, as noted above, is the expression of our deepest spiritual engagement. It is what we are led into when we *know experimentally* how God would wish the world to be, how God would wish human beings to conduct their lives. It is inherently affirmative. It affirms that truth and simplicity and equality and peace are aspects of the divine integrity; they are both incarnate in the world as it is and to be more fully incarnated by us in the world as it might become.

Necessarily, however, in a world which may misinterpret, ignore or even trample underfoot such values, our social testimonies will lead to dissent from much that is promoted by the spirit of the age. That is another of the perceptions offered by the 1998 Swarthmore Lecture, *Who do we think we are?*: 'I am often appalled by the extravagance and complexity of the world around me, including the amount there is in my own life. Countering it at the current time involves swimming very much against the tide'. (N2 in *Who do we think we are?*)

Whenever society accords overriding value to wealth, status, power, possessions, Friends will know that the treasure lies elsewhere than in the primacy of the self. For that reason the choices we make in how to live our lives are always more than they seem. They are a sign to the times.

Testimonies, as John Punshon has written, 'may begin with an act of personal choice, but each of them, if consistently carried out, amounts to a fairly radical departure from generally accepted norms of behaviour.' (*Testimony and tradition*, p.26) Dissent is, therefore, an inescapable consequence of the affirmative, prophetic nature of the testimonies as a calling of us to live within the likeness to God, which has been given to us as a seed.

It is time to dissent from the prevailing direction in which we see society being moved by politicians. We have to be prepared to support each other through the consequences of such dissent. We have to be prepared for the disharmony some of these actions will bring to our worshipping groups. We have experience in our own time of the consequences of actions taken by those protesting at the introduction of cruise missiles. We must tell each other the stories of that dissent. How did we support women who left children while they lived at Greenham and Molesworth? How did we talk with Friends who felt they were wrong to do so? How have we dealt with the meeting 'taking sides' over local issues? Was the presence of homosexual partnerships an issue in the meeting? What were we able to do for Friends who withheld taxes? Were we happy to have our meeting houses used by the wide variety of protesters in that period and by itinerant peace campaigners?

John Southern, in 'Draft social testimony supplement'

Dissent properly arises from clarity of vision, from seeing things as they really are. It is rooted in truth. And it reveals the truth. That was the role of the prophets in the Old Testament. It was also what Vaclav Havel saw as the role of the intellectual in the face of the conspiracy of lies in the frozen communist state of Czechoslovakia. In his book, *The Power of the Powerless*, he tells this story: A greengrocer puts the slogan 'Workers of the World, Unite' in his window. Is he genuinely enthusiastic about the unity of the world's workers, Havel asks? Of course not. But that does not mean the slogan has no significance. 'It really is a sign with a subliminal but very definite message – I am obedient and therefore I have the right to be left in peace.'

Havel's essay invited people to abandon this approach. Instead, they should 'live within the truth'. They should become 'the fifth column of social consciousness'. (Jonathan Steele, 'Crushed-velvet revolutionary' *The Guardian*, 13 March 1999) That should also be at least one of the functions of spirituality, and therefore also of Quaker testimony. Such a function is not essentially negative, arising as it does from a real experience of countervailing values. That needs emphasising as some Friends seem to think that we have to choose between affirmation and dissent, failing to understand that they are the two sides of the same prophetic coin.

Both are vital. Here, Zoe White beautifully and powerfully catches the affirmative sense of this prophetic strand within the Judaeo-Christian tradition:

> ... there have been people in it who have engaged in the task of trying to move out of a Conventional Script into a Quest Plot, who have dared to follow their passion, their vision of a promised Land – a New Heaven and a New Earth.
>
> I am not speaking here of *all* people in the Judaeo-Christian tradition. I am not speaking of those who used the tradition and its structures to further their own ends, or as a means to acquire power over others, or as a way of escaping the radical demands of the Quest Plot. I am referring to those who really went out to the edge, who chose the power of simplicity and community, when others around them were choosing the powers of wealth, domination and competition; who chose to live lives at variance with, if not radically opposed to, the values of society around them. (*Living faithfully with passion*, p.10)

[Mary Lou Leavitt also sees the affirmation in and through the negation.] Although the working out of the testimonies in the world often appears as negative – a refusal to kill, a refusal to swear, to pay tithes, to take our hats off to any but God – their root, with the vision and power from which they spring, is positive. It is not that we would do all these wicked things if we could but that we sternly hold ourselves back and mortify our worldly desires. It is that we live in the virtue of that active, creative, redeeming, healing life and power which makes it simply impossible for us to act – or to want to act – in that way. As Fox explained to the Commonwealth Commissioners when they visited his prison cell, he was 'come into the covenant of peace which was before wars and strife were'. To earn his release from prison by serving in any army was a spiritual impossibility. However inconvenient or costly the refusal, we live in a spiritual reality which gives us a strength, joy and positive vision to act by its rules,

and not by the world's.
'Testimonies in the Quaker tradition', pp.16-17

A powerful example of the prophetic call to Friends came when Witney Monthly Meeting tried to alert Friends nationally to the evil of homelessness and, beyond that, of all that the toleration of homelessness tells us about the fundamental nature of the Society:

> When Witney Friends met again in February they had reached a new sense of spiritual clearness which demanded a DIFFERENT SORT OF SPEAKING. This was not an issue for one or two people in the monthly meeting, it was the monthly meeting responding as a whole with a spiritual concern ... A 'burning issue', not individual but corporate, which has been tested over a number of years. In our politely sanitised way, Friends shrink from prophecy, but Witney Monthly Meeting sees homelessness as a matter for prophecy. NO SOCIETY CAN SURVIVE IF IT TOLERATES THIS SORT OF EVIL WITHIN IT. We can work out principles intellectually, Shelter and the Housing trusts can work practically, but we also need to inspire the will to deal with the problem, TO INSPIRE A SENSE OF OUTRAGE, to make a CALL TO RIGHTEOUSNESS.
> (From a paper based on the presentation to Meeting for Sufferings in April 1992)

I have already tried to deal with the anxiety some Friends feel about the apparent negativity of dissent, by showing that it is the inescapable corollary of a deep conviction about God's calling to the world to live according to God's spirit within us, which leads us to our testimonies. That is, in the first place, positive. That's why it is entirely false to assume that nice people like Quakers shouldn't dissent. The other difficulty that we have in this area is that we are so infiltrated by the sceptical reason of contemporary political discourse that we find it very difficult to keep a sense of the possible realisation of the values of God's commonwealth.

As Rex Ambler writes – specifically of the peace testimony, but it applies to all:

It is surely true that the understanding of human beings we

gain in the Light tells us that the horrors of violence and war are not ultimately necessary, that they arise from ideas and desires that can in principle be overcome. It is therefore laid on us to live in such a way that violence can be avoided, that is, to live as far as possible non-violently. But we also learn from the Light that not everybody is ready for this commitment (not even always ourselves), either because they cannot see its point or because they are not willing to change their lives accordingly. This is particularly true of our collective under-takings in state and society, which are inevitably limited by the moral vision and readiness of the mass of the people. But we can also see, from our own experience of being enabled to see, that people are generally capable of change and that our state and society are ultimately capable of becoming non-violent. This is perhaps a remote possibility, but we dare to hope that it is a real one. It is our dream. And we therefore find it laid upon us to bear witness to this possibility in every sphere of life. We want others to realise not only how they as individuals can be different, but also how, in the long run, the whole society can be different. To communicate this is our testimony.

('The peace testimony today' in *Searching the depths,* pp.55-56)

If only we could keep this horizon of spiritual hope before us always when we deliberate on our responses to the social problems of the day; and in our daily conversations with the pessimism of the Clapham omnibus.

There are also a few aspects of testimony which the particular Harvey Gillman quotation which opened this section, does not cover.

Testimony is demonstrative

As Mary Lou Leavitt writes: 'First of all, a testimony is a form of com-munication, of witnessing *to others*. ... [It] is primarily an outward witness 'to the whole world', actions and words intended to proclaim, demonstrate and convince.' ('Testimonies in the Quaker tradition', p.13) Or, as John Punshon puts it: 'The testimonies are essentially assertive. They proclaim how the world ought to be, and thus, by implication, what other people ought to do.' (*Testimony and tradition,* p.27)

This is not easy for contemporary Friends to feel from the inside. We are weakened by our recent tradition of diffidence about anything that smacks of mission, evangelising, preaching the truth to others, seeking converts etc. The idea of being convinced of a truth to proclaim seems to many Friends tarred with the sin of pride. This means that being explicit about living our lives as a sign of what we have discovered of God's kingdom goes against the grain. We are so aware of the relative nature of the choices that we make that we fail to see that they can still be forms of witness to others. Whether we get rid of a second car, give up an only car, cut down our mileage, swap plane travel for train and so on ... all of these choices are different. But they can still be signs along the same road, and they can yet witness to the same end.

One of our hardest challenges, if we want to know an inward sense of the power of testimony for early Friends, is to live our testimonies, not as a private story, a secret tête-à-tête with God, but as a public sign which points towards an ultimate truth. Just as we have to find the passionate conviction in an undogmatic faith, we have also, in a parallel way, to find the public message in our private lives.

I really want to Lead By Example. But for this, humility is paramount. An arrogant approach achieves nothing and can put people off so much that it has the opposite effect. In trying to achieve a more harmonious world it is possible to create local disharmony, annoying people and causing tensions that negate the overall objective. I don't like the arrogance connected with telling people how they should live, on the basis that I know better. But after years of irritating people with my moralising and being constantly criticised for it, perhaps I have now swung too far the other way. It is nice to hold an idealised notion of myself humbly and meekly leading by example (not that I do) but it would hardly occur to my peers to start boycotting Nestlé after they notice me not using Nestlé products.

If I am completely honest with myself, my avoiding preaching to people because of the arrogance associated with it is in some ways partly to justify my laziness and lack of energy.

N8 in *Who do we think we are?*

Testimony is political as well as personal

If testimony expresses what Friends have experienced of the spirit of God, it must apply to all the contexts in which we live and act. For example, we cannot live out our testimony to equality in our personal relations and at the same time be indifferent to the social organisation of inequality through the class system and the free market etc. We sometimes fail to give a proper weight to this comprehensive nature of our testimonies. This theme is developed in more detail later.

Testimony is not fixed once and for all; it evolves

The testimonies are not fixed once and for all. Their expression is constantly changing as the circumstances that Friends face individually and together also change. 'The spiritual root remains the same, but the practical, social and political consequences quite often do not.' ('Testimonies in the Quaker tradition', p.13)

For example, the testimony against hat honour has virtually lost its application as the social practice of wearing hats as symbols of authority has largely died out. Likewise with plain language, since we all use the 'you' form now for everyone, the invidious distinctions of the 'you' and 'thou' are no longer relevant. Of course the underlying spiritual truths of the need to honour all equally and to say what we really believe remain as applicable as ever.

Just as certain testimonies fade as the circumstances that gave rise to them disappear, so others emerge. For example, our contemporary understanding of social testimony as bound up with the state's role in ensuring that all of us have opportunities for health care, education, employment (so far as possible) and a minimum income, was only able to emerge through the challenge of the industrial revolution, with its need of more highly educated personnel and its creation of much larger amounts of wealth.

Mary Lou Leavitt shows how our testimonies are discarded and new ones formed through the interplay of corporate and individual discernment. She shows how individual discernment is a necessary protection against the rigidity of a corporate position; but that the corporate is also a very necessary check on 'wild enthusiasms and personal whims': 'Precisely because they are *not* creeds or public declamatory statements, the process of challenging, changing or discarding existing testimonies – and of developing new ones – is slow, illogical and complex.' ('Testimonies in the Quaker tradition', p.15)

The testimony against the use of alcohol, which was so powerful throughout most of the nineteenth century, makes an interesting example. The testimony was not so much formally disowned as it faded over time. After the Second World War, a younger generation of Friends, although often brought up in teetotal households, had lost sight of the powerful social motivation of those who had seen the destruction alcohol wreaked on family life in the new urban centres. In that case the issue came to a head through the revision of the *Advices and queries* at our 1964 Yearly Meeting. Yearly Meeting was clearly divided and so could not include a commitment to total abstention with integrity. 'It is not a question of the Society declaring that this or that is no longer the testimony of all; testimonies are what the Society shows to the world as its common belief, and if the Society does not show a common attitude on a particular issue, then that, not any historically endorsed doctrine, is its testimony.' (Geoffrey Hubbard, *Quaker by convincement*, pp.89-90) Testimonies, to remain testimonies, need to be lived. Gradually, where a testimony increasingly fails to command Friends' support in terms of committed witness, it becomes inoperative.

On occasions too, a testimony may fade as its relevance appears to recede, without being replaced. When conditions change, the original concern may resurface and the testimony take on renewed life. That is our recent experience with the testimony against gambling – which is perhaps best seen as an offshoot of the testimonies to simplicity, equality and integrity: simplicity because it affirms the spiritual experience of living in the life and power that takes away the occasion of seeking the power of wealth; equality because it refuses to seek advantage over others; integrity because it sees a fundamental dishonesty in the focus on getting something for nothing.

Many Friends in the 60s, 70s and 80s had got into the habit of seeing as harmless the purchase of the odd raffle ticket at the local fete etc. And there was almost no discussion of the wider issues around gambling, in casinos, at racetracks and betting shops and at amusement arcades, in part because most of these venues were beyond our experience, although there had been attempts to alert us to the damage done to those who become hooked on the activity. Then the Government introduced the National Lottery. Unsurprisingly we had nothing to say because we had ceased to reflect on the testimony, and possibly, in part, to practise it. That's why the frequent criticism of Quaker inaction on this matter was wide of the mark. There was scarcely any recent evidence of sustained corporate Quaker witness or reflection on this testimony amongst the members of the Society at large. We had to allow time for that before any authentic Quaker intervention could be made. The exercise was thorough and enabled us to see that our testimony against gambling still stood. It had been submerged but had not drowned. From discussions in our meetings all over the country the fact that the testimony was indeed in the life came out strong and clear. This enabled us to take the principled – and costly – position that Friends' corporate activities would not seek funding from the National Lottery.

All such changes must be rooted in our spiritual experience, both corporate and individual. The process cannot be codified. There are voices which encourage different approaches; others which affirm a testimony as it has been handed down. Such a dialogue may continue without any crystallisation for a long time. There may be opportunities for that dialogue to be carried on also in the corporate life of the Society; it may be held in the Light in our worship. Eventually a new understanding of what our deepest spiritual belief leads us to affirm may emerge and become recognised in some way.

'Such modifications of testimony come from the life and power of the meeting – from a growth of corporate understanding in the Society which is rooted in our common worship. The process is slow; sometimes painfully so. There is always a strong force towards retaining an old attitude. Many Friends will feel deeply that the particular testimony is an inherent part of our beliefs and that not to maintain it would break faith with our predecessors (many of whom suffered great hardship in maintaining this very testimony). Often, too, the voice of caution and conservatism is heard much more clearly than the counter suggestion that the testimony no longer commands Friends' willing support, and that we are uncertain whether the divine will requires this particular testimony any more. But if the movement for change persists and grows, in time the testimony is modified or dropped.'

Quotation from Geoffrey Hubbard, *Quaker by convincement,* p.89, with additions and modifications by Mary Lou Leavitt in 'Testimonies in the Quaker tradition', p.16

Just as there is no formal process for modifying or laying down a testimony, nor is there for the recognition of a new testimony within Britain Yearly Meeting. Indeed, of late, we have scarcely been conscious of the possibility of this sort of change. That, again, is a sign of our losing touch with the inner meaning and dynamic of testimony in the life of the Society. Nevertheless it does happen and is still happening. How?

I shall give two illustrations of quite different processes.

The first example is about the adoption by the corporate bodies of Britain Yearly Meeting of non-sexist language. As far as I know this has happened gradually, without any formal statement to the effect. It is, of

course, an example of an evolving Quaker testimony. The testimony to
equality has always been applied to the roles of men and women in the
Society. Perhaps the testimony had become taken for granted in the middle
part of the twentieth century. Many Friends felt that the feminist perspective
was not for Friends because men and women Friends were already completely
equal. But, around the 1970s some Friends began to question whether our
complacency was masking from us continuing inequalities in our lives.

It was at that time that I was forced to see in my own life the huge gap
between an abstract claim of equality and my perpetuation of inequality in
my relationship with my wife, Emily. I had for years been dominating her
with intellectual firepower, failing to value properly her more creative and
emotional gifts and, thus, diminishing her sense of self-worth in the process.
I had to learn the acute distinction between the intellect as an agent of truth
and the intellect as an abusive exercise of power.

My awareness was greatly helped when St Andrews Meeting was
challenged by the arrival of two new students with a strong understanding
of the distortions that the long history of patriarchy had created in the relations
between men and women. A concern was sent up from East Midlands of
Scotland Monthly Meeting and was one of the strands that fed into an
exercise throughout BYM on these and related issues. Later we had the
Quaker Women's Group Swarthmore Lecture, *Bringing the invisible into the
light*, in 1986.

One of the issues that Friends wrestled with during that period was the
use of inclusive language. It was raised in all sorts of ways: in letters to *The
Friend*; in personal pleas in local meetings; in requests for the redrafting of
minutes; and, not least, by personal example from those showing how
inclusive language could work. The reception for this concern was often
critical, and sometimes hurtful as many Friends – women as well as men –
could not see what the fuss was about and felt it awkward especially to alter
the time-honoured practice of referring to God as 'He'. Inevitably many
Friends, at local level, still cling to the language they grew up with. And
yet, the climate has totally changed, without any Quaker body having
decided it should. The new practice of inclusive language has become the
practice of our central Quaker bodies in their publications. And many of us
have found that the initial awkwardness has long since disappeared. We
have only to go back to Quaker writings in the first half of the century to
see the huge change that has been made.

This change, to inclusive language, is almost as visible and distinctive as was the refusal of hat honour. It has happened by gentle persuasion. Although it may have seemed to some to be just the result of bees in several bonnets, I suspect it is now widely sensed to have deep roots which go right down into the very spiritual bedrock of our testimony to equality in the eyes of God.

If that is an example of the evolution of a given testimony by processes which are diffuse and implicit rather than formal and explicit, then the developing testimony to all creation (whatever its final title) is much more likely to need a more formal recognition. Certainly a number of meetings have now asked for such a process to be allowed for through the agenda of Yearly Meeting. There is no reason at all why such an explicit recognition should not be made, provided that Friends throughout the several countries of Britain Yearly Meeting are already living out this testimony in their lives. That seems to me to be as much the case as for the peace testimony and, indeed, for any of the other social testimonies.

Recognising and developing a new Quaker testimony is an equally gradual and complex process. It requires pioneering (or prophetic) actions by those who seek to arouse the conscience of the Society, together with the response of those who come to see the new truth in what is being said. It takes place against a background of religious conviction essentially expressed in a spirituality of developing response to God. Moreover, there is a universal aspect to the task of formulating new testimonies – they do not represent a separatist holiness for the elect – they rest on a discovery of the truth applicable to all.
'Testimonies in the Quaker tradition', pp.15-16

The importance of testimony

I hope the importance of testimony for contemporary Quakerism – and for the quickening of our spiritual responsiveness as individual Friends – has been established. But also the difficulties presented by a modern culture which is much happier to see things fragmentedly as different issues devoid of any ultimate horizon. We need to understand these obstacles to know how to rediscover the power of testimony, which is beyond the naming of the testimonies.

Testimony keeps us whole. It is the vital glue which binds both our manner of living and our political action into our faith as integral facets of it. It is an all-embracing spirituality, which has truly overcome the dualism of the spiritual and the political. The testimony to the sacramental nature of the whole of life is in this sense absolutely central to Quaker faith. It recognises that there is no aspect of our lives which is neutral, which does not speak of God or God's absence. That is why the re-energising of our discipleship through the testimonies is one of the most powerful processes of spiritual growth that is open to us.

Testimony is also the foundation for a truly prophetic understanding of the contemporary world, because it never loses the experience of the beyond in the midst of contemporary political, social and economic debate which is all too often conducted within the very narrow confines of immediate, apparently rational, common sense. Testimony's struggle for continued life has to be fought against the all-pervading secularisation of modern life, in which so much is reduced to the simple question of, 'Can I afford it?' Testimony provides an ultimate depth to all the questions that secularisation would assume can be restricted to the shallow waters of materialism.

Having examined the role of testimony within Quaker spirituality, we need to engage with a more practical survey of our specifically social testimonies.

2. What are the Quaker social testimonies?

We need to be clear. There is no definitive list of testimonies in general, or of social testimonies in particular. Some Friends with tidy minds may well regret this but it is clearly the case. I shall not propose such a list either but I will try to offer some ways of thinking about what is generally accepted.

Testimonies and social testimonies

I need to start further back. There is no hard-and-fast distinction between testimonies in general and social testimonies in particular. Some social testimonies such as the testimonies to simplicity and to truth and integrity derive from a spiritual understanding of the nature of God and our relationship to God, in a sense before we apply them to our relationships with our fellow human beings and the creation as a whole. Simplicity, for example, is about not allowing anything to come between oneself and God's word to us; it is about the primacy of our relationship with God, and only afterwards about our houses and bank balances. To an extent that is true of all the social testimonies.

However, our testimony to the priesthood of all believers, although connected with our testimony to equality, is really about the possibility and, indeed, the reality of our relationship with God, unmediated by the paid priesthood. And that is not essentially a social testimony. The testimony against the payment of tithes and that on times and seasons could be seen in a similar light.

The peace testimony and social testimonies

Then there is the difficult question of how to treat the peace testimony. Historically, of course, it has been the testimony which, more than any other, held a dynamic place in our sense of what being a Friend involves. The other social testimonies, in recent times, have struggled to find anything approaching the clarity which the clear-cut decisions of peace or war made possible.

Nonetheless, it is almost impossible to construct a pattern in which the peace testimony is somehow different in kind to the testimonies to equality or to simplicity. It is social in that it deals with how we create peaceful social relations at every level of society, from the personal and the local to the global. That is why it is included in this book as one of the social testimonies. If it does not have here the pre-eminence that historically it has had in terms of coverage, this is not intended as any kind of downgrading of its importance. It has simply, for the purpose of this book, to be seen as one of a series of testimonies.

Social testimony or social testimonies

Some Friends refer to social testimony and others to social testimonies. I doubt whether this is something that should take up a great deal of our energy. I sense that there will be times when we need to particularise the individual testimonies, but there may be others when we wish to stress the rich interconnections of all the social testimonies and their common origin in our understanding of the nature of God and of God's relationship with the world. I have no real problem with that.

Broad testimonies and particular testimonies

The list of testimonies that is covered in this book is a list of broad testimonies, or what Mary Lou Leavitt has termed clusters. We have included all those that were in the document accepted by Yearly Meeting in Aberystwyth in 1997, although some of the names have been altered by us. These are: truth and integrity; simplicity; equality; community; peace and non-violence; a testimony to the earth. We have also included a section on economics, which we see not as a new testimony at this stage but as the place where all the testimonies can be understood from a particular perspective. Amongst this list are two testimonies which might not be held to have been recognised as clearly as the others, although both are included in 'An expression in words of Britain Yearly Meeting's corporate Social Testimony' (reprinted in Part I). They are community and the testimony to the earth. Community, which in 'An expression ...' is treated together with equality, is now given its own independent place.

It has become apparent to those of us working on this book that the testimony to community is justified in that the Religious Society of Friends developed in ways which laid enormous stress on the building up of the meetings in terms of community, including very practical assistance to those in greater need. There has also been a good deal of emphasis recently on community. Some of this has been quite practical in terms of the meeting as a community. But there has also been a good deal of work on community as an essential aspect of God. For example, John Southern's article entitled 'God is community' (*Quaker monthly,* October 1996), in which he writes: 'God is a community consisting in unbroken personal relationships.' Time will tell whether Friends see community as something that derives from the same core spiritual discernment as do the other testimonies. We think it does.

The testimony to the earth, which also figures in 'An expression in words', has not otherwise been officially recognised. However, there is abundant evidence that Friends are living out their concern for the sustainability of all the beauty, variety and abundance of nature quite as much as they are of the other testimonies. Consideration of such a testimony is likely to move onto the agenda of a future Yearly Meeting.

There are, however, particular practices of testimony which are best seen as forming parts of these broader testimonies. For example the testimony against the swearing of oaths is a part of the testimony to truth and integrity; similarly the testimony to inclusive language, which I have argued has recently been recognised, is part of our testimony to equality. It has not been possible to cover all these particular testimonies individually within this book.

Gaps in our coverage of social testimonies

Friends will notice, no doubt, different omissions from the book. These are mostly the result of failing to find the right extracts or of the complexity of covering certain aspects of testimony which seem not easily to relate to the structure of broad testimonies which we have chosen to use.

In some cases we have found ways of incorporating material. For example we have found that 'Community' is a good heading for the material relating to penal reform and the criminal justice system, although there are connections with both equality and peace as well. The testimony against gambling, which has connections with simplicity and integrity, we have included only by looking at the way it has been brought back to life, in the section on 'Social testimony in our corporate Quaker life'.

We are aware that we have been less successful with the Quaker testimony on alcohol, which is currently a testimony for moderation after a long period where the leading was strongly to abstinence. It is not clear to us how this testimony is best considered in relation to the broad categories we have used. Mary Lou Leavitt situates it within the simplicity cluster, but it relates also to integrity in a sense.

We have nothing also on the Quaker understanding of the testimony to equality as entailing the refusal of honours and like hierarchical distinctions of title and address. This has had intermittent airings in the correspondence columns of *The Friend* but without it being possible to sense a widespread unease amongst Friends at the weakening of this testimony. Personally, I regret this. It may seem a small matter, but I believe that that small matter is close to the heart of the whole testimony to equality. Brought up in a Quaker family I was always fiercely conscious that to respond to people differentially according to their social status was wrong. So much so that, rather than hovering around the great and the good, I was much more likely to shun them. I am unhappy that degrees are sufficiently sensed as a mark of distinction to need advertising in *The Friend*. Then there are the honours and the titles of Doctor and Professor, etc. Why does it matter? One of the crucial aspects of Quaker culture is the resistance to treating people differently because of their reputation. It is under pressure within a culture in which such practice is almost universal. It needs to be jealously defended. Or, as R. Melvin Keiser expresses it:

> the inequalities and injustices of society are 'invented by men in the Fall and in the alienation from God' whereas equality is established in the original creation. Honouring social rank rather than the person is a manifestation of sinful flesh; therefore, Fox refuses to bow or doff his hat, honouring one's presumed social betters, and addresses all people 'rich or poor, great or small' with the plain speech of thee and thou. (*Inward Light and the new creation*, p.23)

Rather similarly we have nothing on plain speech in relation to the testimony to simplicity and, indeed to truth. We may tend to view this as an outdated testimony. But is it? Certainly few of us persevere with thee and thou when everyone is referred to as you. But is that the end of the matter? When I worked in ecumenical circles I was quite struck by the way in which the idea of getting one's way by winning the argument seemed to loom larger there. Rhetorical flourishes, many words, exaggerations are all potential hazards. It is true that our practice has somewhat evolved. The sober, emotion-free approach typical of Friends has been joined by forms of expression that can sometimes be more personal, even impassioned. All the more reason to keep our connection with the core experience which is that our language needs to be in the service of truth. That will most often require a degree of simplicity.

There may well be other gaps, consciously or by ignorance. No doubt Friends will let us know.

Problems of what to call our testimonies

The newest of our testimonies, which we have called the emerging testimony to the earth, is the one where there is most uncertainty about how it should be referred to. It has otherwise variously been called the testimony on stewardship, the testimony to sustainability, the testimony to creation. There are problems with all of these. Stewardship in itself is no bad thing but some Friends are very conscious of its role in the Christian tradition in allowing humans to exploit the natural world, seen as subordinated to their needs. Sustainability is too close to technical jargon to make a good title for a testimony. Both the testimony to the earth and the testimony to creation might seem to some Friends to ignore the particular place of humankind as part of the natural world. We have chosen 'Testimony to the earth' as our working title.

3. Faith: inward and outward

'The core of the Quaker tradition is a way of inward seeking
which leads to outward acts of integrity and service. Friends
are most in the Spirit when they stand at the crossing point of
the inward and the outward life. And that is the intersection
at which we find community.'

(Parker J. Palmer, *A place called community*, p.27)

Recognition that faith involves action has remained a unifying feature of
twentieth century Quakerism. We have a precious freedom and strength
from not having to argue for this position. We are corporately convinced
that faith is not real unless lived out in the world. We know that faith is
not a theory and cannot be grasped by the intellect alone. In short, we
know the truth of what John Punshon wrote:

Many people think they are practising religion when they are in
fact only thinking about it. They do not realise that knowledge
of religious truth comes only through practice and is inaccessible
to thought alone. This is because religion is an activity and has
to be done to be understood.' (*Testimony and tradition*, p.75)

We are also clear that no aspect of life – however humdrum or however
controversial – is outside the workings of the spirit of love and of truth.

Learning to respond to the signs of our times, modern Friends have a double
resource in the Quaker tradition of inward waiting and active persistence.
This tradition calls for giving careful attention to the inward guide, in the
inspiration of the individual and in the discernment of the community,
and then matching this inward focus with the hard experience of living
out testimonies that are not at home in the world. The lessons of inward
waiting and outward persistence in the Quaker Way are as applicable
within our meetings as they are to the wider social challenges outside
our communities.
Janey O'Shea, *Living the way: Quaker spirituality and community*, p.64

'So say, so do', wrote George Fox. (*Sundry ancient epistles*, MSS vol. 47, p.36) Faith is about narrowing the gap between what we say about God's love and truth and how we carry that love and that truth into actions. Consistency of word and deed – and word and word – is a fiercely challenging inheritance. It is important to recognise that this is not merely a secular moral command; rather it arises directly from our understanding of the nature of God, who is pure integrity. Without integrity our spirituality is distorted and our relationship with God clouded. This is the foundation of our testimony to truth and integrity. For nothing that leads to God is based on the false or the hollow.

So, when we say that God is love, the integrity of our claim is known by the degree to which it is fulfilled in our lives. Proof of the pudding of our beliefs lies in what it tastes like to those who eat it. As truth requires the fusion of faith and action, so does love. For, as God is love, there can be no spirituality which is not 'for others'. Moreover, since we believe that there is that of God in everyone, we cannot love God without loving our fellow human beings. Our faith cannot be a secret garden; it is a process through which the walls which divide us from our sisters and brothers are taken down.

Even if the dominant cultural association of spirituality is with silence and solitude we have the words of Thomas Merton that such solitude is itself a means of deepening relationship, for 'it is deep in solitude that I find the gentleness with which I can truly love my brothers [sic]'. (*The sign of Jonas*, p.268) Even prayer – especially prayer? – which takes us into the deepest inwardness of the real self, is necessarily an opening up of ourselves to the needs of others. As Elisabeth O'Connor expresses it: 'If prayer does not drive us out into some concrete involvement at a point of the world's need, then we must question prayer.' (*Journey inwards, journey outwards*, p.28) If we could approach prayer in this light it would be as much the business of Quaker work as of Quaker life.

This close relationship of faith and action has not always been understood in exactly the same way, but it has remained in the bedrock of Quaker faith since this was laid down. We should celebrate this persistent witness, which time and again turns to the Epistle of James: 'What good is it, my Friends, for someone to say he has faith when his actions do nothing to show it.' (James 2:14)

I found myself wondering, in a type of examen of conscience, how far my life, worship and spirituality consisted more of concepts and words rather than of deeds and active involvement; more in the cliché rather than concrete living; ...

The curse of the cliché, as I see it, could be found, for instance, in a superb phrase such as 'deeds not creeds', when a rejection of set formulae of belief is not translated into much serious involvement in active testimonial living. I ask myself, therefore, whether my *not* having any fixed credo or set of accepted beliefs really does lead me to show clearly in my daily activities that I do have Quaker values which effectively and obviously influence my thoughts, words and deeds. Where are the deeds that prove that I have no need of creeds and that I have in fact passed beyond any empty profession and recitation of doctrinal and moral tenets into the practical living out in daily life of real Quaker testimonies? What can I point to as peace, simplicity, tolerance, etc. in practice?

Eric Baggaley, *Quaker monthly*, May 1995

Yet, for all its centrality and strength, this tradition is being undermined amongst Friends in Britain Yearly Meeting and needs whole-hearted reaffirmation. It is not so much that it is being explicitly attacked; but, indirectly, it is being weakened. I turn now to examine some of these ways in which faith and action are being divorced.

Being and doing

The first of the ways in which faith is sometimes weakened is about giving 'being' precedence over 'doing'. I shall approach it through a true story.

I was once at a weekend at Glenthorne. In beautiful weather and surroundings we were sitting outside having our final meeting for worship. There was much ministry on the restorative nature of the weekend, which I was glad of; but it came to me that it needed to be put into a creative relationship with the harsh realities of life for many today. As John Punshon put it, 'A religion that cannot absorb the rowdy, dirty and soiled side of life is not worth much.' (*Testimony and tradition*, p.76) After my ministry, a thoughtful Friend was led to respond, also in ministry, that it was all right to let ourselves 'be' rather than 'do' for once.

How would you have reacted? I wrote her a long letter about how I saw the relationship of 'being' and 'doing'. As I wrote, I came to see clearly that, like 'faith' and 'action', it is a false opposition. Like all such pairs of words, it tends to suggest that one can only be *or* do, one *or* the other. This is, of course, nonsense. We are when we do. Sometimes, it is true, our action is mechanical, so routine that it does not feed our sense of creativity nor relate in a vital way to our deepest values. It could be said that we are not truly 'present' – to ourselves or others – at such times. But at other times what we do creates in us states of awareness that heighten our sense of being and are truly spiritual resources – like compassion, or a steady sense of faithfulness, or solidarity with others.

As we 'are' when we 'do', so a state of 'being' is also a form of 'doing': all our more inward 'activities', like thinking, dreaming, reading and contemplating are also ways in which we are created or recreated in our relationship to ourselves, the world and God. They are preparations always; whatever we use our time on renders us more or less fit. And, as with 'doing', these states of 'being' may be authentic or inauthentic, deep or superficial. Our inactivity may be sheer distractedness, may be as mechanical as our activity, or as untrue.

Being present where we really are is what counts; and true presence, in that sense, is a gift which knows no boundaries of 'being' or 'doing'. The spiritual dimension lies in the quality of each. And 'quality' here means attention, integrity and the transcendence of self. Those qualities are not easy to achieve, whether in reflection or in action but they apply to both. Unthinking use of a polarising opposition between 'being' and 'doing' obscures rather than reveals this truth.

I sense a danger here for contemporary Quakerism. To prioritise 'being' over 'doing' is to break apart the unity of faith-in-action/action-in-faith. This leaning towards 'being' indicates perhaps the influence of the personal growth movement within contemporary Quakerism with its emphasis on nurturing one's self. The weariness of years of struggle against damaging social policies may also have created an understandable reaction. But the connection with a privatised spirituality, more at home with the search for personal serenity than with the struggle for justice, is clear. And yet, 'The inner life is not nurtured in order to hug to oneself some secret gain', in Elisabeth O'Connor's words. 'Is not'? or 'should not be'?

Busyness

Secondly, an argument surfaces more and more frequently that Friends are too busy doing things and cannot nurture their spiritual life. This complaint is almost always misconceived. It is never developed to show that Friends who do less are spiritually more deeply grounded than those who do more – and from my experience I doubt whether that could be done. There are certainly Friends who at times are overstretched; but there are equally Friends who may be understretched. The issue should be looked at in a quite different way – whether we're busy or idle. Is the use of our time held in the light? Does our activity or inactivity feed us and do we sense deeply its rightness? Are we preserved in our busyness from all sense of self-importance and in our inactivity from all sense of complacent self-centredness?

Our spiritual responsiveness is not a given quantity. Sometimes a flow of energy can be given to us easing our weariness when we had thought that we were at the limits of our strength; often this will be through a sense that we are in tune with the source of all Light in what we have taken on. Without denying that we all have our different limits, it is striking how our energy may be renewed by the spirit, if we are alive to it. For example, at the end of a long monthly meeting, if we have remained centred, the spirit in the meeting may well help us to overcome our impatience and respond creatively to the concerned Friend with a late message, rather than to bristle with resentment. The spiritual issue is not whether or not we are busy but whether the use of our time is in the hands of our self or the Godself within.

Spirituality as a separate realm

My third instance of the weakening of the mature Quaker understanding of faith comes from a reflection on the renewed emphasis on our spiritual nurture in the last twenty years or so. I am not opposing such initiatives; they have been important for the life of the yearly meeting and the source of much good. It is my conviction, however, that they have had unintended negative side effects: in particular, they have encouraged Friends to place 'spiritual nurture' in opposition to 'social witness', which is then increasingly envisaged as a purely human activity.

This danger has been intensified by the financial crises which have affected our corporate central finances. Faced with the prospect of diminishing resources Friends felt the need to concentrate on the 'essential' aspects of the work of the Society; and the essential was about spiritual nurture, implicitly opposed to witness – as though witness was not spiritual, nor nurture. In the words of a Meeting for Sufferings' minute, which called for larger deductions to be made in corporate witness work than elsewhere: 'we affirm that it is our spiritual life which is the heart and essence of our living witness. We must keep our meetings.' 'Spiritual life'? As opposed to what other sort of life that we have? Surely, our spiritual life is the totality of our dedication to following God; our non-spiritual life is our inattention to the promptings of love and truth.

When we associate spirituality primarily with meeting for worship, contemplation, retreats, states of the soul and the beauties of nature and art, rather than equally with work, inequality, shopping, gang violence, and the rape of our peat bogs, we prise apart what Friends over the centuries have held in unity, the inward and the outward components of faith.

If I were to ignore the way of life of the people I pass in the street because I was more interested in my own spiritual development, I would be just like the priest and the Levite who were doubtless full of sympathy and concern, but had more pressing business with God than helping the man who fell among thieves.
Testimony and tradition, p.78

The roots and the fruits

The final instance I shall give here, to show the danger that certain current Quaker themes present to faith-in-action, is the prioritisation of the roots over the fruits. For this popular metaphor is another way of asserting the primacy of the spiritual, by claiming that we need to grow good spiritual roots first, before we can fruit. The problem with this is that the assertion that we must get our spiritual life right *before* the rest separates out 'the spiritual' from the rest, as though 'the spiritual' was a distinct area of life rather than an understanding of all life in its ultimate significance.

The other problem is that the organic metaphor is taken too literally. Of course roots do produce plants which produce fruits. However, it is the fruits which are the seeds which first create the roots. The metaphor is cyclical not static. And that is our spiritual experience: we may grow through study or prayer, or by committed action or enforced changes of lifestyle or relationship. What really transforms us does not always result from study groups or contemplative retreats. If the emphasis on spiritual development is too 'study bound' we could find that not only is our service weakened by being downgraded in our priorities but that our spiritual life may shrivel for lack of substance. It may remain academic and poetic or bucolic and out-of-touch. Any static understanding of this metaphor is actually subversive of the testimony to the sacramental nature of the whole of life.

And now I've come to realise that this is very similar to what happens when I move towards activism. A bout of enthusiasm or the promptings of friends encourages me to engage with the issues in front of me. And as I take a step, however small, out of my 'comfort zone', I begin to discover what I really think, feel and believe. Activism needs practical and spiritual preparation but I find that I must not let my 'what ifs' disempower me from involvement.

My activism draws on spiritual roots to give it nourishment, grounding and discernment. Meanwhile, through activism, my spirituality comes alive and my inner life is fed with learning and insight.

Change, some say, starts inside people. It is spirituality we need to attend to at this time. Others say we should be active since it is world structures that need to change. My perception is that the tension between inner and outer change can be a creative one.

What I have rediscovered is that spirituality and activism are interdependent. Like the roots and leaves of a growing plant, they depend on each other for growth.

Amanda Wooley, 'Spirituality and activism' in *Making waves* (The newsletter of the *Turning the Tide* programme), No 8, August 1998 p.3

Conclusion

The primacy of the spiritual, whether in the form of prioritising being over doing or the roots over the fruits is, I believe, a real temptation for a number of Friends. Nevertheless it is not yet dominant in Britain Yearly Meeting. Faith-in-action is still clearly a fundamental feature of our Quaker life.

We might strengthen this feature still further if we were more aware of action as sometimes a means of spiritual growth rather than simply a consequence of it. The process of breaking through to new levels of spiritual awareness is by no means always the result of pure thought. It often comes from concrete engagement. Hence Baron von Hugel's advice to Evelyn Underhill was 'more than anything else he could suggest, to throw out the cerebral accent in her religion and to break open her heart to the needs of all, she should devote two evenings a week to "visiting the poor"' ... Do we recognise that we may need our hearts to be broken open if God is to be able to break through?

I wish you could meet some of the people who came to Faslane in August [1998]. I found them focused, dedicated and deeply committed, not just to this project but to non-co-operation with all that is humiliating and hurtful. Their diversity (in terms of nationality and religious tradition, as well as age and social background) was exciting, and their personal bravery inspiring. It was a privilege to be with them and to help them in their task.

We often talk about 'faith into action'. With me it was the other way around; action led me into faith. Eighteen years ago I was deeply into campaigning and running around with banners and all the rest of it. I sought out Friends at the time because of a deep personal fear for the future. Nuclear weapons were proliferating at such an alarming rate that I believed my children would not grow up. Membership of the Society has taught me about the deep interconnectedness of things: that urban violence, bullying in schools, the suffering of refugees and so on, are all linked and that they all come from the same place: a failure to respond to that of God in other people.

Caroline Westgate, 'Trident Ploughshares 2000: Building a culture of peace and non-violence', *earthQuaker*, Issue 28, Winter 1998

My experience of Faith-in-Action

All these words are not just intellectual positions which I have adopted out of pure reason. They are the fruits of my experience. I know that faith can be deepened – even refound – in action. I know that in 'doing' I have experienced states of 'being' that cannot be discovered in any other way.

In all my spiritual journey so far, the most powerful experience of a new quality of Light breaking through came about when I agreed to stand as a local candidate for the Labour Party in what was then a Conservative stronghold in North-East Fife. Previously my political activity had drawn on reserves of stubborn faithfulness just to keep attending meetings; but nothing transformative happened to me – and very little impact was made on anyone else! My engagement was too limited to open me up. However, campaigning had been nurtured into me and I threw myself into election campaigns year after year with tremendous intensity and utterly foolish zeal – since the cause was well-nigh hopeless and what I could achieve for the people of the area was minimal.

But I began to open my ears and eventually my heart to what the people in the old radical paper mill village of Guardbridge wanted to share with me: their sense of loss of political faith, their conviction that no-one cared about them, their cynicism and confusion. As I did so – several times for an hour or more on the doorstep or in people's homes – it was my heart that was opened up by the openness and pain of those who spoke with me. My heart went out to them with a flowing intensity which I had never experienced before. And the experience lasted beyond the particular occasion in an almost physical sense of being 'drawn out towards'. And then it became a way into prayer, which had been very difficult for me without an orthodox sense of a personal God. Doing and being were one.

Eventually I was led to change my job and to work, and later to live, amongst people like those in Guardbridge who had given me something immensely precious. That took time, while my 'creaturely' self wanted to hang on to many tangible and intangible things. As the transformation worked its way in me, reading and meeting for worship also played their part. St Andrews Meeting was a small, lively meeting; we came to meeting for worship and to preparative and monthly meetings to try to discern the things that really mattered. It was as though something transforming might happen at any time in the fellowship of the meeting and in meeting for worship itself.

For me, the decisive shoves occurred when its midweek meeting studied John Woolman, whom I had not read before. Here was a life which demonstrated an inspiring consistency of word and deed. The challenge of that reading shadowed me in meeting for worship. I was led to minister in ways that called me to a position that I had not yet reached, and then demanded a greater consistency between the words I uttered and the life I lived.

So the servant of the Lamb, the spiritual warrior, keeps a balance between the active and contemplative sides of the soul, the religious and the practical. Though we are looking at each separately, we must never forget that in the full Quaker tradition, they are inseparable.
Testimony and tradition, p.84

However that ministry spoke to others, it certainly played its part in changing me. The final nail was driven home by Sewell Harris' ministry at Yearly Meeting in Warwick in 1982 in which he quoted from John Drinkwater's poem, *A prayer*. The final stanza reads:

> Knowledge we ask not – knowledge thou hast lent,
> But, Lord, the will – there lies our bitter need,
> Give us to build above the deep intent
>   The deed, the deed.

4. Testimony as a defence against a secular world

The growth of the secular

When I was appointed to my university post in St Andrews in 1964 I went up there with Emily to look for a house, 'as one does'. I was an active birthright Friend and Emily an involved attender. What did we bring to bear on the search? Our preferences and our dreams: we wanted a house with character, a large garden, secluded and fruitful, and spaciousness to allow for our self-expression. Such dreams were only tempered by what we could afford. And we bought the Poffle, which promised to realise all of those dreams; and we loved our twenty years there. It didn't occur to us to consider the political implications of such a major spending decision. And it didn't occur to us that we needed to take the decision through the guidance of our Quaker faith: the testimonies to community, to simplicity and to equality didn't so much as emerge from the back of our minds. That's where they were vaguely persisting as pale relics of a dated Quaker culture.

Of course, we can see all too clearly now that our purchase of the Poffle was a purely secular transaction. And that, in turn, means that the whole of our life was not lived sacramentally – whatever we believed and said at the time. And, indeed, that was just one area of our life that we lived on automatic pilot, absorbing and acting on the manifold promptings of the spirit of the age. There were others, as it is important to show, not for any confessional pride, but simply because I believe the experience to be representative; almost all of us, at some time, and in some aspects of our lives, will have been living on secular automatic pilot.

If I am right that the example of our purchase of the Poffle is representative for Friends in this country, the first task is to understand it – my analysis will show how the growth of secularism has permeated the members of Britain Yearly Meeting (BYM) from the cultural climate of the age, and how its power to affect us has increased hugely in the three hundred years and more since Quakerism began. The second task is to become more aware that this secularising process saps our spiritual power and undermines our testimony to the sacramental nature of the whole of life; it threatens to restrict our sense of what is spiritual to the so-called private and inner world of the soul. And our third task is to build up our resistance to it.

That, I then conclude, is precisely why testimony is so vital to Quaker experience. Secularisation promotes an accommodation with the times, which destroys our ability to judge them in terms of faith. Testimony, on the other hand, enables us to approach the daily world through the prism of faith.

The cultural overview

'The Church is no longer the central focus of life. One of its functions after another has been taken from it and left it stripped like an autumn tree.' (Rufus Jones, Friends World Conference Report 1937, p.8)

For more than three hundred years in Western Europe we have been living in a culture which has pushed God out of one area of human activity after another; so much so that several times God has been declared dead. This process was, in very important ways, a liberation of reason, science and individual creativity from the shackles of superstition and absolutism.

This human adventure replaced the all-embracing absolutism of the Catholic world view with a more fragmentary, subjective view of truth: it replaced the authority of religion by reason; it subverted traditional wisdom by science and the individual's unfettered right to question. In the process all the old absolutes were undermined. Philosophically, these included truth and beauty and justice; socially they included the organised church, the institutions of justice and the ruling elite. It overthrew the divinely appointed social order, replacing it with representative government and, later, democracy. Its political philosophy was liberalism and its economic order capitalist. And its tendency was always towards secularising human understanding. In other words, its understanding of the human adventure was that of humankind inhabiting a world without any higher purpose: the material world is all that there is. Its end point, then, is the autonomous individual as the sole judge of right and wrong in a world devoid of transcendence and of meaning.

In such a culture how can we truthfully live every aspect of our lives in ways that show forth our knowledge and our experience of the sacramental everywhere?

The economic overview

> Marcuse's *One-dimensional man* ... also spoke more widely of
> the cultural effect of a society geared almost exclusively to
> rapidly increasing consumption. He described it as a society in
> which all the options in life were available within the present
> system, because they could be bought. Television, along with
> other technological media, has penetrated private life to
> provide many of the satisfactions that were previously found
> in church or chapel. (Rex Ambler, 'On looking back into the
> future', in *Agenda for prophets*, p.114)

The development of the economy has, of course, been one of the principal
ways in which secular values have been universalised, with the yardstick of
money achieving primacy in many areas of life. The difference between the
mid-seventeenth century and the end of the twentieth century is immense.
In the past the market place was somewhere to be visited occasionally. But in
modern 'Western' conditions the market place is omnipresent. Its messages
are so all-enveloping that they are woven into the very texture of our lives.

To change the metaphor, it's like background radiation. We are irradi-
ated with information and temptations, morning, noon and night. Much of
it from 'the world of getting and spending'. We are the first society to be
defined more by its modes of consumption than of production; the first
society where shopping has become not a search for the necessities of life
but a leisure activity.

The capitalist market economy reaches into more and more parts of
human life to give them monetary value. It commands everything, including
sometimes sexual relations, votes, life itself. Everything – it is said – has its price.

The capitalist system depends on making people want 'something else';
it has to create wants in order then to meet them. In doing so, it relies on
an elite to lead the process of consumption so that the rest of us can aspire
to follow – you can visit the luxury dream world of yesterday's wealth, on
safari in Africa or sipping Bacardi on that Caribbean beach! The creation of
wants is much more dynamic than in pre-market economies and drenches
us in consumerist aspiration as never before.

Between them, the cultural and the economic factors that make for
secularisation squeeze religion out of most areas of life, leaving it on the
margins as a special activity for a minority. Religious language is little
encountered in business, politics and leisure – except as metaphor; it has

only a marginal place in most educational and media contexts. Although it does still accompany the key stages of life – birth, marriage and death – it does so as a tradition without great vitality. In much ordinary conversation it is totally absent. Secularisation, then, is culturally and economically dominant. We are immersed in an atmosphere in which 'man' [sic] is seen as an 'economic animal' pursuing his self-interest under skies swept clean not only of the 'old man with a beard' but of all transcendence.

The impact on contemporary Quakerism

Friends for much of their history tried to protect themselves from 'the world'. At first they made a clear distinction between living as renewed by the spirit and living in the world's way. Later they kept themselves visibly separate from the world by dress, language and the like. This status as a 'peculiar people' began to be discarded in the mid-nineteenth century. Since then the Society in Britain has moved steadily towards an accommodation with contemporary culture. Quaker spirituality is increasingly stamped with the experimental and rationalist temper of the times.

Most commentators see that change as positive: it seemed to bring to a close the period when Friends were stuck in a backwater, culturally impoverished, intellectually stagnating, and declining in numbers.

At the same time as Friends moved closer to the dominant intellectual framework of the age, they also identified increasingly clearly with the democratic system and its associated aspiration towards social progress and greater equality. They felt that democracy and ethical socialism were steps on the way to the Kingdom of God. Since no fundamental conflict existed between world and spirit, Friends could identify with the former, in its trajectory at least, if not entirely with its existing state. It is this spirit of accommodation which increases the danger of Friends espousing the values of the times without questioning whether they accord with the fundamentals of our faith.

Why have we been so vulnerable to the encroachment of the secular world view? Firstly, if the Enlightenment was the moment when the transcendental and the absolute were tamed by the human and the relative, then contemporary Quakerism is certainly its heir; with our largely immanent faith in that of God within we have little sense of another dimension, little sense of a world beyond our own. The black and white world of prophecy and of early Friends has dissolved into shades of grey.

Secondly, the Society, in its increasing identification with the world, has implicitly accepted the long-standing process of secularisation. We are all immersed in a world of secular interpretations of almost everything. According to Caroline Graveson, 'a larger proportion of our [Friends'] time is spent in secular occupation than ever before'. (*Religion and culture*, p.19) The phrase 'secular occupation' tells a tale. Surely if all life is sacramental, even the apparently secular is in reality sacramental.

What is certainly true is that Friends today spend a far higher proportion of their time in contexts which are secular – work, voluntary organisations, leisure, the media. In the past much more time was spent in Quaker contexts, whether on Quaker business or simply with an extended Quaker family and Quaker friends. What is important in this is the transmission of values. Friends today spend a much greater part of their time absorbing the values conveyed by the secular media and the forces of capitalist consumerism than was previously the case. Early Friends by contrast absorbed the values of their Quaker community rather than those of the world at large.

A letter to *The Friend* aptly illustrated this by complaining of the frequency of its publication and, therefore, the excessive time demanded for its reading. This strikes me as an extraordinarily revealing example of a prevailing Quaker belief that we can be Quakers in a secular world effortlessly. It seems that we are not only wary of indoctrinating others but also ourselves. We are in danger of becoming – to coin a word – 'undoctrinated' Friends.

I have tried to show how the growth of secularism has permeated BYM from the cultural climate of the age. I believe that secularisation saps our spiritual power and undermines our testimony to the sacramental nature of the whole of life. Accommodation with the times destroys our ability to judge them in terms of faith. Before I look at what we can do about this, let's look at our experience of these matters.

Personal examples

I have shown how, in my life, my choice of housing started off as a purely secular matter. Are most Friends affected by this secularising process? Let's see by asking ourselves whether we treat the following issues as spiritual questions. In other words do we approach them from the point of view of our own advantage or the service of God?

- Our paid or unpaid work
- Where we live

- What we do with windfall gains and legacies
- Whether we use private schools or health systems
- Whether we use the car only when absolutely essential
- Whether we buy strawberries flown in out of season or not
- Whether we fly out to Israel on holiday
- Whether we buy organic food, even if it is more expensive

Am I right that many of these decisions are taken in a thoroughly secular way by most Friends – as many others are by me?

Let me give another personal example. Although I have always cycled to work I can well remember using the car freely and easily. In the late 1960s and the 1970s we regularly travelled down from St Andrews to Swansea where both sets of our parents lived. We didn't ask ourselves what the impact of the journey for good and evil would be. We got into the car and went. Now most journeys are open to question: can we go by public transport or walk or cycle? If we can, can we also make the additional time needed (usually!) available, bearing in mind that train journeys can *save* time through reading or writing compared with the car, even if travelling takes longer? We know that the cost of the car is fearful, in air pollution, noise pollution, lost natural habitat, and injury and death to humans and millions of animals. So how do we assess our personal convenience against those costs? Do we do so in the Light?

It is so easy to let habit rule us; we can also be easily swayed by prevailing expectations. Take, for example, the issue of hospitality: do we pay as much attention to the ill effects of our car use on other people as to the face-to-face 'kindness' in offering to drive people about, perhaps sometimes when there really is no need? Transport is, therefore, a question of prayer as well as of politics; both need to be practised in our lives.

It is much the same story with my choice of investments, of food and of holidays. This last is perhaps a good example to take as Quaker sensitivity has not developed so far on holidays as on other choices. Often, when we have held workshops on the topic, its relevance seems not to have been generally understood. Friends talk about where they have been and how they have enjoyed it in much the same way as most people do: food, drink, scenery, comfort, trips. It is a thoroughly secular area of most people's lives. For us too, for many years we simply went to the places we fancied, at home or abroad. Now we try to consider the impact of our travel arrangements, the nature of the regime in the country concerned, the environmental impact and the social impact on the population in the tourist area.

So what was my spirituality when it hardly reached all those parts of my life? It was cramped, partial and unfaithful to the most fundamental Quaker doctrine of them all – that the whole of life is sacramental. (In other respects it still is.) It had been secularised without my being the least bit aware of it. The end result of these zones of exclusion, unless we are very careful, is a sort of private spirituality. We can only avoid this by learning to want to see our actions through the Light shed by divine truth. Sometimes slowly, sometimes much faster, we may come to see where our lives have been colonised by the secular spirit of this time and relearn a different mode of living illuminated by the spirit of God.

Practising resistance

Sharpening polarities

I have argued that secular assumptions have colonised us and that our spirituality is in danger of being confined to the special 'reservations' that are left. I have also argued that the reason why we have proved to be so much more vulnerable to the blandishments of the secular than early Friends is because early Friends had the defence of the doctrine of the two worlds – being *in* the world but not *of* it – which we have discarded for a much more monist view. Have we lost something that could help us resist?

Most Friends today would certainly be strongly opposed to anything that suggested a separation from the world. We want to be in the world. We value the sense of being a part of our communities and bound up with them in the struggle for a world which reflects God's love. The question is this: in our desire to be fully *in* the world do we find ourselves drawn into being all too often *of* it as well?

The values of faith are diametrically opposed to the values of the market. Love, truth, peace, community, equality, point to an other-centredness wholly at odds with the market's relentless appeal to the self. Our faith values, therefore, necessarily stand in judgement on the values of the market, whatever the latter's success in 'delivering the goods'. It is not just that the values of faith and the market differ. The values which are central to our faith are under sustained attack by the economic system as such. I use the metaphor advisedly. Powerful forces are out to persuade us: out there thousands and thousands of people are devoting their intelligence to persuading us to buy what they sell – and to leave our spiritual values behind in the meeting house. Their mission is to change us. Getting us to buy this and that is simpler if we can be persuaded to buy their value system as a whole. And the value system of these modern missionaries of the market is unashamedly materialistic.

We too often ignore the realities of struggle and power; we fail to understand that the world is always an arena in which different value systems are locked in struggle. And that, whatever the complexity of the issues, in an ultimate sense, faith has to take sides. That's what early Friends knew experimentally and that's how they kept the world's values at bay.

And so how we defend our faith values against the seemingly all pervasive and relentless propaganda of the market is not just a social question; it is at the very heart of our faith: can we learn that our struggle to resist the reflex to buy cheap when we can, but rather to buy well, taking into account the impact on the producer, the consumer and the environment, for example – that such struggles are essential to the integrity of our spiritual search? We have to choose: either we acquiesce, more or less uneasily, in the dominant – secular – values, or we emerge from the relative comfort of accommodation into the harsher – but so much more fulfilling – world of dissent.

I suggest that our 'resistance' needs two complementary approaches. On the one hand, the strategic campaign with its implications for corporate stance and action. On the other, the tactical, the slow development of alternative practice, in our daily lives. Each suggests in its different modality the requirement to consciously oppose 'the world' by our lives.

A strategic stance

The nature of currents is that it is easier to swim with them than against them. The currents of market society are very strong. Even if we are swimming against them we may be swept along downstream. But how many of us float on the current much of the time, implicitly accepting its direction, even enjoying the ride?

So the testimonies had a political as well as a personal dimension. Moreover, the spiritual vision of which they were the expression was one of victory. The reflections on the crucifixion with which I began were intended to underline this point with great emphasis. The cross was a means, not an end, but it was a necessary means. The invitation to give up the world's weapons opens us up to insecurity and fear. Only if we

have the power to overcome these natural human reactions will we be
able to resist the pressure to conform to the world's ways.
Testimony and tradition, p.29

Only a polarised understanding of the market's demonic assault on our
spiritual values has any chance of matching the scale of the onslaught. Yet
contemporary easy-osey Quakerism assumes a blurred world in which
divergent values gently jostle for position – quite unlike the sharply delineated
world of *Pilgrim's progress* or George Fox's *Epistles* where Truth and error
contend. There, world and faith are at opposite poles. If the sharp deterioration
in social conditions in our generation doesn't jolt us into rediscovering this,
nothing will.

So far, alas, it has hardly done so. We have responded to that deterioration
fitfully rather than strategically. We have not taken a vigorous and consistent
stance against the forces that destroy our testimonies and our faith –
secularisation, inequality, consumerism, the destruction of the natural
world etc. That is, in part, a matter of taking a public stance, which we are
sometimes too reticent about; and partly of being prepared to plunge in
faith into the areas of political influence and seek to put our testimonies
into practice. We too often remain at home in a world of alternative voices,
not a world of opposing forces.

Daily tactics

But how can we maintain in our daily lives a sense of the ongoing
baptism of the spirit, instead of letting the tide of secularised materialist
values saturate us? The public world of commercial transactions, of advertising
and the rest measures everything on the scale of self-interest. It is true that
Friends, by and large, have not 'bought into' this ideology as readily as into
the cultural processes that have accompanied it. Nevertheless we have not
found a way of creating a consistent stance, still less a practice, of opposition
to it. We seem not to have fully woken up to the enormous power of the
materialist ideology which is exerted over us and of our spiritual need to
resist it.

And that means seeing it as spiritual struggle – the Lamb's War. This
will engage us in a daily skirmishing against the assumptions of the secular
world. And that is about finding ways of liberating ourselves from subjection
to the encroaching and secularising power of the market. Ways – some of
which I suggested in my introduction – in which faith takes over areas of

our lives which were once outside its 'scope'.

> To become a Friend is to opt for a tradition which does this (practice of the ordered life) in a particular and distinctive way. The image of the Lamb's War actually utilises one of the deepest springs of human action, the defensive response to threat. In the ordered life, there is thus an element of self-protection and personal preparation. Making this a source of moral worth and spiritual strength is the great merit of the spirituality of the testimonies.
>
> *Testimony and tradition,* p.84

Elizabeth O'Connor shows how easy it is to be infiltrated by secular values: 'We', she writes, 'who would be shaped by Christ are shaped by headlines and the counsel of friends who do not know Him.' (*Journey inwards, journey outwards*, p.2) I recognise the diagnosis. You can save tax by fictitiously charging your wife or husband for cleaning the room you use at home for an office; your bike is stolen when it was not locked securely and you invent a story to cover your mistake; you charge personal expenses to your business account; you are happy to get that repair done cheaper by paying cash in hand, knowing full well that it will escape the tax net. Almost everyone does that sort of thing at times.

These small daily decisions are in some ways the hardest tests because it is so easy for them to appear to be outside the scope of our spirituality. It is easier to follow unthinkingly the conventional wisdom of the secularised world. That's why we need to be led to consciously exercise our faith in the market place day-to-day, winning back lost ground little by little, reclaiming wherever we can a sense of the materiality of our spiritual lives and the spirituality of our material lives.

That is why I have stressed the importance of our daily lives: litter-picking, shopping, travelling, money and the like. This is what I was given to say to the Manchester Centenary Conference:

> After I get up in the morning and make myself a cup of tea, I go out to clean stretches of road and a corner of the park near my house. It's my round. I enjoy it. It's a tiny bit of exercise. It 'keeps me low', protecting me from any temptation to think that I'm too important for 'that sort of work' ... it feels like a sort of prayer in action. In the tiniest way it's a concern: in my

eyes, accumulations of litter everywhere not only degrade what loveliness there is but speak of an attitude of mind which is locked into self-centredness; and so, in tending 'my patch', I can protest against the individualism of the times. Although I do it in a non-judgemental spirit, nonetheless it is an expressive action which hopes to silently speak to others, especially those who create the litter. Whether it does or not I'm not sure! The younger children show a total incomprehension as to why anyone should ever pick up litter at all! Well, if all it does is to keep parts of the estate cleaner on a daily basis, so be it.

The wonderful thing about exercising our spirituality in these humdrum areas of our lives is that they are always with us. And, therefore, our sense of the sacramental nature of the whole of life is constantly reinforced; our faith values are constantly set against the world's values; spiritual growth has important concrete manifestations as we learn to eat, to travel, to go on holiday, and the rest, sacramentally. Discipleship and spiritual pilgrimage will become real experiences rather than vague aspirations. Our spirituality will be renewed by extending its reach.

That has certainly been my experience.

Testimony as a defence against secularisation

These things may begin with an act of personal choice, but each of them, if consistently carried out, amounts to a fairly radical departure from generally accepted norms of behaviour. In the past they aroused adverse comment and considerable hostility, and could do again. Hence, such principles, and the conduct that flows from them are potentially, and sometimes, actually, socially disturbing. (*Testimony and tradition*, p.26)

Testimony could be a focus of resistance. Indeed, as the impact of a secularising mentality increases, testimony becomes all the more vital. In the end we need the illumination of social testimony to lead us into spiritual wholeness, to a place where all things – from our perusal of our bank statements to our trip to the filling station – are held in our hearts in the Light of God's loving truth.

Let me show how my daily litter picking round is more than it seems – as well as being my half hour's quiet time to start the day. At its most basic it is, of course, just a way of cleaning the streets. But it's more than that: it shows in practical action the need to respect the world, which is becoming a contemporary testimony. It has implications for equality in its acceptance of the menial. It has implications for community in that it implies a rejection of the individualistic self-centredness of the litter dropping mentality in favour of community spirit. It also asserts my responsibility for the public realm over and above the payment of taxes; and, in the context of an estate where the effects of destructive forces are visible almost every hour of the day, it offers a visible sign of an alternative, more hopeful way of living. And, as much as anything, it is a practice of faithfulness in the face of cynics who say, shrugging their shoulders, that 'the litter will be just as bad tomorrow so what's the point'?

Seeing a particular action as testimony deepens its significance. It reminds me that I am testifying to the values of faith which lie so much *deeper* than self-interest, but which can so easily be obscured by it. In this way we become more aware of the sacramental in everything: everything that we do becomes part of a whole faith and not just a series of separate actions on separate issues. And so faith becomes more continuously real. In so far as testimony leads us down below the surface of the dominant social values of our times, it becomes our indispensable defence against the forces of secularisation and individualism, which have become so powerful both in society at large and amongst many Friends.

So, when we reflect on our choice of mode of travel, of food, of holidays, and of everything else can we say 'yes, they are spiritual issues; I haven't reached clarity about them all but I am wrestling with them'? If not, whose message is being spoken by our lives? – almost certainly the message of whatever secular social convention is the norm. The role of testimony can be to bring us to an awareness of the connections between all these aspects of our life and our Quaker faith. It will help us to resist the encroachment of the secular.

> It [religion] has now played out its role as a political ideology, partly because the conflicts in religion have been unresolved and partly because its hopes and promises have to some degree been fulfilled in a secular form, for example in the movement towards democracy and economic equality. But its hopes have

not been fulfilled for everyone, or completely fulfilled for anyone. So for those who are still close to the minority tradition of Christianity it will continue to play at least a compensating role in personal and social life. It is quite possible that as times get harder, as the economic crisis begins to disrupt our long-standing social stability, this personal religion will have a revival, as it did in the mid-nineteenth century. But there is an alternative future which for some Christians still is much closer to the historic impetus of Christianity. In this prospect Christianity can and should be embodied in a prophetic community, accepting its minority role but relating its specific religious practice to a wider secular practice for the transformation of society.' (Rex Ambler, 'On looking back into the future', *Agenda for prophets*, p.115)

5. Testimony: its implications for lifestyle and politics

Introduction

Testimony, as an earlier section makes plain, is the way in which we express our convictions about the relationship of humankind to God and to each other. How can we express these leadings in such a way that they speak to others? The two main ways are: on the one hand, by demonstrating to others what we believe through the multiplicity of choices we are able to make in our ways of living – lifestyle, if you like; on the other, by encouraging society to embody our convictions through adaptations to the policies and institutions which provide the framework for the lives we lead – that is to say, politics.

So lifestyle and politics are equally vital aspects of a fuller practice of testimony. We do not have to choose between them, indeed we must not. Rather we might question the way in which our language works. It seems to suggest an opposition between lifestyle and politics, yet is not politics an essential part of our lifestyle? Or *should* it not be, at least? For the time we choose to give to nurture our vision of the kingdom and to realise it, albeit so very partially, in the public life of the nation and the wider world, is surely a choice which is properly also part of our style of living.

As Mary Lou Leavitt writes – in relationship to the peace testimony, but the point is equally applicable to all other social testimonies:

> Living out a witness to peace has to do with everyday choices about the work we do, the relationships we build, what part we take in politics, what we buy, how we raise our children. It is a matter of fostering relationships and structures – from personal to international – which are strong and healthy enough to contain conflict when it arises and allow its creative resolution. (*The Quaker peace testimony: a workbook for individuals and groups*, p.3)

This essay attempts to show that contemporary conditions require us to respond to the leadings from our testimonies, both in the areas of life in which we can act independently (albeit within very strong influences from historical forces) and in those where we must rely on persuading larger groups to take action together – in lifestyle and in politics.

For when we work to change the whole without seeking to embody in our present lives the values we are striving to incarnate in the wider society, we are divided and without wholeness; the validity of our work for change will be undermined by its contradiction in our way of life.

On the other hand, to work only on the life choices within one's own – albeit partial – control, whilst ignoring the controlling context set by government measures, is to limit our awareness of how our testimonies are powerfully affected by public policy. This is certainly the greater danger for Friends.

It is my conviction that, if changed lives contribute to changed policies, it is also true that changing policies changes the ways we live our lives. That view is shared by Grigor McClelland, who argues that *Witness to Truth*, the Truth and Integrity in Public Affairs publication, is wrong to see personal transformation as a precondition for social change, to assume that the heart must always be changed first; and he quotes the phrase, 'It is precisely and only from each person's integrity that ... the transformation of our ... institutions' will follow. (*Witness to Truth*, p.16) His view is that we should not oppose structural reform and personal spiritual regeneration and prioritise one over the other; instead we should see society and the individual as mutually shaping each other.

So, let me be more concrete and take the example of genetically modified (GM) foods. Let us, for the sake of argument, assume that such foods are, at least in the context of present knowledge, an unpredictable risk both to our own health and to other species. If so, it will surely be obvious that the attempt to adopt a GM free diet will be successful only if the framework of law enables it. Unless there is a governmental strategy to ensure that individuals who are opposed to GM foods can avoid them – by labelling and other measures – it would be almost impossible for an individual to do so. Moreover, even if government ensures that individuals are able to keep to a GM free diet, that is absolutely no guarantee that the use of GM foods won't endanger wildlife for everyone, those refusing to eat GM foods and those eating them equally. Clearly lifestyle without politics is not enough.

We need to be reminded of this because Christianity has unfortunately been more at home in the ethics of personal relationships than in public policy. We can see this distortion at work through the usually individualistic and philanthropic interpretation of the story of the Good Samaritan. This is my reworking of the story: 'Leaving the theatre one bitterly cold night in 1995, a Good Samaritan comes across a distressed young woman huddled in a doorway. She learns the girl is seventeen, has run away from home and, after begging all day, has just been robbed of her earnings. She takes her back to her comfortable and spacious suburban home, gives her one of her three spare bedrooms, feeds her and, next morning, takes her to a homelessness agency.' (Adapted from the spoken version of my Swarthmore Lecture, May 1996)

That's more than most of us would do. She seems a 'Good Samaritan' indeed. But, at the last General Election she had voted for the party that ruthlessly cut the housing programme and stripped almost all sixteen and seventeen year olds of the right to benefit, and, therefore, to housing. She pushed hundreds of youngsters onto the streets, and helped one.

Our Good Samaritan's face-to-face practical love is inspiring; but she hasn't seen the connection between the spirit of her act and the political world. Nor, one could add, has she seen the connection with her lifestyle – she is part of the problem because she is taking more than her fair share of the nation's available housing provision.

Here we have the three ethical contexts: direct personal help in the name of love; the way in which one lives one's life – lifestyle – in the name of love; and one's contribution to the organisation of society as a whole – politics – in the name of love. These three are indivisible because a love which we express in one context and deny in another is a less than whole love. My Good Samaritan is so on the first count. But she is a Bad Samaritan on the other two.

In suggesting that restricting testimony to those lifestyle decisions which are in our direct control is an inadequate basis for testimony, I am not suggesting that they lack importance. On the contrary I believe that we should see them as a key part of our spiritual development. Every time we shop with our conscience, every time we hold an investment decision in the light, every time we consider whether to use the car or travel in a more humane way we are rediscovering the critical distance between our faith values and the values of the market and of secular society. Every time I think: 'Shall I use the car tonight? ... it's raining and I'm dead beat – but I've got good rainwear and good legs ... no I'll not give in to the siren voice of comfort' (though at other times I doubtless, and sometimes rightly, will), I am testifying to who I am and, through that, testifying to something that lies much deeper than my material advantage or comfort. Such decisions, whether I'm faithful or whether I succumb to convenience or whim, are the stuff of prayer. Every tiny decision, taken in the light, reclaims the world of secular, routine practices, for God.

Implications for lifestyle

When I became a Traidcraft representative in Mount Street Meeting in Manchester it was a creative discipline which helped me to realise that the way I lived, the way I spent my money, expressed the values that mattered to me, whatever I *said* they were. I had been brought up to live frugally and to buy cheaply. What Traidcraft taught me was that I needed to pay more, not to flaunt my purchasing power, but to be just a little bit fairer to those people producing the food – otherwise what did the Quaker testimony to equality amount to? Buying cheaply was only superficially responding to the testimony to simplicity if it exploited the labour of others. So, gradually, I began to buy from my own stall more and more of the things I needed, no doubt helped by the fact that it was 'my' food going out of date if I didn't! I even bought the Chinese dates, which at that time were dry and tough, rather than better quality and cheaper ones in general commerce. But that made me realise how few Friends saw it as an opportunity to shift their purchasing power and use it as a spiritually informed influence for right relationships on a global scale. It seemed more like a charitable gesture of support. I used to ask myself: Do they not eat or drink many of those products? Is it just that they can't easily afford to? – as I could. I knew that was true for some. But others seemed just not to have made the connection: they were content to make a gesture towards fairness; but, in reality, the coffee they liked from commercial sources, or the dates or whatever, counted most.

There is no part of our lives which does not depend on the chain of cause and effect linking us to the whole world and its resources. Consider how your smallest everyday choice as a consumer can touch the lives of faraway people and the earth itself. Inform yourself as fully as possible about these effects in order to make conscious decisions responsibly.
Redland Meeting, Environment Worship Sharing Group 1987, taken from *And the creation was opened unto me*, 11.25

But, of course, I was and am in essentially the same situation. In other respects I was just as insensitive to the impact my purchasing decisions were making on life on earth. I didn't buy *everything* I could have done from my own Traidcraft stall; I'm sure I still reserved some bulk buys for the cheaper supermarket shopping when the price differential seemed particularly great. Take another example: at the same time as I was feeling critical of my fellow Friends for not shifting their purchasing on principle into Fair Trade, I was buying non-organic foods. It's only recently that I've overcome the resistance to the price differential, even though I have been aware of how damaging contemporary farming methods are and am amongst those who could easily afford to do so. Or again, I'm only just getting past the feel-good factor at buying natural fibres rather than synthetics and am belatedly and slowly realising that my cotton purchases too need to be organic, because cotton growing involves a far greater use of chemicals than almost any other branch of farming.

I think that's what the experience of trying to live more closely in harmony with our testimonies is almost always like. We do something that feels right, but something else, which also feels right, we don't do, or don't do yet. We probably know someone else who does. Yet other areas of enlightenment have not even registered with us as questions. And this is true of us all. The Catholic tradition calls it the solidarity of sin, which forms a stratum of equality for the whole human race. But these bedrock strata contain also the universal urge to keep trying to get things right. None of us lead lives which are absolutely consistent, let alone in full harmony with all our testimonies. What matters is the direction in which we face and the movement we make to bridge the gap.

Lifestyle is, then, just shorthand for the way we live, and the way we live is the demonstration of how real our testimonies are. We create our testimonies day-to-day by the cumulating decisions that we take, which offset – to a greater or lesser extent – our self-interest with the will to truth, to simplicity, to peace, to community, to equality and to harmonious co-existence with the other elements of the natural order. As such it is integral to our sense of how the testimonies work through our lives.

Many of us live in the more prosperous areas of large cities, or within commuting distance of them. The accumulated decisions of all our neighbours help to determine what life is like for the people who live in the inner areas of those cities, and in the large isolated housing estates on their edges. Decisions about where to live, what forms of transport to use, where to spend money, where to send children to school, where to work,

whom to employ, where to obtain health services, what to condone, what to protest about, business decisions, personal decisions, political decisions – all these have an effect. Our first and greatest responsibility is to make those decisions in the knowledge of their effect on others.
Martin Wyatt, 1986, *QFP* 23.49

There are, of course, thousands and thousands of decisions we can take to make the world a more fulfilling and truly human place for all. Opportunity or burden? It is possible to feel overwhelmed by the range and the complexity of them. How can we cope with them? Certainly not with all equally and not all at once. Indeed, perhaps not all at all. We have to examine a few things closely until we have developed a practice that is automatic but not unthinking, leaving space for the next opportunity.

Sometimes too we may lack knowledge and sometimes we will lack the will. Sometimes our lack of will leads us to avoid the knowledge that would enlighten us. But a prayerful approach will help to find a direction through both uncertainty and complexity. This area has to be one of the central focuses for the exercise of our spiritual discernment. It is so, precisely because these decisions in all their ordinariness are routine parts of our daily life. They are inescapable. They are part of the continuous texture of our lives. They are not encountered in special places of spiritual retreat but are everywhere. So if they give us spiritual exercise, they will give us spiritual challenge and spiritual training all the time. If we do our shopping 'in the Light' we are likely to do most things likewise. And then we will know inwardly and not by rote what the sacramental nature of the whole of life really means.

I have written elsewhere of how we urgently need to recolonise the secular world for the spirit, and what better place to start than with the many decisions of getting and spending where the power of secular values is most awesome. That means discerning what it means for our relationship with God when we choose home-made sandwiches rather than take-aways; flasks not cans; water for the garden from the washing up rather than the tap; foodstuffs from Traidcraft and/or organic suppliers; bank accounts at Triodos or the Co-op. And so on. It is my experience that the greatest help is to know that we have made a start; that some areas of our lives have been held in the Light and that we have been shown things that should change and have changed some of them. The more the Light is followed, the deeper the joy and the readier we may be for a next step. If there is one spiritual virtue that, more than any other, comes to be known in this adventure it is the priceless one of faithfulness.

I offer this experience, which may connect with yours. At the end of the ten years wondering whether to change my career and move into the city, we asked for a meeting for clearness in our monthly meeting. It was a very useful occasion, where the Friends chosen to be with us asked us gently probing questions. One of the ones that I was asked went something like this: 'Are you sure you won't waste your particular talents by becoming a facilitating community worker? You have gifts of leadership which, as a community worker, you will have to hold in check; you can be a powerful speaker and you won't get the opportunity to exercise that gift. Wouldn't you be more useful to the people at the margins by being their advocate in the political world, or amongst Friends?'

I could see the power of this argument then, and I still do. The best use of one's talents has a good Biblical ring to it. And yet, what I have come to see is this: *I needed* that experience of working at the grass roots with so-called 'ordinary' (ugh!) people, often doing quite humdrum things. I needed it spiritually. It taught me so much about faithfulness. (And, ironically, in the end, it made possible my Swarthmore Lecture, which, otherwise, would have lacked the visceral sense of the challenge that the contemporary world has thrown down to our testimonies and might have drowned in the abstraction to which my mind tends to gravitate.) We may not always be led to do what is seen as what we do best.

The experience of living in Ordsall, choosing to be in community with the excluded, through a good deal of thick and some thin, has liberated me spiritually. It has been an apprenticeship in faithfulness. Yet faithfulness is something we all know in part. Let us be thankful for the measure we have been given so far, for faithfulness always calls us beyond where we have reached. I believe that the experience of faithfulness is perhaps more important than almost anything else in enabling us to accept God's nagging in those areas where we are dragging our feet for the time being.

That faithfulness – in living alongside people, absorbing some of the same shocks that come from the harsh individualism of street practice, or in the Quixotic faithfulness of the litter picking round, or whatever *your* practice may be – is also a quiet subversion of the values of the age, in the name of deeper values: those which, as Friends, we call testimonies.

In the face of the power of the values of the secular world, the key spiritual resource we possess is the accumulated and constantly enriched tradition of our testimonies. When we consider whether to buy cheap or to buy fair we have our testimonies to simplicity and to equality to guide our approach. When we consider whether to travel down to London by car or by train we have the testimony to the earth to help us. It is the testimonies which give us the possibility of standing aside from the spirit of the age, because through them we believe we are in touch with something underlying all human experience and which partakes of the nature of God.

The experience of each one of us will be different. My experience of a powerful progressive leading in these areas of life is offered, not at all as a model, but as one person's spiritual path. Like all such stories it has to be selective and is transparently not the whole truth, although I hope it is nothing but the truth.

In our case – and perhaps this is not representative – the shake-up in our lives, which increasingly forced us to ask how our lives reflected our Quaker beliefs, seems to have come not so much through the little everyday decisions, but rather through being shaken over the big questions of job, house and money.

I touched on my leading to change my job in the final pages of 'Faith: inward and outward'. I wrote that the change 'took time, while my 'creaturely' self wanted to hang on to many tangible and intangible things.' That phrase underplays the fearful resistance I put up against the leading. Indeed, such were my insecurities, I have to admit that I will never know whether I would have followed my leading, though it was strong and clear, if the University had not offered me a voluntary severance package. Yes, I know the reality of fear and the hands that close not in prayer but clutching insistently at material security. The thought that I might have refused the offer of the adventure that has so enriched my life – and, for a handful of gold, or rather the certainty of a comfortable pension, – is a central part of my story. I have learned several lessons from that leading. They include the following: you don't have to be perfectly ready to follow even a far-reaching leading; but, when you are prepared enough, all your anxieties in advance can be magically transformed into serene acceptance; when the leading is followed the strength has been made available and the challenges can be met in a – generally! – untroubled spirit.

It is a similar story with our choice of where to live. Let me remind you of what I said about our choice of the Poffle in Strathkinness, before progressing to the moves we have subsequently made. When I got a job in St Andrews University in 1964 we simply bought the cottage with character

and potential that we fell in love with. That decision was taken in a purely
secular way. We didn't consider the effect of our decision on the local
communities; we didn't consider whether our choice would tend to the
polarisation of housing according to class or not; whether it was part of a
process of deepening housing inequality; we didn't consider whether it would
increase our need to use the car, thus increasing pollution and worsening
global warming; we didn't explicitly consider the testimony to simplicity –
though, on reflection, the more ostentatious houses were ruled out.

Twenty years later when we moved from Strathkinness to Manchester,
where I had found my first community work job, we knew that the decision
was one which needed to be spiritually grounded. After all, my motivation
for my change in career clearly related to our testimonies to equality and to
community. I wanted to be with those who had increasingly become
marginalised. Once again, our response to that leading was slow and faltering.
We convinced ourselves that we couldn't face too much reality all at once;
so we decided that our daughter needed the only school in Manchester that had
something approaching the social mix of the neighbourhood comprehensive in
St Andrews. We bought a large Victorian semi-detached house in Didsbury.
(Ironically, that wasn't enough to get our daughter a place in the school;
she went to another school with a much less favoured intake and survived
– thanks to the presence of the daughter of Labour-supporting doctors, who
had on principle refused to buy their way out through the well-developed
public school system; and also to some dedicated teachers).

So we lived in Didsbury, and I worked first in Wythenshawe and then
in Ordsall. How could I be unaware of the paradox of our privileged
housing when I worked in Ordsall and lived in Didsbury; when I rode back
in the evenings and realised that I didn't need to scan the windows to see
whether they had been put in? There was never any doubt about the Light
and what it showed; the only doubt was about whether I wanted to be
shown. That's why it took ten years before we made the move into the
inner-city estate of Ordsall, in Salford, from the affluence of Didsbury. Now
Ordsall figures frequently in the news as a symbol of lawlessness, the sort
of place no-one in her or his 'right mind' (now there's a phrase worth
spiritual reflection!) would want to live in. Estate agents clearly did not
believe we had chosen to move in that direction; there must be a financial
crisis, a separation, a repossession story. Water doesn't flow uphill and people
don't choose to move to Ordsall. It's not in their interests. Self-interest is a one
way climb upwards. That is the anti-testimony of secular values, with which

our testimonies contend. I have never seen it more starkly demonstrated.

Why were we so slow? As usual it was fear: we were afraid of the greater prevalence of violence, which exercises power by ensuring that no-one ever witnesses against any local person in court, the hassle of having one's car stolen or vandalised, etc. Afraid, too, of not being able to sell the house once we had bought it. (Here again, we were in the privileged position of being able to buy elsewhere even if the worst came to the worst.) Living watchfully – and rarely in pubs! – some of these fears turned out to be exaggerated. Indeed, although our car was touched on the first night, and once since and we have had a couple of bricks through our windows, and the door kicked in, we have only spent small stretches of time in acute anxiety. However, there are few days when I don't see the evidence of fresh acts of crime or vandalism; I'm either intervening directly in or reporting a couple of hundred incidents a year. So we have had to learn to stay centred while being on the alert.

Yet we can honestly say that the whole experience has been an opening ... despite the plethora of railings and bars! Perhaps we needed to wait those ten years to reach the point where we were prepared for a move which cuts right across the expected trend of always upward social mobility. It is important also to acknowledge that by this stage there was growing reflection on our Quaker social testimonies, and that helped us to move in this and many other areas of our life much further and faster than would otherwise have been the case.

The other thing I learnt from those ten years waiting was that I needed to be nagged. And I think it is important to try to describe that experience. For those ten years I knew that our house was not in accord with the testimonies – possibly not to simplicity, nor to equality, but, more crucially, not to community. Increasingly housing was being polarised by income and council estates were becoming ghettos for the poorest and most disadvantaged people in our society. It didn't feel right to be part of that process. Of course it wasn't my family that was nagging me, nor my friends, still less – sadly? – Friends in my meeting. It was something else. It was quietly there again and again and again – part of the very fabric of our lives. It never let me go. It wasn't threatening. It wasn't paralysing. It wasn't a command. It was an inward conversation which always ended with my being shown how my lifestyle was inconsistent with my professed beliefs. It was infinitely patient and quietly persuasive. It was the Light in spoken form and it nagged me lovingly into something which I knew in my heart of hearts that I wanted to do, however long my resistance. It's like the problem of the noise that intrudes into meeting: it can destroy all intentness and communion if it is resisted; but, once accepted, it can be embraced in the silence itself. The nagging is needed; but it has to be accepted – and that means loved – if it is to work creatively in us.

There was never any doubt about what the Light showed; the only doubt was about whether I wanted to be shown.

The third major area I want to write about is money. I also don't want to write about it, because I know that, in this respect particularly, my life is still very divided. As Martin Luther wrote, 'There are three conversions necessary: the conversion of the heart, the mind, and the purse.' Many of us find this last particularly difficult. I do. In some respects I have followed the Light; in others I have dug my heels in and pleaded that I'm not yet ready to move. I know that I am still not fully clear in my response to the legacies and lifetime gifts and windfalls I have received; nor in my intentions as regards our own disturbingly substantial wealth.

At the outset let me explain that the wealth we have has not been largely derived from legacies nor high salaries but from a combination of thrift, a double trading down in the housing market and a £30,000 voluntary severance payment – coupled with the iniquitous ability of money to breed in the stock market, even in its ethical form, to the advantage of the rich. And let me acknowledge that this makes it much, much easier for us to take the steps we have.

Now let me share again something of my unfinished business in this area.

We took our first major decision to question our ownership of what we had been given when we left Strathkinness for Manchester. We tried to sell our house to a sympathetic purchaser who would have maintained its environmental resources; and, for him, we were prepared to forego the value of part of the site as building land. When that fell through, we sold the building land separately and gave away the gain to environmental and social projects. However, we did not give away the part of the value from the sale of the two cottages which derived from improvement grants which we had taken advantage of previously – grants funded by general taxation, including tax receipts from millions of people much poorer than us.

We have largely avoided taking substantial sums from legacies. For example, I used the legacy from my mother to help in the family's purchase of additional land to add to the Semerwater Nature Reserve and in a specific piece of woodland for the Woodland Trust. Of my father's considerable wealth distributed in his lifetime, my portion was largely directed – tax efficiently – to the Society of Friends and other charitable bodies. However, we have also enabled some of my parents' money to reach their grandchildren and great grandchildren. And we have reserved a part of our inheritance as things stand at present for our children, none of whom is secure in a profession or well-off in other ways.

As for the windfalls from privatisations, I tapped into them as a form of protest: I bought shares in the companies that were being privatised, then sold them at a profit as soon as possible and sent the money as a donation to political organisations working for a fairer economic system. When it came to the windfalls that we couldn't avoid, because we had funds in a particular building society, we were immediately clear that the money we were being given was not in any way ours. It felt absolutely right to give it away and to continue to do the same on each subsequent occasion. This is how I put it, speaking to the Manchester Centenary Conference:

> Some days correspondence brings something to chew on. One day a letter telling me that I had gained over £2,700 by magic, because Lloyds Bank had absorbed my Cheltenham and Gloucester Building Society account. £2,700 for nothing! What to do? I'm well enough off to be able to afford anything I might reasonably want as well as many things I might want unreasonably. Nonetheless I'm tempted to keep it. It could be useful if I fall ill or need nursing care in my old age, or to give to my children, who show no signs of financial security. In the end I was glad I wrote to *The Friend* hoping that others in the same gravy boat would see it as money that they had no right to and should give away – it meant I couldn't forget to actually do it as opposed to merely intending to.

However, some Friends have gone much further than we have in their use of money, including giving away most of their capital in their lifetime. That is a standing invitation to us all. But it only works as an invitation once we have taken the issue down into our spiritual core – to where we can find the place where we are not defined by what we have. And to the place where fear of insecurity has been overcome. Only if we have come to realise that all the brainwashing of our current economic system cannot finally prevent us from coming to know – and know experimentally – that what is mine is not ultimately mine but God's.

As yet I have only come to know that in part. Curiously, what has helped me to reach to the fringes of that insight – apart from nineteenth century French socialist thinkers and John Woolman – has been our move into Ordsall. All sorts of bases of self-interest have been overturned here. To start with I'm paid for only half the hours I choose to work; this is a deliberate means of bringing my wage rate down to something more realistic for the area. Then there is the fact that gardens are so tiny and I'm a very keen gardener, whereas the local authority is not so keen on paying to keep *its* gardens in good order – so I have loads of scope gardening in the park in the middle of the estate. I'm also able to contribute quite a lot financially to the local community in largely unseen ways. In my way of life in Ordsall, money, time, skills, property have all been partially 'republicised'! It's a wonderfully subversive experience, running counter to all that the modern market economy seems to understand.

However, I need to take up an earlier theme and make clear that lifestyle is not only about the great issues of house, job and financial resources, though money is rarely far away. Indeed the wonderful thing about lifestyle is that it covers almost everything. It is made up of thousands of decisions that we make daily or weekly. All the decisions we make about whether we keep any spare money, and, if so, where. Which bank? Which building society? What sort of investments? All the decisions we make about what we buy. Do we need it at all? Have we considered where it comes from? The nature of the regime; the transport implications? The fairness or otherwise of the trade? Whether the firm has a good record in terms of employment policies, environmental responsiveness, etc? Is it wasteful in packaging? etc, etc. Then there are the decisions we take about our use of energy in the home and through our decisions about using transport. Private car or public transport? Train or plane? The decisions we take about how often and how and where to go on holiday. What impact for good or ill does our part in the tourist trade have on the country concerned? Should we offer our financial support to an unacceptable regime?

Rather than finding the range of these issues daunting, I see them as one of the most accessible vehicles for the contemporary adventure of the spirit. I know that I have found the omnipresence of these issues a schooling in the real meaning of the sacramental nature of the whole of life; my spiritual discernment is under constant exercise so that it becomes a second nature – or perhaps a rediscovery of our first? I know also that this discernment grows as we practise sifting out what our testimonies would have us do from the secular values of the times. It is a process or an adventure. No-one does everything that could be done. We all have to start at one area of decision making and move on to others. And we benefit all the time from those who have pioneered the way – who have raised the questions and alerted out consciences. I know that those who have given up their car or foregone their wealth are a signpost to me, even if I have not yet taken their route – or even if I never will.

Despite all the failings and the stubborn resistances, I can say that my lifestyle has changed quite fundamentally in the last fifteen years. I have come to understand it as a progressive *centring down* of my life, strangely akin, despite the difference of timescale, to our centring down in meeting for worship. And the changes have been a confirmation of George Fox's wonderful Epistle 10: 'And earthly reason shall tell you what ye shall lose. Hearken not to that, but stand still in the Light, that shows them to you, and then strength comes from the Lord. And help, contrary to your expectation.' (Cecil Sharman, *No more but my love*, p.4) Those renunciations which seemed to diminish our security, our comfort, our opportunities have, for me, proved once again the essential truth of the Christian message. Much of this is expressed by Richard Foster's *Celebration of discipline,* which is quoted in the Introduction to Part III.

So, how we live is not a vague consequence of our faith. It is not an optional extra for some of us. It is an inescapable expression of our faith. And, what we continue to express is also what really creates what we are, what our faith is. Our social testimonies need us to be constantly reflecting on our lifestyle to see what is of God and what is just creaturely. If we neglect this area it will expose our spiritual phraseology as mere hot air.

Implications for politics

The necessity of political action

I begin by a reminder of why personal changes in lifestyle are not enough. Let's look at transport. Personal lifestyle decisions on how we should rightly move around the country cannot be effective without playing their part, along with conventional politics, in changing public policy in this area. Our own decision to contribute less to global warming – by walking, cycling, using public transport or travelling less – will not, of itself, preserve us – or anyone else – from that outcome. Such a decision certainly needs to be taken from a deep inner conviction but it also has to invite others – whether implicitly or explicitly – to join in the witness, so that the context for a progressive public policy becomes more favourable. And it needs to be accompanied by more direct political actions to persuade those with the power to change those policies, to do so.

We speak of the power of the Spirit, and our need to be open to it. But when it comes to other forms of power, to our response to secular 'authority', we are more uncertain. And as for the exercise of power ourselves, I hear expressed the feeling that 'power' and our testimonies and methods are mutually exclusive. We work towards equality and unity rather than the imposition of our wills.

But we all exercise power in our daily lives. We have power as consumers, we have power in relationships, we can use the power of protest. Some have more power than others, and many people feel disempowered, cynical, frustrated. But whether we are 'in power' or on the receiving end, we need to be aware of the power balances (and imbalances) in our lives and in society in general. We also need to be aware of our responsibilities, whether they involve the ethical use of power or working for change.
Harry Albright, *The Friend*, 6 August 1999

I cannot see a way of stopping at any point on this continuum: we have to be involved in all three stages. Being solely concerned with a person-to-person approach is just a sentimental cop-out. Putting all our eggs in the lifestyle approach is blinkered; throwing ourselves into political campaigning without working on how our own contribution is being made to the problem or the solution – or both – makes for a certain hollowness, even hypocrisy. Witney Monthly Meeting's paper on homelessness from 1992 addresses this last issue of the awkwardness when we campaign against a social evil to which our own lifestyle might be contributing: 'Part of the guilt which some Witney Friends feel when they consider their concern comes from self-questioning about whether our own way of life contributes to the very evils which we deplore. Could George Fox's advice to William Penn be applied to our choices of lifestyle and social behaviour? "I advise thee to live in thy comfort for as long as thou canst." '

And so, if politics puts into practice values which are either more or less compatible with our testimonies, how could we possibly be detached from that? In conditions where the values of faith and the values of the world have radically diverged, our faith groups need to be also lifestyle groups *and* campaigning groups. Our values need to be campaigned for; our vision of society needs to be placed before our fellow men and women as an alternative vision of what life is all about.

As Quakers we are involved in nothing less than building the Kingdom of Heaven on earth, and today this means working for a new society as well as changing ourselves. Our understanding of Quakerism, particularly its emphasis on a positive, critical approach to existing structures and practices in society, and its concern for working together practically through our day-to-day lives, leads us to consider community living.

'Towards Community: A Statement' (This statement was drawn up by the Towards Community Group in November 1974.) [It is worth noting that, in addition to the political emphasis, this extract points towards an extension of lifestyle to the development of corporate models of living which strive to embody the values of the kingdom and are expressively set over against the prevailing values of society.]

I am not saying that we should come out as a church group in support of a political party. What I am saying is that there are positions which we need to fight for. And positions that need to be present in the public debate; sometimes positions that the politicians may be wanting to hear, to help them move beyond the apparently limited horizons of what seems to make pragmatic sense. As Paul Oestreicher has written: 'The alternatives politicians face are real, but always limited. Yet not quite as limited as it seems to them. People and pressure groups are necessary to help them expand the vision of what is possible. Yet the extremest options are not always the most radical, do not always get to the root of the problem. To help politicians to do that will not make for popularity, but that is what Christian prophecy is about: pointing out reality, however unpalatable it may be. Nor will the middle ground necessarily provide the answers. Jesus, and this bears repetition, would never have been described as a "moderate".' (*The double cross*, p.38)

And that oughtn't to mean simply expressing our view to the Government. It should involve real work as a religious body, mobilising its adherents, to get an alternative view across in every way possible and positively seeking publicity for it. In the words of Grigor McClelland:

'Should Friends campaign? It is of the essence of democracy that citizens should try to persuade one another, and I believe that campaigning, in one way or another, is not only a right but a duty. This applies to both single-issue and party-political campaigning.' (*The Friend*, 21 February 1997) That quotation refers to Friends as individuals, perhaps, but it is equally applicable to our meetings, albeit not in terms of party-political activity. Campaigning needs to become as simply associated with our spiritual life as praying. Indeed we should expect our prayers to feed into our campaigns and our campaigning to nourish our prayers – or, better, that our prayer life will be engaged and our campaigning prayerful.

As we persist in trying, by whatever means we can, to raise the level of caring and sharing in our meetings there will, if we are faithful, come a point when members no longer feel alone and impotent, but know that they are together, and that they can do something that will make a real difference in the world. There will come a point where our trust and confidence in each other and in the Spirit has made us into a real community, living more often in the life and power that takes away the occasion of all wars, able to witness to the truth not only in ministry, at demos and on petitions but in our lives also.

Audrey Urry, 'The meeting community'

Friends have for a long time known that testimony involves working towards the expression of their testimonies in the structures of public life. The campaign to end hanging as a punishment was something Friends felt deeply about because it brought the state a little closer to our peace testimony. The emphasis Friends have developed on working to remove the causes of social evils is also inescapably political, because the causes are generally structural. And in BYM we have recognised this political responsibility repeatedly in our sessions of Yearly Meeting. For example, our minute on Justice, Peace and the Integrity of Creation in 1989 states that this concern

> grows from our faith and cannot be separated from it. It challenges us to look again at our lifestyles and reassess our priorities and makes us realise the truth of Gandhi's words: 'Those who say religion has nothing to do with politics do not know what religion means'.

Another indication of the breadth of this understanding of faith is shown by the fact that the work of the Parliamentary Liaison Secretary has also been very highly valued by large numbers of Friends.

And yet, despite all this, many Friends sense a diffidence and, sometimes, a hostility amongst us, regarding any concrete manifestation of a political dimension to our faith. Why should this be so?

Firstly, there is a strong trend within the Christian Church for the separation of spirituality and politics. That tendency is aided and abetted by a poor understanding of the distinction between politics in general and party politics; politics gets a bad press and is the subject of very negative stereotyping amongst the general public, and this intensifies the huge gulf between the idealised world of spirituality and the demonised world of politics. Such trends, whilst not dominant amongst Friends, almost certainly affect to some degree or other a significant number of us.

Secondly, we have created a debilitating division of functions between our local and our national bodies. Many Friends probably tolerate, at least, the political education and persuasion engaged in by our central departments. But relatively few meetings fully understand this as a dimension of their spirituality at a local level. Hence we lack a widely diffused experience of a corporate response at the local level to the structural problems of the political world. A large part of this reluctance to engage locally has to do with a fear of divisiveness and that, in turn, seems more real the less good practice there is to point to.

Thirdly, the individualism of the age fosters the sense that faith's political responsiveness has to be exercised at an individual level rather than a corporate one (a fuller discussion of this point follows). And that effectively takes the political out of our meetings.

However, local corporate political action is possible. In fact it is much more widespread than many Friends have realised. Let me see what I can list off the top of my head in a minute: vigils against the West's bombing of Iraq and Serbia; participation in the Jubilee 2000 Campaign; corporate membership of the Churches National Housing Coalition; buying adverts in the paper about the Quaker position on poverty or the National Lottery; lobbying against the growth in the number of women imprisoned; working with the Real World Coalition towards the last General Election. No doubt there is much more.

In Hardshaw East Monthly Meeting we have set up a Social Justice Group which is empowered by the monthly meeting to help Friends witness to the social testimonies, including by political persuasion. In the course of the last General Election campaign, we held a vigil outside Mount Street Meeting House to express our dismay at the narrow terms of the political debate and our conviction that government has to face up to the fundamental long-term issues. One of the elements of this group is that it is a campaigning group, which will have a little paid help, with funding from the monthly meeting. A worker will work with us to encourage us to exercise our faith in the political realm, among other ways by bringing the concerns that are surfacing in our national corporate work into closer connection with local Friends – and vice versa. Our testimonies certainly give us ample scope for bringing our understanding of faith to bear on current issues, such as: the indebtedness of the world's poorest countries; widening inequalities in Britain; controlling the runaway engine of free trade at the World Trade Organisation (WTO); the loss of habitat for wildlife; the car and the problem of global warming. These need not be approached in a party political spirit nor dogmatically; if we are open and sensitive and ground our campaigns in our testimonies, there will be a very real sense of unity amongst Friends.

That is certainly the experience of Hardshaw East Monthly Meeting; we have had no problems with divisiveness; we issued a statement on the General Election, which monthly meeting found acceptable; we are trusted by MM to act responsibly and we can raise with MM anything we have any reason to think might cause any difficulty. This experience, which has now lasted for four years, is very encouraging and should diminish the nervousness which some Friends have been afflicted with, which tends to paralysis in the expression of our social testimonies. It could also be helpful in linking local Friends and national concerns, thus diminishing the perceived gulf between the two.

In recognising the importance of taking political action corporately as Friends towards the Kingdom of God, we need to be aware that the rhetoric of political change can be cheap. It is extremely easy to criticise others, but we would find it hard to act creatively and rightly if we were given political power. Prophecy is needed; dissent is needed; but also humility. And we knew that humility should be natural to us as we know that we ourselves often do not do what we should do even when it is something within our own direct power to do.

That does not make me despair of politics any more than I despair of people. The macro- and the microcosm are intimately related. There is nothing in the politics of my nation that I do not recognise in myself. How do I weigh a costly home insurance policy against the needs of a young struggling mother with three children who has no home at all, not in Capetown, but within half a mile of my house? Or running a car? Or even buying a cinema ticket?

Personal responsibility and public decision-making are not of a different order. How does one weigh the equipment of hospitals for expensive surgery against the use of finite resources for preventative medicine? It can be argued that the personal answers are easier than the political ones. Do our lives bear that out?

The double cross, p.36

What sort of political action?

If politics in general causes Friends some anxieties, there remains the vexed issue of the spiritual and political legitimacy of different forms of political action. Namely, conventional politics and non-violent direct action.

I am not convinced that the differences of opinion on this question are always deeply rooted in our Quaker faith. We have to be careful that we do not simply follow the agenda of the mainstream, which asserts that conventional democratic political action (meetings, lobbying, demonstrations, letter writing etc.) is always the only legitimate form of political action. Friends may be prone to that assumption for three reasons. Firstly it is the reflex of most of those of their age and social position; secondly, the liberal Christianity of BYM in the twentieth century was extremely closely inter-woven with the extension of political democracy; thirdly, Friends have developed a desire for respectability, partly justified by the hope that it will increase the influence of Friends' good name, even though this is completely at odds with the character of our origins.

In terms of principle, we have to start from the certainty that the law of God cannot be identified necessarily with the will of the people. The legitimacy of the ballot box has ultimately, for Friends, to be subject to a higher court of appeal. The question then becomes: if I/we are fully clear that some governmental action or law is inconsistent with our understanding of God's will or that it forces us personally into actions that are against our conscience, is it *ever* right to resist the law?

Clearly the answer to this has to be, 'Yes, it may be right to do so'. It clearly was right for individual Friends to refuse conscription to the armed forces. Very few Friends would argue that the individual refusal to pay tax for war purposes is wrong, whatever may be thought about its effectiveness or otherwise. In this sense direct action is wholly in tune with our understanding of testimony as expressive action. And this is true regardless of whether the state is a democracy or not. We have never agreed to allow the will of the people, however expressed, to constrain our conscientious convictions of what we have to do.

How many 'bad' laws have been repealed because people wrote to their MPs? Was the ancient law mandating every adult male to do at least one hour of archery practice every First Day repealed (only in the last couple of years) because people campaigned, or was it repealed because almost every adult male in the country broke the law every week?

'The law' is the servant and protector of society, not the master of it. If we feel by our conviction that to oppose something we must break the law, then, so long as we are prepared to accept the consequences, so be it. If we feel the law is more important than our testimony, then what value is our testimony? Are we more concerned with appearing to be respectable than maintaining our integrity?

Simon Gray in *The Friend*, 28 August 1998

The legitimacy of a democratic government's actions does not in the final analysis rest solely on its election by the people: it is quite possible for such a government to exercise power illegitimately, and sometimes illegally. Many democratic countries have resorted to torture as an instrument of state policy: for example Israel has done so systematically; our own country used methods that amounted to torture in Northern Ireland. The USA was clearly guilty of crimes against humanity on a massive scale in Indochina. The question then arises as to whether the threat of use of nuclear weapons, or the threats of global warming through the unchecked expansion of our usage of the internal combustion engine, or the threats to the environment from the revolutionary and extremely rapid development of GM crops... whether any or all of these involve actual or potential damage to the world's environment, including potentially widespread death and destruction, so that they are also crimes against humanity and an illegitimate exercise of power.

The understanding that the use or threatened use of nuclear weapons could never be justified under international law is certainly one of the principal motivations of those involved in Trident Ploughshares 2000, the non-violent direct action against nuclear weapons in the UK. Indeed, as

Caroline Westgate wrote in *The Friend*: 'People who appeared before the sheriff three times were remanded in prison ... and the hope is that their trials will test in Scottish courts the opinion of the World Court that nuclear weapons are illegal under international law.' ('The cook's tale', *The Friend*, 18 September 1998) In the autumn of 1999 three members of Ploughshares 2000 were indeed acquitted by the sheriff on this basis.

So far, so straightforward. It becomes, more complex, however, in a number of ways, some of which it may be helpful to touch on. Let's start by giving a range of very different instances of direct action, which will serve to show that this is not an area where rights and wrongs are easily defined.

A   Action to destroy experiments in growing genetically modified crops

B   Action to damage nuclear delivery systems

C   Reclaim the Streets Motorway Parties

D   Newbury Bypass direct action to prevent/ impede the construction

E   Holding up traffic to persuade the authorities to put in a pedestrian crossing

F   Pulling up bindweed in council owned roadside shrubbery – without asking

G   Getting around arms embargoes by falsifying documentation

H   Failing to declare income for income tax purposes

I   Failing to warn asbestos workers of the danger their employment caused them

J   Mass boycotts of unpopular measures: e.g. the Poll Tax

K   The NATO led bombing of Serbia in 1999

L   The involvement of secret services in a plot to destabilise the Wilson Government

M   Breaking the speed limit

It should be immediately obvious that there are many different forms of action which in one sense or another take the law into their own hands. They vary in at least the following ways:

1.   whether there is an appeal to a higher law or, just a resort to self-interest

2.   whether the authority being 'addressed' is legitimate; in

particular, whether it has a democratic legitimacy

3. whether the action is an attempt to flout a decision taken legitimately, by a legitimate authority; or to enforce a change of policy or persuade of the desirability of a change in policy

4. whether all other avenues to change the situation have been exhausted

5. whether the action is violent or non-violent

6. whether those involved are: an individual; groups of individuals; organised groups; companies; governmental agencies; governments or groups of governments

7. whether the action involves only individual Friends or whether it seems to involve a corporate endorsement by BYM as a whole.

I am well aware that many Friends will say: 'We know what we mean; we mean a group of people who take the law into their own hands and try to frustrate the will of the people.' But it isn't so simple. Let's try to sift out the examples which Friends generally would not accept as legitimate.

The first consideration is whether the reason for the action is deeply enough founded on something higher than self-interest. If not, those examples can be dismissed – this would cut out G, H, I and M at least. For Friends, it goes without saying that self-interest will not be a justification for non-violent direct action.

The second consideration might be whether enough other measures of persuasion have been tried and have failed. This is often held to be the case. Few of the examples would be cut out for this reason – although, there must be a question mark over the bombing of Serbia in 1999, example K. There is considerable disquiet now about the Rambouillet ultimatum, which seems to have been designed to make it impossible for Serbia to accept. In that sense it is by no means clear that negotiations could not have succeeded in some measure. This is not always an easy criterion to apply, of course. Much depends whether you believe that unlimited time can be afforded for conventional persuasion or not.

For example, there have been several instances of local people forcing onto the political agenda their concern to have a pedestrian crossing put in on a busy stretch of road which needs to be crossed to get to a park or whatever. Often they have failed to do so by conventional political action.

They have only succeeded when they have blocked the road by forming a continuous procession across it and back. They might have poor local councillors; they might not know very well how to use all the normal democratic processes; and, if they voted in local elections – which is rather unlikely, may well have voted for parties which had not been asked whether or not they would approve. Most people would take the view that occasionally such expression of deep feeling, which the formal voting mechanisms cannot get at, are an acceptable part of the whole complex play of different forces which determines how opinion and then policy and action is shaped.

It is also really important to refuse to judge the conspicuous pressure of non-violent direct action as though it is the only pressure on our elected institutions of government. There are also all sorts of hidden non-democratic pressures on government. Money is often a very powerful form of direct action. Multinational companies may exert very significant power on government behind the scenes; that exercise of power may exert more leverage on government than the occupation of the Newbury Bypass site by dozens of direct action protestors. You only have to look at the negotiations of the World Trade Organisation to get a sense of the immense power wielded by such unaccountable and unrepresentative commercial bodies. Ordinary people, combining together, are much more visible. They may defy the law more blatantly. That shouldn't, of itself, make their exercise of power pernicious. Those without power have always had to use the power of numbers.

I shall now look at the most controversial aspects of the issue for Friends. These seem to be:

- when an action is engaged in, not because personally one could not rightly carry weapons etc, but to prevent what is seen as an evil policy being carried out
- when an action involves the destruction of property
- when the action involves Friends corporately and not just an individual following his or her conscience.

> When an action is engaged in, not because personally one could not rightly carry weapons etc, but to prevent what is seen as an evil policy being carried out.

The first aspect is to do with whether the action is an attempt to directly force a legitimate power to back down on its position, rather than only to refuse to be personally involved in what is seen as an evil policy. This seems to be the case for A and D and possibly E and J, but these also are designed to ensure that the debate is carried on openly rather than just by the establishment. This is how one of the Quaker participants in the Newbury Bypass NVDA protest put it:

> We know now, looking across the landscape where once was forest and that now looks like the moon, that we cannot stop this road, but maybe we can change people's minds about the necessity of roads, for the future, and then all the Government's billions won't be able to buy the help of these poor souls (the road builder's security guards) on the other side of the razor-wire. (N19 in *Who do we think we are?*)

It is into this category of actions that the animal rights actions to protest against the export of live animals, the occupations of sites of new roads and runways, and the actions against genetically modified foods all fall. Because, unlike the actions of conscientious objectors, the aim is to change a policy that has been decided on, this is always a harder category for democrats. However, even those Friends who are most reluctant to interfere with the due democratic process surely cannot dismiss the possibility that this might in some circumstance be necessary. For example our much prized democratic system was engaged in secret chemical experiments on individuals and whole communities over large tracts of the country during the Cold War. If we had known this at the time, would an occupation of the runway from which the spray planes took off, have been wrong? Surely not.

When an action involves the destruction of property.

Some Friends object to the fact that the actions are not completely non-violent, as they understand it. They see hammering the controls of a Hawk jet or cutting the wire fence around Greenham Common cruise missile base as an exercise of destructive power – even although there is absolutely no threat to human life. This is surely an unrealistically demanding interpretation of non-violence or pacifism or the peace testimony. For all sorts of legitimate reasons we may destroy things. The bailiffs who clear the direct action protestors from road sites also destroy things. Friends who have a new kitchen will usually in the process destroy the old. In doing so, we may reflect on the testimony to simplicity but we are unlikely to focus on the peace testimony. There are certainly issues about the legitimacy of the exercise of force, but surely not about the peace testimony as such. It is hard to imagine any Friend refusing to cut off the padlock of a gate, on the grounds that this was violence, if it had been possible by doing so to allow the inmates of a concentration camp to escape. What we have to measure in our consciences is the relation between the harmfulness of the existing power, its legitimacy, and the nature and extent of the force required to resist it. This is how Caroline Westgate justified the intention to physically damage 'our' nuclear submarines:

> One of the big stumbling blocks for Friends has been the determination of the activists to physically attack the submarines. But this is not a gratuitous act of violence. The protestors' aim is to do enough damage to land up in a Crown Court with a judge and a jury, and to test out the principles of our government's duties and obligations under international law. These are the same laws under which the Nazi war-criminals were judged at Nuremburg and the same laws which are currently being used in Rwanda and the former Yugoslavia. The damage is not to people or even to private property, but to the most destructive weapon ever devised by humanity. In upholding the peace testimony we 'refuse to fight with outward weapons'. This begs the question: what weapons are we prepared to use? You may well say 'Not hammers!' I would argue that it is possible to wield a hammer non-violently. The first rule of NVDA is to remain personally non-violent at a deep spiritual level. I can assure you that the people who are part of this project are completely committed to non-violence.

Much will depend on the context into which we can place the individual action. Nigel Dower helpfully offers us a wider view than that of the personal use of force against other people: 'Violence comes in many forms: at its root is the idea that what is violent damages, degrades or destroys what is of value. As Johann Galtung reminded us at the QCEA seminar in March 1993,

> ... there is in addition to the active violence of individuals (like

killing, assault, rape, stealing), the violence of institutions and structures (capitalistic structures which oppress, land tenure regimes, censorship), but also 'cultural violence' which, Galtung explained, is the pattern of legitimation for the other forms of violence (e.g. standard economic theory which legitimates selfishness, or, I would add, standard international relations theories which legitimate nation-state interests).
('Development, violence and sharing', p.10)

In approaching this question we need to be very careful not to adopt a very pure definition of violence to condemn these largely symbolic actions in the name of the peace testimony, only to find that we are complicit with all sorts of violence – verbal, structural and even physical – ourselves.

Direct actions such as cutting fences only become part of a non-violent protest when other forms have been tried and failed, and when there is a huge imbalance of power in which the weaker side is not heard. In this case the balance is so uneven that Trident Ploughshares 2000 activists became aware that they would not be heard if they did not take direct action.

Other non-violent methods being used which mark Trident Ploughshares 2000 out from other direct actions include openness and accountability. To ensure openness, several weeks beforehand a copy of the handbook was supplied to the base commander with names and addresses of activists and dates of intended actions. To ensure accountability was clear, when engaged in an action such as cutting fences, activists neither resisted arrest nor ran away.

Throughout my stay there was a very respectful attitude on the part of all Trident Ploughshares 2000ers, with everyone involved being treated as individual human beings.
Zee Zee Heine, *The Friend*, 4 September 1998

When the action involves Friends corporately and not just an individual following his or her conscience.

When a Friend refused conscription, this was – primarily – an individual act and it was a refusal to comply, without attempting to frustrate the war effort others were engaged in. Refusing to present Quaker publications to the censor in 1917 was a corporate act in defiance of law. If the authorities lacked democratic legitimacy such actions would clearly be easier to accept. However, they cannot be ruled out even where the law has a democratic legitimacy.

The most recent example for Friends in BYM was the vexed question of BYM being asked to withhold the part of taxation attributable to military expenditure on behalf of a number of its employees. The consideration lasted several years and seemed at times to be leading to corporate unity to carry this out. In the end, however, that unity was shown not to have a sufficient depth and embrace, and the action was changed to one of trying to persuade the government to change the rules. Passions ran very high and clearly corporate defiance of law will only come from an issue which engages Friends with great power; even then, the quality of our thinking on the importance and the limitations of the law, even in a democratic state, will need to be improved.

What sort of political action? Conclusions

I have deliberately not attempted to produce a simple answer. The fact is that it is a very difficult area for us to be clear about. What I hope to have achieved, however, is a position where it would be very difficult to dismiss out of hand the actions of Ploughshares 2000, the GM crop protestors or the anti-roads campaigners. One could only take up an absolute position against such actions if one was prepared to condemn out of hand those helping runaway slaves in a democratic country where slavery was countenanced by law. Let me take that as the archetypal example of a situation where conscience might lead to defiance of a law, which, while unacceptable to conscience, was legitimately in force.

I would then suggest that the examples which I have given above – whilst open to much deliberation as to the nature of the evil which they oppose, as to the extent of the damage that they might cause, and as to the depth of the conscientious conviction that has given rise to that non-violent direct action – are, in essence, of the same kind.

Some Friends might argue that, while it may be right for individual Friends to follow their leadings and defy the law, corporately we should not do so. I think everyone would accept that for BYM as such to find unity in some form of defiance of the law would be harder. The issue would have to be central to our faith and thoroughly worked through in our meetings. However, it cannot reasonably be ruled out. The Yearly Meeting's defiance, in 1917, of the Government's regulation requiring the submission of pamphlets to the censor during the First World War is an excellent example of what may become necessary. Its statement concludes: 'We realise the rarity of the occasions on which a body of citizens find their sense of duty to be in conflict with the law, and it is with a sense of the gravity of this decision, that the Society of Friends must on this occasion act contrary to the regulation, and continue to issue literature on war and peace without submitting it to the censor. It is convinced that in thus standing firm for spiritual liberty it is acting in the best interests of the nation.' (*QFP*, 23.90) Certainly the prudential need to protect our 'good name', or our charitable status, cannot possibly be an overriding priority for Friends.

Other political questions

However, the challenge to our testimonies does not only arise from the issue of non-violent direct action. I shall briefly raise a cluster of rather different issues. At the centre of this cluster is the question of whether the very nature of democratic politics is compatible with our Quaker values. Political activity, particularly but not exclusively in party political affairs, will provide us with some severe tests of our testimonies. It is integrity which will be most under pressure and which we will need to hold fast to. This is not to say that the compromises that political life involves necessarily destroy our integrity. Compromise happens in all families and all communities, including Quaker meetings. Groups of people have to negotiate a common approach, which means some individuals agreeing to drop or postpone particular goals. This happens inevitably in political life as well, but need not be any more destructive of integrity.

However, the inability of politicians to clarify what their personal viewpoint really is and to explain the reasons why it is not being pressed may affect one's integrity. So may the constant pressure to put a favourable gloss on realities, the constant pressure to rubbish one's opponents and the pressure to say rather different things to different groups of people. Canvassing, for example, requires an exceptional honesty if one's views are not to be at all inflected towards the perceived position of the person whose vote you are asking for.

It may be helpful to relate this discussion about political integrity to the long-standing Quaker reflection on the prophet and the reconciler, which usually refers to the peace testimony. The issue has multiple facets. It relates to absolutism and relativism. It approaches the difference between what we might individually be called to do and what is right for others, or for society in general. There is room here for dialogue and understanding between those who look to a politics which is close to their ideals, for some through the Green Party, and those who struggle for progress in the mixed and messy reality of, for example, a Labour Party in power. There is clearly something attractive about being able to identify wholeheartedly with the political party one supports because it seems to be very close to our Quaker testimonies. However, where important political change can be realised now by supporting a party which only goes a part of the way towards those testimonies, others may well decide that this is the right course of action.

Rex Ambler's approach to the peace testimony illuminates this dialogue very usefully:

> The original version of the testimony ... had a double reference: it indicated the resolve of one group of spiritually-minded people to live by the truth that had been revealed to them, and it bore witness to a future possibility for all people to live by that truth, if and when they came to see it and respond to it. It might help us to resolve our own dilemma with the peace testimony if we could recover this double meaning. ('The peace testimony today' in *Searching the depths*, p.55)

Political life is, indeed, a challenge for Friends, both in terms of its ends and its means. However, the political both results from prevailing values and impacts on them in turn. We cannot afford to be too precious and to turn our backs on it to keep our hands clean. It would be too easy to stand aside and feel smugly superior. Our testimonies are strong enough for us to live them out in the hurly-burly of political life, with integrity.

That is no reason for being complacent about the current political culture. Rather we need to be clear that the creation of an informed and sensitive culture of political discussion is a deeply spiritual priority. It is helpful to begin by realising that politicians, too, feel imprisoned by a public opinion which is understandably, perhaps, but mistakenly vengeful in penal affairs, which is inclined to look at politics in terms of narrow self-interest and which refuses to contemplate much limitation of its present so-called freedoms for the sake of the world's well-being in the future. If we are aware both of the long-term physical damage of this approach and the spiritual damage of all such narrow self-interest, we must surely be at work to enlighten the political culture of our time.

This is, I think, close to what Michael Bartlet, BYM's Parliamentary

Liaison secretary had in mind when he wrote:

> What we need to see developed in the first part of the next
> century is a vigorous concept of *consent* and *responsibility*. We also
> need to see that each one of us is part of a network of reciprocal
> relations where we cannot be alone and we are mutually
> responsible to each other. The vibrancy of a community can
> only be fed by the currency of good will generated by forgiving
> relationships. I believe that in our process of decision-making
> and work, we have something valuable as Friends to offer the
> wider political process. ('Faith in today's political world',
> *Quaker monthly*, February 1997)

We may need to look also much more intently than we have done for a
long time at how we work politically, and not just in terms of whether we
are for or against non-violent direct action. Indeed, as Christine Crosbie has
argued, we may need to put more stress on 'initiating and developing
dialogue between groups' rather than 'on providing the "right" answers'.
('Towards a "post modern" politics', *Quaker monthly*, April 1996) She makes
it clear that she is not suggesting we should stop being involved individually
with party politics, writing letters to MPs, campaigning through single-
issue groups, etc. But she argues that we should be involved in 'other forms
of action which consciously seek to find common ground between different
groups in society, particularly groups which feel they have little in common
or much to fear from each other'. Are there more personal ways than we
have yet found, of speaking to individuals and groups who exercise power?

The corporate dimension

The virus of secular individualism has so affected large numbers of
Friends in BYM at this time as to cause a serious failure of nerve in relation
to the corporate nature of Quaker faith, and specifically, of our testimonies.
Time and again, Friends suggest that each of us can only know what is
right for her or himself. The conclusion drawn from that is that we are too
different now to engage in actions together; and that we should simply
each express our version of Quaker faith in our own individual way. This is
summarised as 'no two Quakers think alike' or 'no two Quakers act alike'
and treated as a joke. And the sub-text of the joke is that we can be rather
pleased to be known for such originality. This somewhat proud laughter is

more dangerous than it seems. It weakens positive conviction and broadcasts loss of nerve. In terms of our theme it pronounces a death sentence on Quaker social testimonies, because, as I have already shown, they are in essence *common* understandings of the direction the Light shows us. Some Friends have gone so far as to suggest that, as there is no longer any possibility of common understanding and action on social matters, BYM should pull out of this area of work lock, stock and barrel. What that means is that, corporately, we would have nothing to say about peace, about poverty, about sustainable development, about racism or international debt. The only action we could take would be as individuals. This is a counsel of – or temptation to – despair.

There are further implications of this position. It would exclude all issues of corporate social responsibility from our business meetings; in turn this would make it even harder for them to find a place in our worship. So Quakerism would have been cut off from its history of social concern, cast loose from its bedrock in the sacramental nature of the whole of life. In short, the shattering of Truth into myriads of individual opinions, after destroying the coherence of our system of belief, would have destroyed the basis of Quaker testimony. All that would be left is our shared practice of silent worship. It is doubtful whether the Society would survive on that sole basis.

Sometimes this position is buttressed by apparently more sensible arguments about lack of time and energy, or the need to work ecumenically instead of trying to do everything in Quakerly isolation. Clearly there are issues here which need to be recognised. We cannot do everything together – the organisational problems really would be oppressive; so we have to act as individuals more often than not, even when we are following Quaker testimonies. We would be mad not to work with others where we have common ends or a common approach, because to do so will strengthen the impact we have. Time also is a problem for almost all of us and that creates further limitations; yet many of us will find the time for things which seem to connect to the flow of divine energy. Is it not first and foremost a question of whether the corporate work we do leaves us fulfilled because it seems essentially 'right', perhaps even 'given'?

Whatever the intellectual and practical difficulties, it remains true that Quaker testimonies are corporate and they cannot be kept alive without corporate exercise. It is not enough for this to happen through national committees. For many Friends that is surrogate witness and does not exercise hearts, minds, spirits where we live and work and worship. The practice of testimony, I believe, must be a focus of our spiritual life and learning at this local level. That will mean discerning the things which will help us to grow into a more faithful experience of the social testimonies, and acting accordingly, corporately where this is appropriate. For this to happen, the preconditions seem to me to be these:

- a full understanding of the implications of the testimony to the sacramental nature of the whole of life
- a reaffirmation that one of the crucial contemporary Quaker understandings is that we need to search for the causes of social evils and work to overcome them rather than simply to offer bandages to those who are hurt by those evils
- an inner conviction that the individualism of the age runs counter to Quaker values. The economic, social and cultural means by which we are persuaded of the primacy of the individual encourage us to remain in our personal spheres of action and to undervalue corporate action in our local meetings or through our national institutions. Resisting individualism will open us to the desire to be part of a corporate Quaker body working – locally and nationally – to express publicly, in word and deed, our testimonies to truth, peace, simplicity, equality, community and to the earth.

These positions are still a dynamic part of our Quaker inheritance and can be further strengthened. And this in turn suggests that the corporate is an essential part of our experience. We are not as different as we think. Our approach to social and political issues has real and essential elements of unity, which could only be strengthened by a fuller rediscovery of testimony. That means going deeper. This unity of social values needs to be experienced as something more than the chance agreement of our various subjective social opinions. The deeper question is rather whether our coming together to worship brings us into glimpses of Truth which we need individually for our journey towards God, which the Society needs corporately for its sense of relation to God's ultimate loving purpose and which the world also needs for its wholeness. Otherwise corporate action will seem arbitrary and inessential when the language of priorities is spoken. Does our faith, then, cast Light on society in ways that convince us that the Light is not mere subjective preference? That it leads us into unity?

I believe it does. But I know many Friends will be sceptical. So, let me add that I am well aware that reaching corporate unity on social problems will be no simple matter. I do recognise that not all Friends see eye to eye on everything! We do not agree about Quaker schools, the right to strike, abortion and much else. But we will experience greater unity when we start from testimony, not policy. Let's take the example of unemployment. Our starting point is our testimony to equality. On that basis we will share a conviction that unemployment in general is unjust: it is a way of sharing work and income that is radically unfair. We then need to discuss our differing perspectives on how the problem is to be tackled.

Some may emphasise long term changes in the organisation – and understanding – of work; others may argue that work should be more fairly shared now, through a variety of expenditure and taxation proposals. But it can be a dialogue on the common ground of our testimony to equality. With deep unity at that level, attitudes towards particular policies will become more manageable. Sometimes we will reach unity; sometimes we will fail; sometimes our differing proposals may rightly coexist. But our starting point must be unity through our testimonies.

Let me use the recent example of the National Lottery to show how our unity on our testimonies remains a reality. Remember that it was an issue we had done little corporate work on for several generations. The exercise throughout the yearly meeting produced minutes from more than a hundred preparative and monthly meetings and other Quaker groupings. Despite some differences of emphasis, the overwhelming impression from that exercise was of the Society as a body of people firmly united in their opposition to organised gambling in general and the state run National Lottery in particular.

Let us take heart from this. Our testimonies are evidence of our unity at a deeply spiritual level. The housing concern, the Yearly Meeting sessions on poverty in 1987, the encouraging unity over international debt relief, for example, reveal a great reservoir of agreement amongst us. Like the half full rather than half empty reservoir, we should start celebrating the amazing fact of our Quaker social unity.

Or, again, consider the peace testimony. Of course differences of opinion exist amongst Friends on the Second World War, the Gulf War, the bombing of Former Yugoslavia, the use of sanctions, UN peacekeeping forces, liberation struggles etc. Nonetheless we have the testimony and a clear corporate approach to issues of peace and war. We can hold vigils as corporate acts of opposition to the war in the Falklands, the bombing of Iraq or the bombing of Serbia. Quaker Peace and Service is able to act corporately on our behalf even if not every Friend is in agreement.

Friends are no more divided on truth or equality or simplicity than they are on peace. I believe we are broadly united on the following propositions, for example: inequality should be reduced through taxation and benefits policies and raising low pay; there should be greater openness in government; ever harsher penal policies are not only ineffective but wrong; car usage should be discouraged. It would be wonderfully strengthening if we learned to approach social problems on the common ground of our testimonies, so that even the differences stand out against a common backdrop.

It's here, at the core of our Quaker spirituality, that we come to know a unity which is not afraid of difference. When we look at social issues from our understanding that there is that of God in everyone, we know at a very deep level that the highest and deepest realities of human life – which are of God – are being crushed all around us, and sometimes in our hearts too. We see this in the humiliation and oppression in so many ways of so many of our sisters and brothers: for example, those who internalise the 'worthless' judgement that society places on them because their 'economic worth' is least; those who live in fear-ridden urban deserts; those crippled by asbestosis in the name of profit; and so many others. We may not agree about every detail of a remedy, but we do not, I believe, sense such judgements as mere subjective opinion.

If our discernment of what we should do in lifestyle and politics is more than a rationally argued choice, and more than mere personal preference, if it is discernment through our faith values, are we not under a spiritual imperative to live it out in our corporate life, as well as individually? That is what our testimonies should help us do. As we practise them, they become a means for building up our corporate life. Rediscovered and practised more deliberately they could recreate a corporate Quaker identity, a sense that, together, we have been given something vital to do.

If the serious practice of our testimonies could reinvigorate our corporate life – as well as our spirituality – how can this be brought about? We cannot rely on the prevailing currents of society. They are flowing still in many ways in an opposed direction. However, many Friends are paddling upstream in all sorts of craft. The beginning is to become more aware of that and to celebrate it. Then we need to reflect on our testimonies and discover ways of sharing our successes and our failings as we strive to witness to them. That is what I shall cover in the next sub-section on mutual accountability.

Conclusion to implications for politics

No religious body is in a better position to unite around its fundamental values, our testimonies, and offer them to a world which is more than ever deprived of radical vision. That is the distinctive contribution Friends could make. We could be of service if we faithfully contributed to the public debate, seeking out much more actively than at present opportunities to share the vision inherent in our testimonies. The Leaveners are a splendid example of that dynamic in one context. We may not all be actors but, with encouragement and support, we could become more effective agents of change.

I expect to meet resistance from Friends for whom the Religious Society and pressure groups seem incompatible. Many are also very wary of public statements. Certainly we should speak when we are clear (which may not be when we are unanimous). Certainly we should speak out of the real experience of our lives and do our best to avoid the hypocrisy of calling on others to do what we have not been able to do ourselves. Certainly we should speak to our testimonies.

But speak we should. It is a question of need. Christians have been prepared to prioritise the spirituality of responding to the needs of the hungry by feeding them. Friends have for a long time declared that we also need to rid society of the causes of the hunger. That is also a need, although much less widely recognised as an equally important aspect of faith. But BYM has had long enough to grow up. We cannot practise faith other than fragmentarily if we do not recognise the crucial influence of national policy on how life is lived.

A decision to contribute more to public, political debate – to do the small amount that a body like ours can do to encourage openness, fairness and the values which make for true community – would also be an aspect of testimony. As Tim Newell wrote in *The Friend*: 'The power of preparative meetings to inform local debate must not be underestimated. From that forum, individuals take strength to exercise leadership in presenting alternative visions of how things could be.' (21 February 1997) I cannot emphasise too strongly that for me this would be a deeply spiritual path. It could only be done in faithful unity by a people of God. It would be a further stage in the proper response of religion to the development of democracy.

Testimony, I have argued, is the key link between the preceding sections on lifestyle and politics. Approached in terms of testimony both are integral to our faith. For testimony is the way in which we express in our lives our understanding of what human beings are meant to be: loving, truthful, peaceful and centred not on self but on God and therefore the natural world and other people. It is because we have neglected it that we have allowed our faith to fragment, so that our corporate witness no longer seems to some essential to our spiritual quest. It is because we have neglected it that we are too diffident to believe that our lives are lived as signs to the world. The rediscovery of testimony is crucial because it is the place where individual and corporate merge, fusing together lifestyle and politics, in faith.

Mutual accountability

'I found that there was no book that could substitute for what I most desired as a seeker – a sense of connection with other seekers, a community of mutual support and devotion that would enable me to practise my faith more meaningfully in the world.' (Keith R. Maddock, 'Spiritual guidance among Friends', *Friends quarterly*, July 1999)

Whatever we call it, the practice of sharing our spiritual journeys with each other, in an atmosphere of trust, encouragement, challenge and adventure, is surely an aspiration which, in theory, we share. Yet, as we have seen, practising our faith involves us in living our testimonies; and testimony inescapably implies twin approaches to embodying our values in the concrete realities of our world, through lifestyle and politics. It also implies corporate action by Friends on both these aspects of life, both locally and centrally. Yet Friends, for whom testimony is a fundamental inheritance, are still paradoxically diffident or uneasy about both politics and lifestyle. If that is the case we clearly have a great deal of essential work to do. If testimony is to be fully rediscovered as a living power in our lives it must embrace both these areas, overcoming the specific fears and inhibitions which mark each of them, and which discourage us from sharing our experience in the depths where we are spiritually nourished. How can we be a spiritual community unless we share with one another how we understand our faith-in-action? Our stories of how we have been progressively led? As Sandra Cronk put it:

In gospel order, those gathered into the church community have a covenant with God. It is a living relationship of trust, listening and responsiveness to God's call. They also have a covenantal relationship, comprising the same qualities, with

each other. They are accountable to God and each other for
maintaining those relationships. (*Gospel order*, p.22)

What has undermined this covenantal relationship of trust and disclosure?
What are the reasons for our nervousness about a greater sharing of our
experience of following – and not following – the Light in our daily lives?
In terms of lifestyle they arise essentially from the fear of being exposed to
the experience of others, which, it is often felt, would throw a disturbingly
revealing light on the inadequacies of our own lifestyle. In terms of political
involvement we are frightened above all because we fear the conflict with
other Friends that might be aroused by our differing discernment, potentially
giving rise to disunity within our meetings.

This double inhibition is extremely destructive. Both to the living power
of testimony in our lives and, therefore, also to our spiritual power both as
individuals and as a Society. It is particularly destructive because it leaves
our spirituality and our testimonies in the realm of the abstract. In that
lotus land it is just too easy to muddle along. The real challenges to our
spirituality come in the very concrete circumstances of our day-to-day lives,
in the constant reassessment of what love requires of us. And in the equally
sharp and finally equally concrete arena of political choice. Easy generalisations
simply won't do here. So the attempt to rediscover our social testimonies
has to be the attempt to rediscover their power to rule our lives and their
relevance to the development of social policies for the whole nation. And it cannot
be stressed too often that such a rediscovery is necessarily a spiritual journey.

There are all sorts of other reasons why we flinch away from mutual
accountability but none of them, I believe, is spiritually grounded. They all
stem from fear or from the adoption of values derived from the secular world
rather than faith, including from the culture of English reserve. I shall
examine these other reasons as well as those outlined above in greater detail.

Firstly our culture favours individualism. This individualism suggests
that we are responsible for our own life and resents the 'interference' of
others in it. There is nothing very Christian about that. I know the strength
of this position. Despite a Quaker upbringing it took me years to see – and
still doubtless only in part – that my self-reliance, for all its virtues, was also
a very effective way of shutting God – and other people – out. In this respect
the influence of the contemporary culture of individualism constantly
undermines our testimony to community.

Secondly because our spirituality is so weakened we resist being offered too directly and too concretely the Light that is refracted through our fellow Friends, for fear that it might convict us; that it might enable us to see what we have not yet seen. Then we would be faced with the choice of changing our lives or denying the Light. The invitation to change some of our practices might well scatter some very uncomfortable spanners around the cushions of our comfort. This fear of being disturbed, of being asked to change some aspects of our lives, is a strange fear for a religious people, since one of the main themes of religions such as Christianity is that our lives can be and need to be transformed by the workings of God's Light and love in us. We may say the ritualised: 'Strive to know each other in the things which are eternal' but really we don't want that if the things which are eternal turn out to be incarnated in the nitty gritty of political campaigns or of attempts to put the car in its place. All too often we respond to the witness of our fellow Friends, not in terms of joy at their response to the Light, not in terms of an open-hearted wondering whether there is some illumination for us, but rather by a paralysis which manifests itself as a refusal to listen and to see.

Thirdly we have to ponder whether John Punshon was right to question whether contemporary Quakerism is prepared for a spirituality based on a 'transforming power'. Easy words to say, less easy to actually live. Indeed has our Quaker faith become, as he puts it, a therapeutic confirmation that we are all right as we are, rather than a revolutionary agency to effect our transformation into a fuller inheritance of our nature as children of God? This is what he writes:

> Thus, I detect a tendency for contemporary Quakerism to become a needs-centred movement with an essentially harmonising and reinforcing role in the lives of its members. Traditional Quakerism, on the other hand, performed a challenging and transforming role which had quite a different effect. Crucial to its challenge were its testimonies, then incapable of severance from its doctrine of God. (*Testimony and tradition*, p.42)

This is a diagnosis of very great insight. The modernist culture of 'personal growth' is terrified of the prophetic, of anything which suggests that we need to reflect on our falling short. Affirmation clearly has its place; but spiritual maturity is prepared to allow the Light to show us what there is to see. Denial of what the Light shows will be a betrayal of truth. As I wrote in *Beyond the Spirit of the Age*: 'the nurture of self can all-too-easily become an end in itself, which is an end to true spirituality ... The self which we nurture, is it our self-willed self, or the Godself within?' (p.59)

Fourthly contemporary Friends clearly have a deep-rooted problem with guilt. Our excuse for denying the Light is all too often that guilt is bad for us. I have written about this in my Swarthmore Lecture and the passage bears repeating, I believe:

> It seems to me that we need to return to some robust common sense. If we accept ourselves as we are without reservations then guilt will not arise; but surely we cannot be as self-satisfied as that! If we do not see, or feel, any need to change our conduct, from where will the motivation come to change it? If we do feel the need to change our conduct in certain respects, then we are conscious of a gap between what it is and what it might be. Whether in our daily lives or in wider public questions, that gap is the spur to change. This experience is at the heart of religious experience and it is the source of the prophetic voice. It is that gap which creates guilt.

Of course I understand that the word may carry associations with experiences that are not at all positive. Especially where the experience of the gap is not the result of an inward illumination, freely assented to, but rather the result of a standard of judgement that seems externally imposed in some way. 'Nonetheless, the essential experience of being convicted by the Light cannot be forsaken without almost irreparable damage.'

In short our fundamental Quaker reliance on the Light creates the dynamic which leads to our sense of falling short; that sense, which some of us want to term 'guilt', may be a spur to change or a paralysis preventing change. I still believe that the most important factor in accepting the falling short as an invitation to renewal is an understanding of the underpinning forgiveness of God. There is no paralysing guilt where the experience of that forgiveness is deep enough.

What mutual accountability asks of us is whether we can share, without pride and without paralysing guilt, our stories of following the Light and the stories of our failing to follow it. It should not be so hard, because we all share the fundamental experience of following in part and not following in other parts.

It seems to me that our response to the Light can be characterised in one of these ways:

- the Light is so overwhelming that you immediately follow
- the Light is so frightening that you refuse to acknowledge that it is showing you anything; indeed the merest glimpse and you turn your back on it and it can be as though no insight has occurred
- the Light shows you something that you would rather not see; sometimes the Light is a bit stronger and you may begin to respond; sometimes the creaturely resistance prevails.

It is this last scenario which is the one we know most of the time. It's the intimate dialogue of feelings, of hopes and fears, in which God – the illuminator – nags us often gently towards what we know to be right. Well, if nagging isn't right for you, it might be cajoles or inspires! What is important here is the realisation that the Light which we appeal to is, at one and the same time, the Light that shows us our darkness and leads us out of it. It is the diagnosis and the cure. As William Penn wrote: 'The very Principle, that is Light to show him, is also spirit to quicken him, and grace to teach, help, and comfort him.' ('Primitive Christianity revived' in *The peace of Europe, the fruits of solitude and other writings,* p. 243)

Once again we are able to see how reflection on testimony is bound tightly up with our spiritual condition. What is preventing us from risking the experience of mutual accountability is what is weakening our spirituality. It is at least arguable that the most direct route to a deepening spirituality would be for more and more of us to share with each other how it affects every aspect of our lives. I wrote about this daily experience of the search for rightness, for the Manchester Centenary Conference:

> Such are the small-scale daily decisions of most of us. Decisions or just automatic reflexes? If decisions, does taking them feel like a meeting for worship moment by moment? Do we sense all these – and every other area – of our lives to be places where our spiritual discernment is exercised? I've not used much special spiritual language in writing about them. Yet we need to be centred down in those decisions as in meeting for worship.
>
> Then they won't be decisions to feel anxious about, still less to push away out of guilt. Of course sometimes we fail to do things which *could* rightly be expected of us; all the time I

fall short but the effort and the failings are alike offered to God in the hope that I will be guided to be more faithful in due course. And that is my experience.

If all the decisions of our daily lives are an essential part of our spiritual struggle, how could we possibly keep them out of our worship and ministry, our meetings for learning and for clearness? If only we dared to trust we might come to know in each other the inspiring, loving, cajoling and forgiving spirit which is of God. And, yes, even the gentle nagging that kept on reminding me that our lovely Victorian house in Didsbury wasn't the right place for us; that we really could in one little respect swim against the tide towards a closer relationship with God.

Let me give an example which I believe is encouraging. One of the contributions in part IV describes the experience of the Lifestyle Group in Hardshaw East Monthly Meeting. I was a member of that group and experienced it as both supportive and challenging. Not separately. The challenges were supportive. And the support was challenging. In describing our experiences of trying to live out our faith, none of us laid down the law, assuming that our experience would be necessarily right for everyone; rather the challenge lay in the illumination of truth, so that we came to see more clearly in some particular respect, because the experience of others made sense of an area of greyness or mistiness in our own.

It could be enormously helpful if such groups became widespread. It would complement the work done on the expression of 'our spiritual journeys'. (Once more that pitfall of language: our work on our spiritual journeys was perhaps never properly completed, or even conceived, because it didn't clearly enough recognise that our spiritual journey is the way in which the whole of our life relates or doesn't relate to God.) So, that should be where our mutual accountability is exercised. It doesn't, of course, always need a special long-term group. A meeting for learning could easily incorporate an aspect of this into its programme for the year. But it does need time and trust and good facilitation in varying combinations. There is also very good reason for a similar approach to our political choices. If we had to explain them to our fellow Friends this would surely encourage us to see that choice as a faithful one that can be shown to relate to Quaker testimonies. Once again, careful planning and facilitation would be needed. But again our sense of the relevance of our spirituality to every aspect of the world's agenda would be strengthened. The sacramental nature of the whole of life could become much more real to us all.

Conclusion to
Testimony: its implications for lifestyle and politics

I have tried to show that testimony necessarily supposes that we show what the Light has disclosed to us. Lifestyle and politics are two vital ways in which that disclosure is reflected outwards to others. So, lifestyle and politics are areas of life that we need to live under the guidance of the Spirit as it constantly renews our understanding of testimony. We still have work to do in our meetings to fully appreciate that such work is properly a deepening of our spirituality and connects crucially with all our institutions that focus on that, albeit at present, often in too special and compartmentalised a way. Elders, for example, have as yet rarely grasped that the spirituality of our active life is every bit as vital as the spirituality of our contemplative times, and just as much a part of their work to nurture.

I have argued that our local meetings need the experience of corporate discernment of what the testimonies call them to do; and that, unless this corporate discernment is exercised sufficiently at the local level, it will atrophy. Also the corporate work at central level can only effectively be sustained by those who see the importance of corporate work in their own areas. Without that consonance, we will have a widening gulf between the centre and the periphery, to the detriment of us all.

Finally I have appealed to Friends to really live adventurously and for us to share our experience in groups where we can celebrate the different ways in which we are trying to live more simply, more equally, with more sense of the part we play in local, national and global communities, more peacefully, with greater integrity and with more care for the whole planet. If only we could be brave enough to listen to and share and wrestle with each other's experience in a kind of challenging supportiveness! How much our spirituality could be strengthened. We have so much to contribute and so much to learn. All the rich variety of our experience of following the spirit in the heady range of day-to-day decisions which we all make and which help to build bad, better or good relations with all those whose lives touch ours through the myriad interactions of our now global society. What a responsibility. But also what scope for following to the best of our faithfulness the promptings of love and truth which are the foundations of our testimonies and should be the ever strengthening foundations of our lives.

6. The action of faith: conclusions

Despite the ways in which they have been weakened, as I have shown, our testimonies are yet alive. They are still implicitly – and perhaps increasingly explicitly – central to the faith and practice of BYM. We must not be complacent, however, and we must be prepared to hear the hard message that our responses are not good enough.

How well do we live our testimonies?
How far have we rediscovered the meaning and the power of Quaker testimony and of our social testimonies in particular?

It is really difficult to assess how fully engaged are Friends generally with our social testimonies. Some of us clearly see glasses that are half empty; for others, they are half full. Yet others of us are wondering if our glass is even a quarter full. I doubt whether it is possible to make a definitive judgement on the totality of our responses to our social testimonies. But it may be helpful to look broadly at the different emphases that lead to the half full and the three quarters empty glasses. Or are they the cisterns of living water, of which Roger Wilson wrote? (1976, *QFP* 23.08)

If our glass seems half full, it is because we know Friends who are living out their testimonies in far-reaching ways: they are resigning from well-paid jobs because of a conflict with the testimony to truth and integrity; they are giving up the car and using other methods of transport as a response to our environmental crises; they are choosing to live in the inner city alongside the most socially excluded; they are giving away large amounts of capital in ways which further the testimonies; they are living lives which minimise their ecological footprints; they are working as a vocation, building up society rather than serving their own self-interest.

Of course none of us is doing all of these things; and many won't be doing anything on that scale. However, they may be practising all sorts of more humdrum ways of living out the testimonies: saving electricity by switching off unnecessary lights; having showers rather than baths; not buying flashy cars or lottery tickets ... the list is endless. Taken individually each of these specific actions will seem totally insufficient in relation to the challenges our world is facing. Yet, where there are many such minor actions we may well feel more positive. If we look at Friends in the round the testimonies certainly do seem to be real. However well-off a good many Friends may be, there is what I call an inflection of the lives towards equality, simplicity and the rest.

Often we disparage the small first steps people make, and this is a mistake; it destroys the opportunity for the small step to be a practice for greater things.

Some months ago, during the opening worship at monthly meeting, this thought and feeling came to me, though at the time I was not ready to share it out loud:

'Do not be dismayed if you only seem led to do small things, for little things give practice for greater things and even in little things peace can be brought about, and the will of God done.'

Nick Langley, 'Contributions to building peace', *Quaker monthly*, January 1993

Yet we have to return to that question: how *well* are our testimonies?. Faced with the testimonies as a spiritual imperative – and, indeed, faced with the Cross – and with the social and ecological crises at home and abroad, it is only too clear that our lives do not match the challenge of our testimonies to find ways of living in gospel order; nor can we see our response as adequate to the world's needs.

In asking, 'How is our practice of social testimony?', we have to take account of the context. In other words does our practice of testimony measure up to the gap between the theory that we are all children of God and the contempt, the neglect, the abuse, the exploitation which is the reality for so many? Does it measure up to a world in which global inequality grows ever deeper, with its bitter harvest of malnutrition, disease and death? A world which is wiping out habitats and species wholesale in its worship of unfettered economic development? A world in which, for all the talk of community here in Britain, the reality is in many parts a terrible disintegration of community: it's youngsters in packs marauding through the streets with hammers and iron bars; it means a week in which, within two hundred yards of my house, a young black woman has been driven out of her home by masked youths wielding iron bars. Two women in another house had bottles through their front window while they were sitting in the room; thirty yards of wooden fencing has been ripped up and piled against an empty property and set on fire; those boarding up a damaged empty property at night have been passed by a gang of balaclavad young men hissing 'grass' and 'we'll get you grasses out one by one'; fire engines have been stoned and young children of primary school age have retaliated on a group of nuns who came out to ask them to behave, with paint poured all over their front door. And that is just a selection from, admittedly, a bad week.

If faith were about trundling along in a middling sort of way, then our practice of the testimonies might do. But does not faith ask more of us? Of course, faith expects failure and weakness. And forgiveness is at work. Yet faith is also generative of expectation – it looks towards God's common-wealth of love. It is here that many of us have to acknowledge that our faith has been muffled by our comfort. We know, for example, that we live lives that may well condemn dozens of peoples in low-lying islands to lose not only their homes but their very homeland in part through our profligate use of fossil fuels. Our lives say that that is less important than the ease and speed of our travel regime – even when our spoken faith says it cannot be.

The question, then, is whether our practice of testimony measures up to the scale of the problems we face, locally, nationally and globally.

Our weakness is that much of the time we are only vaguely conscious of our testimonies and only live them out in very selective areas of our lives. Many of us perhaps see the testimonies more as the expression of our personal values than as a corporate adventure of the spirit, a discipline or a discipleship. And nationally, more is needed of the Society than a piecemeal approach in which we flit from the growing inequalities in society in 1987 to the iniquities of the National Lottery in 1995. It is not enough to consider each issue on its own. We need the underlying sense of direction that a renewed social testimony would help to create.

It is easy to show that most of us fall very, very short of the discipleship required to live out our testimonies in total integrity. I certainly do. That shouldn't really need any individual to point it out for us to recognise it. We only have to hold the world and our lives in the Light for it to become clear. However, some Friends have tried particularly forcefully to help us to see the gap between what we profess and how we live. Barbara Forbes, John Southern, Jack Richards and John Cockcroft are amongst those who have striven to alert us to this prophetic gap. The charge is that, while we are prepared to go some way towards matching our deeds and words, we balk at anything which carries a significant cost. The general claim is that, while we may adjust our lives to respond to the problems the world presents to us, they are rarely radically transformed. We believe in equality but will not live on an average income; we believe in community but will not live amongst those left behind in the sink estates; we believe in peace but largely live lives outside the areas of most persistent violence; most of us still use our cars as though global warming and the rest was scarcely a real threat. And so on. The charge is that our faithfulness is cost-free; that we only give, of our time and our money, what comes easily.

We are right to be worried that in spite of clarion calls from concerned and influential Friends, and in spite of the work of so many who have quietly got on with witnessing through service, we have merged closer and closer to the common image of middle class respectability. Although we regained some of our reputation for social challenge during the cruise missile campaigns of the 80s the majority of Friends were uncomfortable at the thought of meeting houses used for overnight resting places and as communication centres for itinerant unemployed campaigners, and of members appearing in court for breaches of the peace.

Let us not be deflected by the slightly sexist language of our Yearly Meeting's statement: 'The Eight Foundations of a True Social Order' (which can be found as 23.16 in *Quaker faith and practice*). I want to see us carry the concern of those Friends of seventy years ago into the sitting rooms and garden patios of suburban middle class professional Friends and ask again why they can spend more on cat food than on the central work of the Society.

John Southern, 'God is Community', *Quaker monthly*, October 1996

It seems to me that there are three powerful forces which are at work on us, making it more difficult to respond with wholehearted spiritual integrity:

- We do not live lives that are truly adventurous because we do still cling, in our different ways and to different extents, to our comforts and our material securities. Some of this is linked to our middle class position.
- We are imbued – to some extent at least – with the individualist, secular and materialist ethos of the contemporary world.
- We have not found ways of being a vibrant spiritual community in which we can be mutually loved into greater faithfulness.

So our practice of our testimonies takes on the character of our charitable giving. It is measured out so as to avoid any personal discomfort. And because of that it lacks too often the authentic hallmark of transformational witness, seeming rather to be a partial conformity to something that has been handed down.

Yearly Meeting 1997 recognised that a real re-discovery of our social testimony would lead to transformation: 'we are moving to a new place of unity in our understanding of the inter-relatedness of spirituality and action ... Steadfastness and prayer and love and risk are asked of us as we go through the painful process of feeling the call but only partially discerning it; then full discernment, perhaps terror at what is being asked of us.'

Terror – how often do we admit, as Friends, to feeling terror? Can we feel collective terror? Does our particular interpretation of the Christian faith provide the sort of challenge which can lead us into uncharted territory where the only thing we are sure of is that we have 'felt the call'?

Some time ago, I came across Hermann Hesse's definition of bourgeois: preferring convenience to justice, comfort to love, and a moderate temperature to the deadly inner consuming fire. I immediately recognised myself and many of my Friends. Why is it that, amongst Quakers, I feel a dampening down of any remnants of 'inner consuming fire'? Why does being a Quaker, and meeting with Quakers, no longer give me spiritual energy? Are we in danger of using Quakerism as a comfort blanket – something which will keep us moderately warm, rather than fanning our inner fire? If I take any steps towards a more radical life, one which is led in greater solidarity with the oppressed, why do I feel that I do this in spite of, and not because of, being a Quaker?

As Friends, we believe in 'Faith in action' and 'letting our lives speak'. Where, at the end of the twentieth century, is Quaker action which challenges us in a way which will lead to our spiritual transformation? Are we even interested any longer in spiritual transformation which goes beyond a warm feeling of comfort and well-being? Do we no longer recognise ourselves in the words of St Augustine, that our hearts are restless until they rest in God? Quaker faith should be a challenge as well as a comfort; at the moment, I confess, I feel that it is neither. We have become bourgeois: preferring convenience, comfort, and moderate temperature. And what is more: we are proud of ourselves for being thus. We regard it as unQuakerly to be passionate; we prefer moderation in all things, including our hunger and thirst for righteousness. Inner fires, like real fires, can go

out quite easily, if they are not fanned. As Quakers, we claim that we do
listen to our inner voice. But our response to our inner voice is made by
us as people who are too much influenced by society and the siren calls
of conformity and the main stream.

Barbara Forbes, 'An inner consuming fire', *The Friend*, 26 June 1998

Can we hear Jack Richards in this passage?

'As a corporate body we seem to lack spiritual fervour. It is as
though we are no longer driven by our current strengths and
resources, but travelling on stored momentum. We are part of
rather than distinguishable from the mores of Western society,
which since the Industrial Revolution has become catastroph-
ically separated from nature, and whose greed and selfishness
are destroying the planet. Limitations to these ills are such as are
forced upon us, rather than arising from our sense of rightness.
It is safe and comfortable to assert that personal example will
eventually effect change; reformers who recognise that the
world simply cannot wait will be willing to pay the price of
their own discomfort in many senses, including the scorn of
others. We need to redefine compassion and what it asks of us.
    It should be our greatest care to avoid such accommodation
to society's values that we lose our own. We are for justice,
peace and the integrity of all creation; any specialist skills and
concentration judged to be necessary – such as in the area of
conflict resolution, emergency relief, criminal justice and
many others – do not alter our belief that all the world is holy.
Quaker organisations should clearly reflect that paramount
unitive principle. In the apocalyptic global crisis which can no
longer be denied, Quaker Green Concern strives to raise
awareness of its mainly ecological elements. Such action is in
essence not separable from the current re-visioning of Friends'
structures and objectives. What, then, is the purpose of the
Religious Society of Friends, and how does that purpose relate
to the world in its anguish?' ('Re-discovering our Social
Testimony', *earthQuaker*, Issue 19 Summer 1997)

All this is, of course, true. We need to hear the prophetic voices which call us to greater faithfulness. And we need to understand that the original Quaker and Christian message contained much of what we need if we are to live adventurously rather than simply comfort our mediocrity with a tired metaphor. John Punshon has been enormously helpful in this. We know that, just as Peter betrayed Jesus, none of us live lives wholly illustrating God's love and truth.

And so, I believe we need simultaneously to affirm the faithfulness which we have been given, as a grace, *and* to hold our unfaithfulnesses in the Light which shows them for what they are. Then we should pray that the clarity shed leads us bit by bit into a more whole hearted discipleship.

However empty or full our glasses may seem, we can still ask the question as to whether they are filling or emptying. And, here I think it is right to be encouraging. The Rediscovering our Social Testimony (ROST) process has made a difference. It is possible to point to some directions of change:

- many more Friends are now familiar enough with the word to use it in speech and on paper. Testimony has become part of our contemporary Quaker language again
- the peace testimony is no longer isolated as the only contemporary Quaker testimony, as it tended to be. It is also more easily seen in its essential relationship to the other testimonies
- we have an agreed form of words which expresses our understanding of Quaker social testimony at this time – the 'Expression in Words' (see Introduction)
- we are beginning to be more aware of the evolution of testimony and, in particular, of the periodic need to recognise new testimonies or new applications of existing ones. In particular we are beginning to find ways of considering a new testimony to creation
- we have begun in some meetings to share our lifestyle decisions with each other and to talk about money
- there are signs here and there of local Friends seeing that their spirituality necessarily leads them to need to take up some broad political positions and to campaign on them.

The fundamental question beyond all of these is whether the testimonies are helping Friends in BYM to lead more faith-full lives. That is much harder to answer in a very definite way. Yet there is enough anecdotal evidence that a significant number of Friends have been led to take action that is more adventurous and more costly than would have been the case without the ROST exercise throughout the yearly meeting. This is reason to be thankful.

But it is nothing to be complacent about. Individually and corporately it remains the case that our witness only palely and fitfully reflects our belief that the ultimate reality of our humanity lies in its divine attributes of truth, simplicity, equality, peace and community.

Either way, what is most important is that we strive to be more open together and to share with each other the ways we have felt led to live out our testimonies in our lives. We need to develop what I have called a 'culture of mutual accountability'. That kind of sharing, about money, about our use of resources, about personal integrity, about our expression of peacefulness and sometimes its opposite, is something we need. We don't need it only to develop our awareness of the things we should be doing but aren't – helpful and important though that is – but also because it will enlarge our spirituality by widening its scope to every humdrum aspect of our lives. It will also help us to practise a rejection of the individualism which has such a strong grip on us, even when we know that it is a distortion of God's emphasis on our being members one of another.

The challenge for us of this balance of the corporate and the individual is to find in it the spiritual power which is often associated with dogmatic certainty. The maturity of the Quaker way lies in our refusal to accept that only dogmatic certainty gives rise to the faithful witness of true discipleship. But we need to prove it by our lives.

Part III – Living our Quaker social testimonies today

Extracts and personal testimonies by many Friends

1. Introduction

Witnessing to the essential things

In their beginnings, Quakers didn't think of themselves and their testimony in terms of a new faith, but as witnessing to the essential things, illuminated by the same light as was in the prophets, in Jesus, in the apostles and the early church. Quaker worship and way of living resulted from, and also recalled people to, following this light, this continuing thread of testimony, expressed in the language and social context of the time – wherever truth, equality, simplicity, God's light in each person was being denied in relationships, but also in the institutions of church and state power.

By reflecting on how this developed over the centuries, it's possible to trace, with hindsight, how the thread of testimony was lost, sometimes for lengthy periods, though hosts of Friends held quietly to essentials in private life and inspire us today by their faithfulness – which at times the Society followed in corporate witness.

What has seemed lost or undervalued for periods has been one or other of the essentials of testimony, leading to a loss of wholeness and connectedness, e.g. the preserving as a unity, spiritual and material, faith and politics, being and doing. On that latter 'split' there's no more telling comment (authorship forgotten) than this: 'testimony is not so much doing more as being more faithful in what we do'.

But though hindsight can be salutary, the essence of testimony – spiritual discernment carried into practice – is derived from love of God and our neighbour calling us to be and to do now.

David Turner, *Scottish Friends*, Summer 1997

The social order and the whole of life

We Friends take the whole of life to be sacramental because we believe in the light of God in every person. The social order is part of that life; and love must inform all our notions of justice – in Britain and throughout the world. We therefore affirm:

- that all people are to be valued for themselves, not merely for what they contribute
- that all people are entitled to quality of life, and to opportunities for growth, not hampered by unjust economic conditions, or by inequalities caused by prejudice
- that our responsibility as stewards requires that all resources are to be used for the good of everyone throughout the world, for the generations to come, and in harmony with the environment.

Tim Newell, in *Quakers and the General Election*, 1997

Wigton Meeting discusses our social testimony

We share the deep dissatisfaction with the structure of modern society expressed by London Yearly Meeting in 1987 and recorded in *Quaker faith & practice* at 23.21. This refers to the knowing polarisation of our society into the affluent and the 'have-leasts' which led London Yearly Meeting to find itself 'utterly at odds with the priorities of our society which deny the full human potential of millions of people in this country'.

The core of our social testimony is our belief in the fundamental equality of all humans and our duty to work for a society which cares for the needs of all its members irrespective of social status. We distinguish between the underlying needs of people and their wants or preferences. We believe that the satisfaction of genuine need of all people should take priority over the satisfaction of wants which may themselves have been artificially stimulated. We do not think it will be helpful to attempt to list exhaustively what human needs may be, but they will often be distinguished from wants by being able to identify a serious harm that will be done if a need is not met. Needs will include not only those things necessary to sustain life but also the knowledge and skills needed to make informed choices in life and equal opportunity to set about achieving them.

We recognise that the health and wellbeing of people will often be better assisted by preventive action taken at the level of the structure of society rather than by attempting to cure ills after they have occurred. We assert the value of equal quality of education, of health care and of opportunity to shape the course of each person's life so that each may achieve a sense of dignity, self respect and achievement.

We further believe that value and achievement cannot be measured solely in terms of money, possessions or political influence. Each person should have the opportunity to consider and determine their own values and they should not be penalised for rejecting those of materialism. Social life must recognise duties to others as well as rights and we support the spirit of the eight 'foundations of a true social order' set out by LYM in 1918 and reproduced in *QFP* at 23.16. In particular, we find principle vii relevant to our situation today: 'Mutual service should be the principle upon which life is organised. Service, not private gain, should be the motive of all work.'

ROST Co-ordinating Group, *Rediscovering our Social Testimony: Responses & Challenges,* 4.1 (The QSRE paper 'Rediscovering our Social Testimony: a developing statement' was considered by a study group of Wigton Meeting on 6 September 1995. These notes arose from that discussion and were considered by Wigton PM on 10 September.)

Merging our Quaker testimonies

If an answer were to be devised to the question 'What is Britain Yearly Meeting of the Religious Society of Friends for?', it would embrace in principle the entirety of what we see as our responsibility towards the world as a single entity. Whilst our concerns are for wholeness, however, the complexities of modern life tend so to break it down into specialist areas that many people become correspondingly fragmented, and suffer loss of a sense of identity and purpose.

The term 'social responsibility' might imply separation from that of 'peace', yet just as it would be artificial and valueless to ponder whether the motive for a given action were religious, political, moral, or whatever else, it is likewise pointless to try to establish whether our responses to vast convulsions such as those of central Africa, former Yugoslavia or Northern Ireland should be designated as concerns about peace, or of social responsibility. Our lives need to express such unity of faith and purpose as will look towards a merging of Quaker testimonies, encompassing the totality of our concept of right conduct, and of our corporate responses to the Earth's sufferings.

As a corporate body we seem to lack spiritual fervour ... It is safe and comfortable to assert that personal example will eventually effect change; reformers who recognise that the world simply cannot wait will be willing to pay the price of their own discomfort in many senses, including the scorn of others ... It should be our greatest care to avoid such accommodation to society's values that we lose our own.

Jack Richards, *earthQuaker*, issue 19 summer 1997

Towards a social testimony for the twenty-first century

We affirm that everything in our world is from God and that the light of Jesus Christ is in everyone; therefore we are both trustees and channels for the gifts of the Holy Spirit: peace, love and justice. These are essential to a true social order.

In that social order we believe that paid employment should be shared equitably by everyone of working age. We advocate job-sharing. We need maximum as well as minimum wages and reformed taxation to achieve this.

A political, social and economic environment to encourage the best in people calls for a well-funded, comprehensive system of inclusive insurance, responsible to government, for sickness, disability, unemployment and pensions.

Land, air and water are sacred; their purity must be protected. Their value must be for the community, not for private profit. Policies for sustainable development are necessary to protect future generations.

We will work for economic as well as political democracy, believing that we are able to learn the ways of co-operation and to apply them in the common interest.

We seek a new commonwealth, in which the stewardship of communications, transport, production, distribution and exchange is for the common good and is accountable.

Our religious faith leads us to conscientious objection to the unaccountable power and influence of capitalism.

Quaker Socialist Society, September 1995

A road to Damascus

It is now many years since I felt the need to make a double commitment – though at the time I didn't connect the two elements together. I had lived my short adult life in a comfortable sort of agnosticism. I'd been a more or less successful West End actor for a couple of years, and was now working for independent television.

What is it, even in such unchallenging and unchallenged circumstances, that gnaws at us with its own sense of dissatisfaction? In the space of a couple of years I resigned from my job and attended my first meeting for worship in Euston Road. The malaise at the time – if that's the right word – was personal and generalised. With the stretch of our lives ahead of us, I felt there had to be more to it than a modest kind of TV glamour and a political and religious indifference. I wrote to [the Labour Party at] Transport House and was taken on as a journalist. This really was, for me, a Road to Damascus – ironically occurring in the political arena, while the spiritual pull took its time.

I remember my first meeting for worship well. In particular I recall an awkward, shy man, well on in years, who dropped in while waiting for his train. He stood to speak, nervous and hesitating, placed a sad bunch of flowers on the table, then apologised for leaving early to catch his train. The incident taught me that meeting is open to all.

For thirty years, then, I have been a member of the Labour Party, a councillor and Parliamentary candidate, and a more or less regular attender wherever I have been or lived. I've asked myself over and over again why was it easier to 'take the plunge' into socialism than into Quakerism? I suppose one answer must be that it is easier and more comprehensible to 'fight your corner' for socialism in the Labour Party than to fight a corner (for what exactly?) in the Religious Society of Friends. Would one wish to 'fight' there anyway? For me, the decision to become a Friend would/will be the second most decisive decision of my life (my marriage, the key and secret of most of what I am, is the first). In writing I feel that I can divulge, confess even, more than I have ever put down before. The irony of my own choice is that it has taken the wretched afflictions upon society of the last couple of decades to make me see clearly that my religion and my politics need each other for strength, like the entwined coiling of a rope.

I was at meeting for worship yesterday and almost rose to speak. What I would have said would have been this: 'In its long history the Religious Society of Friends has never been more needed than it is today. The peace testimony and slavery were enormous challenges. Today's challenge is even harder: it is a global, sweeping and invasive philosophy of primary self-interest that makes the alleviation of human misery impossible because people are accepting it as a fact of life. Gross wealth and huge misery co-exist in many minds as immutable features of the universe, ironically and metaphorically as "acts of God"'. I would also perhaps have reminded Friends and myself of Christ's instruction to let our light so shine before others that they may see the meaning and value of good works, and, by so doing, glorify that which we believe to be God. I have come finally to the conclusion that, as with politics, commitment and conspicuous conviction are desperately needed in the modern world. Perhaps my socialism has waited too long to be united to its heavenly twin of faith.

Ian Flintoff, *Quaker Socialist Society*, Spring 1999

Experimenting with Light

Two dozen Friends met with Rex Ambler on an 'experiment with Light' exploring what he had found in his four years of studying George Fox's writings. Light, we were to discover, is both within and without, and has the characteristic of searching, showing, lightening (as in enlightening). It can be comforting and warm, but often it has fierce power, like a laser or a flash of lightning. Margaret Fell had warned that 'the light will rip you open'. Indeed, declared Fox, the Light 'will let thee see thy heart', 'it shows you when you do wrong', 'it will reprove you', and yes, it hurts to see these things. But 'if you love this Light it will teach you', 'it will lead you in the way of peace'. Yes, there is hope and healing too.

Some of us queried the emphasis on Light and we were aware that Light can be used in a hurtful way, as if darkness is evil ... We use the word with humility and were very conscious also of the goodness of darkness, where the seed grows safely, where labour and birth so often take place, where one rests and dreams.

Another word is Truth, not just truths, facts, but something that seems like another understanding of the divine. Truth is always practical, to be lived, for 'there are too many talkers, and few walkers in Christ'. The Truth shows recognisable facts about ourselves, for example lust, drunkenness, violence. Truth leads us to be whole people, without deluding ourselves, without hypocrisy (as moderns would say, with integrity) or as Fox said, 'being single before the Lord'. We need to tread and trample all deceit under foot in ourselves, then 'things may be spoken in nakedness of heart one unto another'.

Each has a measure of the Light, enough, and what is right for that person, but partial – hence our need for each other, so each measure of the

Light complements the other. I think one could say this also of cultures, faiths and even meetings. Each has a measure of the Light, we are responsible for our own measure, and it is ours to respect and develop, but also we should know that our Light complements and enhances the Light of others.

The Light shows us the Truth that we need to know, each one of us in our own situation. When we see truly, then we can know what we must do next.

When we are open to 'the wisdom of God and the life of God in ourselves', we will 'do rightly, justly, truly, holy, equally to all people'. Quakers are not the only people to see a unity in faith and works, of course. Nonetheless, prayer as Friends understand it is completed in service, or rather the prayer and the service are one. Unless we care, witness and serve, we cannot say we have a spiritual life.

Anne Hosking, *The Friend*, 19 February 1999

First seek God's kingdom

In a particularly penetrating comment on this passage of Scripture (Matthew 6: 25-31), Søren Kierkegaard considers what sort of effort could be made to pursue the kingdom of God. Should a person get a suitable job in order to exert a virtuous influence? His answer: no, we must first seek God's kingdom. Then should we give away all our money to feed the poor? Again the answer: no, we must *first* seek God's kingdom. Well, then perhaps we are to go and preach this truth to the world that people are to seek first God's kingdom? Once again the answer is a resounding: no, we are first to seek the kingdom of God. Kierkegaard concludes, 'Then in a certain sense it is nothing I shall do. Yes, certainly, in a certain sense it is nothing, become nothing before God, learn to keep silent; in this silence is the beginning, which is, first to seek God's Kingdom.'

Focus upon the kingdom produces the inward reality, and without the inward reality we will degenerate into legalistic trivia. Nothing else can be central. The desire to get out of the rat race cannot be central, the redistribution of the world's wealth cannot be central, the concern for ecology cannot be central. Seeking first God's kingdom and the righteousness, both personal and social, of that kingdom is the only thing that can be central in the spiritual discipline of simplicity.

The person who does not seek the kingdom first does not seek it at all. Worthy as all other concerns may be, the moment they become the focus of our efforts they become idolatry. To centre on them will inevitably draw us into declaring that our particular activity is Christian simplicity. And, in fact, when the kingdom of God is genuinely placed first, ecological concerns, the poor, the equitable distribution of wealth, and many other things will be given their proper attention.

As Jesus made clear in our central passage, freedom from anxiety is one of the inward evidences of seeking first the kingdom of God. The inward reality of simplicity involves a life of joyful unconcern for possessions. Neither the greedy nor the miserly know this liberty. It has nothing to do with abundance of possessions or their lack. It is an inward spirit of trust.

Richard Foster 1978, *Celebration of discipline,* pp.106-107

2. Truth and integrity

Testimony to truth

The issue of lying, when we say what we believe to be untrue, is another order of 'apartness from godde'. I have lied many times to avoid awkward situations, and I know this is a fundamental falling short of my testimony to truth, and I feel it hinders me from belonging to the wider community. The issue of truth for us as Quakers is at least partly one of identity. Being truthful means being honest about who we are, individually and in whatever groups we belong to.

In withholding truths or telling falsehoods we place a barrier between ourselves and others. It is hard to love across such barriers because they prevent us from being wholly present. Our place in a family of all people requires us to (aspire to) engage deeply and lovingly with whoever we meet: difficult enough anyway, near impossible when we don't involve our true selves.

G9 in *Who do we think we are?*, 1998

Truth and Integrity in Public Affairs (TIPA): the first stage

When a group of members of Warwickshire Monthly Meeting peace action group began to identify a concern that things were not as they should be in public life, the primary issue for us was the dishonesty and deceit involved in a covert surveillance of private individuals by the police and security services. One of the most disturbing elements was, and is, the indefinable nature of 'the establishment'. Who were they? On whose behalf, or by whose authority, did 'they' keep tabs on 'us'? We began to research what E. P. Thompson had dubbed 'the Secret State', adopting this as our working title. An abuse of power seemed to be involved. When Stephen Donil and Robin Ramsay published their book *Smear!* in 1992, showing how the security services had spied on Harold Wilson as President of the Board of Trade and later as Prime Minister, it was obvious that this wasn't just an abuse of power, but a usurpation of power. The real power holders, it seemed, were unelected, and indeed kept elected 'power' holders under surveillance!

Gradually the whole business came onto the political agenda. The Freedom of Information Campaign, Statewatch, The Campaign for Press and Broadcasting Freedom, and many other groups were becoming increasingly vocal and visible. Legislation was enacted which acknowledged the existence of the security services, and brought telephone tapping under statutory control. The tide of openness began to spread to local government with the passing of the Local Government (Freedom of Information) Act in 1985. True, the controls were weak, and the habitual secrecy of the British state machine ensured that the Interception of Communications Act gave little remedy as long as official secrets legislation was so tightly drawn that individuals could not gather evidence! Slowly, however, came the realisation that we (the TIPA committee was established after yearly meeting united with the concern at the beginning of the 1990s) were one of many groups pushing at a slowly opening door.

What was the role of Friends amongst all these campaigning groups and amidst all this change? TIPA was popular with Friends. I remember as I nosed my car down a country lane in search of one of the many meetings which had requested an input, my fellow speaker remarking that the whole thing had done wonders for her geography! We were part of a broad movement for change, and we had come to realise by now that government and administration, even including local government, was only a small part of the Secret State. For me the most important realisation over these last ten years has been that what we tend to refer to as 'TIPA issues' covers not just politics but commerce, education, community affairs, industry and so on. They affect our social testimonies, including our involvement in justice issues, education, interfaith matters, and our peace testimony. Although TIPA has, rightly in my opinion, dwelt little on the internal life of our yearly meeting, there is also an implicit challenge constantly to examine our own processes, as well as our personal integrity.

Political attitudes towards official secrecy, confidentiality and account-ability have changed considerably since concerned Friends from different parts of the country first came together a decade ago. The first stage is over. The issue is on the political agenda, and there is a serious ethical debate about such issues as the limits of freedom of information.

Our political processes (in the very broadest sense) are imperfect, and our use of them is imperfect, but what matters most for Friends is an act of faith. How can we express in practical ways that we believe that right processes will lead to right outcomes – and, since perfection is likely to remain exceedingly rare, that better processes will lead to better outcomes?

John Cockroft, 1999

Truth & Integrity in Public Affairs: the work goes on

Although the name of the project, Truth and Integrity, is the right one in terms of reflecting the strong relationship with Quaker testimonies, it is helpful to think about the work of the committee in terms of power, and in particular unaccountable power. The so called 'commanding heights', or levers of power, which drive the key decisions affecting millions of lives, are what the TIPA committee is interested in, especially the intersection between political and economic power. The role of the multinational companies is crucial in this context, as it is through their activities that capitalism is often seen at its most brutal, with political power on the ground colluding with economic interests thousands of miles away. It was through an ecumenical body, the Ecumenical Council for Corporate Responsibility, that the TIPA committee work began to move in this direction. Working in conjunction with Quaker Peace and Service, the committee began to address Friends' concerns in this area, bringing together work on ethical investment and corporate responsibility.

It is important to recognise that truth and integrity has to begin in individual lives, and then move to wide arenas, from the family through local government and then to the international stage. The TIPA committee, however, had felt from the outset that work on individual truth and integrity, and that of the Society of Friends as an institution, was beyond their remit. The committee was also clear that local issues were best addressed by those near to them, leaving the committee and secretary to address issues which can only be worked on centrally, or internationally. Thus local government is clearly of great importance, as are the educational and medical worlds, to give but three examples; however, the limited resources available meant that we must rely on local initiatives to deal with most of these concerns. This leaves the committee and secretary to continue focusing on the accountability of the intelligence and security services, freedom of information, and the European institutions. Beyond this, the work on economic power has expanded considerably, now working in close co-operation with Quaker United Nations Office in Geneva as well as the American Friends Service Committee.

In the ten years of the existence of this piece of Friends' work it has gone from being a relatively narrowly focused project, dealing with the secret heart of government, to a project whose essential purpose remains the same, but whose focus has shifted to the 'commanding heights' – in other words the levers of power, which are largely economic. Work in relation to the intelligence services carries on, and this relates to the economic work, as one of the principle reasons for the existence of the agencies is 'to protect the economic well-being of the UK'.

Robin Robison, August 1999

(Britain Yearly Meeting is a member of the newly reconstituted Ecumenical Council for Corporate Responsibility (ECCR), and Robin Robison, who works as Secretary to the Truth and Integrity in Public Affairs (TIPA) Committee, is currently honorary secretary to ECCR. More information can be obtained from him at Friends House.)

Ethical investment and monthly meeting treasurers

A few years ago, as members of our monthly meeting peace committee, we raised a concern about the investment of monthly meeting funds. We felt that our Quaker testimonies for peace, equality, honesty, integrity and simplicity should be expressed in all areas of our corporate lives as Quakers, as well as in our individual lives.

Our monthly meeting responded to our concern and made some changes in its investments. However, when we were asked to become treasurers of our monthly meeting in 1997, we were still concerned about two things. The bank used for day-to-day transactions had a doubtful reputation with regard to third world debt and no ethical policy over use of its funds, and we also had considerable sums invested in CAFcash and Charibond.

We wrote to the managing director of the bank in question asking about its current position with regard to third world debt. We received a detailed reply. The bank was 'scarcely involved in Sub-Saharan Africa' but 'with over fifteen million customers, staff and shareholders' they had to strike a balance for conducting their business.

We were not convinced that we should continue to use the services of this particular institution as their policies concerning the use of funds deposited with them could not meet our requirements. We wrote to the local branch manager explaining the reason for withdrawing our money, at the same time thanking him for the good service we had always received at the branch. We felt that our attitude towards banking and investment should not be negative. Although there were definite areas to avoid there were also opportunities for promoting renewable energy, social housing, fair trade, organic food and farming and micro-credit facilities for small third world businesses. We found that Triodos Bank satisfied our requirements.

The next thing was to consider long-term investments. Our monthly meeting had been advised to invest in CAFcash and Charibond as they are common investments funds specially set up for charities (CIFs). However EIRIS published a disturbing analysis of a number of CIFs in 1996 which led us to question the investment policies of CAFcash and Charibond. So we wrote to both of them and received sympathetic replies, but we felt that neither of these CIFs had an ethical investment policy at that time. So we withdrew our money.

As we knew we were not qualified to set up our own investment portfolio we sought the advice of an 'ethical' financial adviser who advertises in *The Friend*. We explained that we no longer wished to hold government stock as some of the money could be used to fund the production and export of armaments. We also wanted to support care for the environment, recycling initiatives, animal welfare, care for people in developing countries and to encourage good employment practices everywhere. Our adviser sent us a list of unit trust managers whose policies would suit our requirements and we went ahead from there.

Since we were withdrawing our money from the CIFs which count as 'special range investments', we had to make sure that all our funds were distributed in the correct ratio between 'narrow range' and 'wide range' investments. It is very useful to keep our repairs reserve fund in readily available cash, so this money is held on deposit in several different building societies; this counts as 'narrow range' investment. We have found one society, the Ecology, which lends its funds with particular concern for the environment and for community projects, which again satisfies our concern for positive investment.

As treasurers we are happier to be working with funds invested in companies who support Quaker concerns. Throughout the period of change and re-investment we received advice and support from our monthly meeting trustees. When we had the complete programme of our banking and investment plans, we took it to monthly meeting and were very encouraged by their favourable acceptance.

Just recently we have received several calls from members of other monthly meetings who have heard about our 'ethical' policy and sought our advice. Some of them have problems with Friends who believe that trustees are bound to invest their money for the maximum return. This is not true. The Charity Commissioners have no authority to insist on investments which contravene the basic concerns of the charity. It is sometimes said that our very old meeting houses are so expensive to maintain that we must look for the highest rate of interest or dividend. But do Quakers really believe that beautiful buildings are more important than people or the future of our planet? On more than one occasion we have heard a treasurer say that the local high street bank is the only one he or she can conveniently use. We can say from our experience that our present banking arrangements are no trouble at all, either for paying out or depositing money.

We are always aware that not all of our members are active supporters of Quaker witness in the world. However, for many Quakers, an essential part of their Quakerism is an outward expression of the compassion and concern for justice and peace that they find deeply rooted in meeting for worship. Thus there has always been a strong Quaker presence on marches and at vigils supporting the anti-apartheid movement and CND, and opposing wars in Vietnam, the Falklands and the Gulf. Just last May the Bull Street Meeting House in Birmingham was filled with Friends from all over the country who had come to support the Jubilee 2000 movement, calling for cancellation of unpayable third world debt.

It seems to us that Quaker money should be supporting those ideals that find expression in our witness and in our testimonies and not working against them. [The article concludes by raising questions about some of Britain Yearly Meeting's investments as they stood in 1998, but these have been omitted as policy changes over time].

Anne Brewer and Audrey Garnett, *The Friend*, 11 June 1999

Contributing to the problem

I am privileged to live on the edge of open countryside where by day I hear the wing beats of passing geese and by night the screech of owls and bark of foxes – the sounds of silence. I chose this home – and Quakerism – because I crave silence.

The new M8 extension has thrust harsh reality into my tranquil oasis. It passes several miles from my house, but on still days – and nights – the drone of traffic is clearly audible, where before I heard silence. On the day the new road opened, I stood by my window puzzled by the sound. When the truth dawned, I was horrified. Not just because my peaceful place is being invaded by a disturbance I am powerless to control, but also because I am as responsible as anyone else for the problem.

The opening of the new road coincided with the decision to become a two car family, because my new job involves a lot of travelling and my partner was having to cycle fourteen miles to work whatever the weather, clearly unsustainable through a Scottish winter. The noise from the road suddenly intruding into my life seemed like instant and justifiable retribution from Mother Earth.

In addition, there was the awareness my new job has given me of the blight the bypass around the city has brought to many areas. Not only the constant noise, air pollution and ugliness of the road, but also the way it cuts several communities off from their countryside – no pedestrian bridges were built, people are expected to take a deep breath and run for it. Even once they escape into the hills, the noise follows, audible for miles. Ironically, in my work with these communities to improve the environment they live in, I use the road that damages them every day. If the bypass had not been built, I probably would not have taken the job, because the travelling time would have been too great.

Tess Darwin, *Quaker monthly*, July 1996

Dilemmas of living in truth

The practice of our testimony to integrity is still about honesty, veracity and trustworthiness. It also seems to include being open, not underhand or secretive; and also open-minded, seeing the other's point of view, even if not agreeing with it; being reliable, keeping confidences; and not deceiving people by word or deed. One of the difficulties with which we may be confronted is in discerning what is true and, having discerned it, finding ourselves unsure how to express it with sensitivity.

When we are confronted by a choice between two equally difficult alternatives, moral justification can be adduced for choosing either alternative and the choice, when made, may well attract moral condemnation from those who disagree with it. Every dilemma is two-edged and can suggest complicity or disapproval. It is no protection to be 'right' morally, but discretion and a refusal to be pushed precipitately into things can be a strength. Corder Catchpool wrote: 'Conscience ... commands loyalty to the voice of God in the heart. I think this is the same thing, whether it be called religion or morality.'

If we have made a practice of attempting to resolve minor dilemmas by a careful weighing of moral arguments on either side, instead of a course which is the most expedient or convenient to us; if we have already tried to live without the petty wickedness of gossip, prevarication, dissimulation and all the other little deceits acceptable in modern life: then we may develop a power of discernment which will assist us also to resolve the major dilemmas of living in The Truth. To Friends, this more simply means offering such dilemmas, both small and large, to the searching power of the Light.

John Goodbody, Sarah Scott, John Hudson, *Quaker monthly*, August 1994

Integrity and commitment

Friends warm to the idea of 'caring and sharing' as an expression of social witness. But there is another 'pair' which I believe is equally significant. This is the combination of integrity and commitment.

By the 'integrity' of our own actions I mean the way we see certain kinds of action as matters of principle: acting peacefully, truthfully, justly, respecting people's rights – all important dimensions of the idea of 'living the kingdom' now.

By 'commitment' I mean further action well beyond what is required if we are to act peacefully, truthfully and so on, namely promoting or pursuing peace, truth, justice, rights. This many Friends do with great energy and commitment. But it is something quite different from what is ordinarily understood by the integrity involved in following moral rules. There is a world of difference between acting non-violently and promoting non-violence, acting justly and promoting justice or combating injustice and so on.

Friends are very much into doing both, but this in a way is what separates us from many others, for whom there is a tendency either to stick with the one – dutiful action – or to go for the other – hot pursuit, with little or less regard for the first. Thus, when others are tempted to weigh consequences, we appeal to principle, for instance over questions of non-violence or integrity; but when others might rest behind what strict duty requires of us, we feel the call to go beyond that, to play our part in 'mending' the world – not as a call of duty (against our inclinations) but with a love for and care for humanity that involves our whole being.

Nigel Dower, *Friends quarterly*, April 1996

Staying committed

Perhaps the most important thing in my life is to try to achieve a unity between the personal, social, political and spiritual responsibilities I have assumed and my corresponding intuitive commitments. I feel out of touch, unconnected, distant from God when I find myself with responsibilities I do not believe in. I have promised myself to remain in any job only as long as I believe in that job and would do it without pay or in spite of inconvenience. The moment my heart is not in my social responsibilities, I try to reduce them and shift my burden into areas for which I feel passionate commitment.

N1 in *Who do we think we are?*, 1998

Living as truly as I am able

I was born in 1943 in Portsmouth. The bombs which terrorised my parents have been replaced in my life by a threat and a promise far more poignant and dangerous. To live my life as a gay man and to celebrate, at the same time, my fatherhood and my profession, demands a toehold balance which terrifies and enthrals me.

I was honest with my wife and told her about my sexuality before we were engaged. Eventually the crisis came. I would not like you to think I capitulated to despair without a struggle. I tried to pray, took advice, kept myself wickedly busy, and tried so hard it felt as if I were bleeding. I went away for a month to think. I stayed for a while in a monastery where, for the first time in thirty-five years, someone when speaking of homosexuals said 'we' instead of 'you'. I could have wept.

While I was away I was encouraged to take a hard look at the things I still did like about myself – my ability to care, the way I relate to my children, my honesty and my intuition. It dawned on me slowly that all these things spring from sexuality. By putting the lid on my sexuality I was effectively closing down all that was worthwhile in my life. In a very real way I had chosen to cease to live.

But I kept on retreating. Surely to live my life 'in the service of others' was a preferable (and more comfortable) way than to stand on the edge of acceptance for the rest of my life. Somewhere in the midst of this turmoil it became obvious that I could never love, not really love, until I had learned to love myself a little. As it was, even my dutiful fathering of my children was based on a lie.

Leaving my family is the hardest thing I have done so far. I make no attempt to let things seem like they used to be. We occasionally have tea together as a family since that comes naturally, but I have had to find a new way of being a father.

Being a gay parent is like much else about being gay. Nothing is received wisdom. Everything has to be thought out from a starting place of zero. But unnerving though this is, it feels more real than trying to live out the parameters set up by the nuclear family. Some time ago, I found myself writing in my diary, 'I am now living as truly as I am able.' Being real, being alive and being vulnerable again has set me tingling.

Peter Martin, *Meeting gay Friends*, 1982

Freedom from duplicity

Simplicity is freedom. Duplicity is bondage. Simplicity brings joy and balance. Duplicity brings anxiety and fear. The preacher of Ecclesiastes observes that 'God made man simple; man's complex problems are of his own devising' (Eccles. 7:29). Because many of us are experiencing the liberation God brings through simplicity we are once again singing an old Shaker hymn:

Tis the gift to be simple,
Tis the gift to be free,
Tis the gift to come down where you ought to be,
And when we find ourselves in the place just right,
Twill be in the valley of love and delight.

When true simplicity is gained,
To bow and to bend we shan't be ashamed.
To turn, turn will be our delight
Till by turning, turning
We come round right.

The Christian Discipline of simplicity is an *inward* reality that results in an *outward* life-style. Both the inward and the outward aspects of simplicity are essential. We deceive ourselves if we believe we can possess the inward reality without its having a profound effect on how we live. To attempt to arrange an outward life-style of simplicity without the inward reality leads to deadly legalism.

Richard Foster, 1978, *Celebration of discipline*, pp.99-100

Other pieces which examine the social testimony on truth & integrity are:

3. Simplicity

An Experiment in Riches, 1988

How difficult it is to imagine the misery and destructive limitations of poverty, when we live in affluence – though that has its own destructive attributes! To descend permanently into voluntary poverty is unhelpful, and presumably not right for most of us. Are we then to continue in affluence?

Three members of our meeting, discussing 'An Experiment in Poverty', discovered that we already practise many of [these] abstentions. We do not have central heating but heat only the room in which we are spending most time. We do not run cars, having chosen in our retirement to live in a town small enough to offer, within walking distance, all that we usually need. Most books we read are from the public library, as we know our personal books too well by now. We all spend less than £12 a week on food for ourselves and our guests – very easy for the two of us who are vegetarians – but the garden contributes, so perhaps that is not a fair comparison.

All three of us have incomes that would enable us to live much more expensively. So why do we not? Is it masochism, or laziness over changing from the tight economies of our youth? Or is it an obsession with the concept of simple living? We ourselves attribute it to our particular sense of fairness, our conviction that it is not for us to spend on ourselves more than our share of the world's resources. If we take more than our share, someone else must have less. We have to bear some responsibility for those living in deprivation.

Deciding on our 'fair share' is not easy. The traditional assessment is the national average disposable income, but in this country that is now over £80 per week per person, man, woman and child. So another possibility today is to try to live nearer the *world's* average income, what everyone in the world could enjoy if incomes were to be distributed equally (and if incentives, based on social commitment or even on status instead of income, successfully kept up production). The world average is now perhaps as much as £50 per week per person – and here no allowance need be made for the house one owns; houses play a very small part in the incomes of most inhabitants of the world.

Having accepted what seems a fair income, we have freedom of choice in how to spend it. We can let ourselves be extravagant in one direction so long as we cut back in another. Our own choice is to take a daily paper, *The Friend* and *The Economist*, but not to have a television – though I suspect this is to save time rather than money and perhaps one day we shall want one after all!

A major advantage of this way of laying out our income and expenditure is that it leaves us – and surely a very high proportion of the Society of Friends – with money to give away to charities, or to the poor whom we know personally, if we can persuade them to accept it. Or we can use some part of it on pressure groups or political parties, trying to persuade our rulers to deal in a more Christian way with those in need. If enough Friends decided thus to curtail their own spending, we should have a splendid lever with which to try to move the government.

So what about trying this experiment for a year or two and discovering how truly rich you feel?

Maisie Birmingham, *The Friend*, 11 March 1988

Simplicity in the modern context

We may think of simplicity as one of those old-fashioned Quaker ideals: good enough for a bygone age, when life was slower, quieter, relatively uncluttered. The modern world we live in is getting more complex by the day, with its administrative jungles, its gadgets, and more gadgets. How does simplicity fit into that – and what kind of 'social testimony' can it make? What kind of social relevance does it have?

One could argue that the very complexity of modern life frees us to pursue higher interests, do better things than engage in mindless drudgery: let those clever machines wash, cook, compute, practically write our letters for us. We can use the time saved to study, to meet people, do things for others, or to contemplate the mysteries of the universe, if we like. In theory this complexity makes life simpler: it gives us the space, the time to rise above the humdrum level of life and take note of deeper things – rather like the silence during meeting for worship. In theory. In practice, what we tend to get is not so much a helpful contemplative 'silence' in our lives but what I would call the ceaseless chatter of things: Mend me! Polish me! Check me! Switch me on/off/over! Replace me, I'm worn... or outdated... In the end it's only too easy to find ourselves not freer spirits but ever more enslaved by the material things of life. Bearing witness, through all we own, to the consumerist ethic that dominates our society, an ethic that clearly puts things above people and their concerns.

The other point of course is this: can it be right for me to own so much when there are others who have practically nothing, or very little? It's not an easy question to answer, either. There is such a thing as pretend poverty, false simplicity, related to 'champagne socialism' I suppose. But there is also such a thing as true solidarity – not just spoken, but lived. And lived openly: as if to say 'Look, let's not overindulge while there are still so many who can't even live in modest comfort.' But then how much, of what, can I in good conscience allow myself? How does one interpret 'simplicity' in the modern context, and make of it a positive statement?

This is something I ask myself often. And maybe it's in the 'asking myself often' that the answer lies: not in a dogmatic kind of abstinence, not in publicly wearing a sort of life-style uniform – not, in other words, in doing the thing to the letter, but in the spirit of always renewed inquiry: Do I really need this? If not, will it at least be shareable, give pleasure to others as well as myself? Is it genuinely labour-saving, or just another noisy, demanding toy that gobbles up energy, wastes resources, has been produced by virtual slave labour in some underprivileged part of the world? So much to think about, find out about. Looks like this modern simplicity is terribly complicated!

There's one more aspect to this though: increasingly, in our society, we run our daily lives like stage managers and film directors – pushing buttons to produce whatever effects we choose. I call it the 'putting a record on' attitude to life. Very tempting, of course! But there is a big difference, in terms of joy/enjoyment between *making* your favourite piece of music ring out where and when you want it, or *finding* it given to you, chancing across it as you switch on the radio. That difference I think is summed up in the one word: gratitude. In our 'advanced' culture we've forgotten how to be grateful; we want things on demand. And from our attitude to things it is maybe only a relatively small step to our attitude towards people.

Angela Arnold, ROST *Responses & challenges* 1996

My living out and not living our testimony to simplicity

I grew up in a Quaker family which was moderately well-off but lived modestly. We had our treats on occasions but we were not ostentatious in dress, furnishings, holidays or gadgetry. There was money for games, books and occasional concerts or theatre. And we had our birthday and Christmas treats. That was forty or fifty years ago. Looking back I see it as a satisfying lifestyle and I don't remember feeling deprived of anything or desperately longing for things I didn't have.

For a long time simplicity was not something that I thought about a lot. I tended to live very cheaply as a young man for nine-tenths of the time and 'splash out' pretty extravagantly on some special occasion. Perhaps the Yearly Meeting session at Warwick in 1993 was one of the first times that I had really considered what was involved in the testimony. My understanding is that the core of the testimony is to do with the spiritual imperative to 'let go', to practise 'detachment' from everything. That has not been easy for me in theory or practice.

In theory, I have always been against the detached observer in favour of the committed participant. Yet I have come to understand the wonderful simplicity of the position: that perfect freedom is to be found in letting go. Because, when we don't cling on, we are really free to follow God's leadings. The testimony to simplicity, is, then, at the heart of our faith. But I have also found it difficult to put into practice.

I struggle with possessiveness and also covetousness and the need for security. Let me give a trivial but revealing example, which, in terms of the testimony to simplicity, cuts both ways. I virtually never buy snacks when I'm out or travelling. My parents managed without doing so. It has crept into our lifestyles and becomes one of those things which we need the money to be able to continue to do. I've always set my face against it. It's partly a streak of meanness or asceticism (which goes with the occasional splurges); it's also a deliberate effort to live more simply in terms of money and the use of resources such as packaging. So I take my own bottles and flasks and supplies of all sorts. I almost always take too much and bring some back. There must be in that a part of me which is clinging on to a security which oughtn't to be so necessary.

What about our standard of living? I do lean against the spirit of consumerism in a lot of ways. I may be found in a caftan with the heating off; I have some resistance to jet setting around the world ... though I may go and visit my daughter in South Korea; I try not to go to restaurants at all frequently; I still assume that taxis are for tycoons; I wear my clothes until they are full of holes; we have relatively few of the white goods. Here we have inherited a washing machine and a box freezer but in Didsbury we had neither, nor dishwasher, microwave, television or video; we spend very little on furniture and decorating.

And yet we spend more than my parents did in almost every single category with the exception of housing: food, drink, transport (both car and rail), clothes, entertainment, telephone, heating (they had no central heating), etc. Our simplicity is very relative. We spent £16,500 last year excluding estate agents' fees but including all the other extra costs of moving; excluding also donations – all in all probably around two to three times the standard of living we would have on benefit.

The ratcheting up of expenditure is almost irresistible. But others are left further and further behind. In the two-thirds world as well as at home. So we drink our wine and eat out in restaurants and the rest, secure in the knowledge that others are starving or cannot find twenty pence for a youth club entrance. Simplicity is also needed if the Testimony to Equality is to be taken seriously. Moreover the Testimony to Truth will be a dead letter if we say we treat everyone as our sisters and brothers and treat them by our additional consumption as of no importance.

We don't like to talk about our lifestyles. But we have to. Our faith, our spiritual health requires that openness so that we can stimulate each other to greater resistance to the market and encourage each other in our acts of resistance, however small.

Jonathan Dale, ROST *Responses & challenges* 1996

Part of a talk to the Treasurers' Conference, 1998

I go 'over the top' with family finances, having written down our spending every day for over twenty-three years, using about twenty-five categories. My thrifty husband, reared in great poverty as a Strict and Particular Baptist, has begun to accept the monthly facts I force upon him, and to enjoy what we have been able to do recently. We lived very carefully for nearly twenty years, then our pensions began and we downsized from a cottage with land to a town flat, and we now have £60,000 capital – mainly in the Triodos Quaker Social Housing Account, I hasten to add! And now our only child, Alice, is twenty-two and actually earning her living, no longer receiving twenty per cent of our income, as in the last five years.

In January 1998 and also in January 1997 we have spent the previous year's surplus by dividing it in two, and each deciding how to give away our half. My husband's £1000 the first year, and £1,500 this year goes on young people in our area whom he first got to know when he worked as a home tutor, and whom he still knows through the vagaries of their visits to the courts and to prison, and in helping their families. I think he goes over the top, especially as the bulk of his so-called pocket money also goes in their direction. But this decision has taken a tremendous strain out of our relationship and accounts, now that we can afford such a decision. My giving tends to be simpler, going direct to Britain Yearly Meeting, or Mediation West Cornwall, for instance. The chance to really make a difference is exciting, and as treasurer I can always do it in perfect anonymity, of course, if it is one of 'my' charities.

We have now decided to give away all our surplus each year, so in fact we are ignoring the effect of inflation and letting our capital shrink. Why not? We have pensions and the flat we own, and our daughter is independent. We make sure we are living at a level one of us could sustain on one set of pensions and the savings income, and last year we increased our 'giving away' which includes gifts to the Quakers and to charities (partly via the Charities Aid Foundation) and to friends and relations, from twenty-three per cent in 1996 to twenty-seven per cent in 1997. If the government is being slow to redistribute wealth we can make a start ourselves!

We scrutinise the changes in our spending from year to year and try to simplify. But I perpetually lose the battle over the car. Martin maintains he needs it to be socially useful, to give lifts to his young impecunious friends, to get them to the probation office on time, or whatever. And they can obviously more easily accept the lifts than payment for railway tickets.

When our preparative meeting discussed lifestyles a year ago I confessed to many, many failures over simplicity. We are just about vegan, but spend a lot on birthday cards and newspapers. I have more clothes than I need but only two pairs of shoes, blue and brown. You all know the picture. But, the main point is that we know our financial position, and make decisions and revisit them several times a year. What probably keeps us sane is 'pocket money' which we each spend as we wish; £10 a month for many years, but now up to about ten per cent of our income. This gives us each some privacy and independence, to buy presents for each other, or a book, or coffee in the town, or even to give more away.

I think I am hoping that an understanding of financial audit will lead on to a wish for a social audit. Do you remember that in Jonathan Dale's Swarthmore Lecture he said that we might consider the possibility of an annual review, with other Friends, of our lifestyles and our spiritual condition? This would require openness and courage, but I believe it would lead to real spiritual growth and to faithfulness to our social testimonies.

Janet Lynch, *Quaker monthly*, November 1998

Some inner attitudes and controlling principles of simplicity

Freedom from anxiety is characterised by three inner attitudes. If what we have we receive as a gift, and if what we have is to be cared for by God, and if what we have is available to others, then we will possess freedom from anxiety. *This is the inward reality of simplicity.* However, if what we have we believe we have got, and if what we have we believe we must hold on to, and if what we have is not available to others, then we will live in anxiety. Such persons will never know simplicity regardless of the outward contortions they may put themselves through in order to live 'the simple life'.

To receive what we have as a gift from God is the first inner attitude of simplicity. We work but we know that it is not our work that gives us what we have. We live by grace even when it comes to 'daily bread'. We are dependent upon God for the simplest elements of life: air, water, sun. What we have is not the result of our labour, but of the gracious care of God. When we are tempted to think that what we own is the result of our personal efforts, it takes only a little drought or a small accident to show us once again how utterly dependent we are for everything.

To know that it is God's business, and not ours, to care for what we have is the second inner attitude of simplicity. God is able to protect what we possess. We can trust him. Does that mean that we should never take the keys out of the car or lock the door? Of course not. But we know that the lock on the door is not what protects the house. It is only common sense to take normal precautions, but if we believe that precaution itself protects us and our goods, we will be riddled with anxiety. There simply is no such thing as 'burglar proof' precaution. Obviously, these matters are not restricted to possessions but include such things as our reputation and our employment. Simplicity means the freedom to trust God for these (and all) things.

To have our goods available to others marks the third inner attitude of simplicity. If our goods are not available to the community when it is clearly right and good, then they are stolen goods. The reason we find such an idea so difficult is our fear of the future. We cling to our possessions rather than sharing them because we are anxious about tomorrow. But if we truly believe that God is who Jesus says he is, then we do not need to be afraid. When we come to see God as the almighty Creator *and* our loving Father, we can share because we know that he will care for us. If someone is in need, we are free to help them. Again, ordinary common sense will define the parameters of our sharing and save us from foolishness.

When we are seeking first the kingdom of God, these three attitudes will characterise our lives. Taken together they define what Jesus means by 'do not be anxious'. They comprise the inner reality of Christian simplicity. And we can be certain that when we live this way the 'all these things' that are necessary to carry on human life adequately will be ours as well.

[And so I] suggest ten controlling principles for the outward expression of simplicity. They should never be viewed as laws but as only one attempt to flesh out the meaning of simplicity for today.

First, buy things for their usefulness rather than their status. Cars should be bought for their utility, not their prestige. Consider riding a bicycle. When you are considering an apartment, a condominium, or a house, thought should be given to liveability rather than how much it will impress others. Don't have more living space than is reasonable. After all, who needs seven rooms for two people?

Consider your clothes. Most people have no need for more clothes. They buy more not because they need clothes, but because they want to keep up with the fashions. Hang the fashions! Buy what you need. Wear your clothes until they are worn out. Stop trying to impress people with your clothes and impress them with your life. If it is practical in your situation, learn the joy of making clothes. And for God's sake (and I mean that quite literally) have clothes that are practical rather than ornamental. John Wesley writes, 'As ... for apparel, I buy the most lasting and, in general, the plainest I can. I buy no furniture but what is necessary and cheap.'

Second, reject anything that is producing an addiction in you. Learn to distinguish between a real psychological need, like cheerful surroundings, and an addiction. Eliminate or cut down on the use of addictive, non-nutritional drinks: alcohol, coffee, tea, Coca-Cola, and so on. Chocolate has become a serious addiction for many people. If you have become addicted to television, by all means sell your set or give it away. Any of the media that you find you cannot do without, get rid of: radios, stereos, magazines, videos, newspapers, books. If money has a grip on your heart, give some away and feel the inner release. Simplicity is freedom, not slavery. Refuse to be a slave to anything but God.

Remember, an addiction, by its very nature, is something that is beyond your control. Resolves of the will alone are useless in defeating a true addiction. You cannot just decide to be free of it. But you can decide to open this corner of your life to the forgiving grace and healing power of God. You can decide to allow loving friends who know the ways of prayer to stand with you. You can decide to live simply one day at a time in quiet dependence upon God's intervention.

How do you discern an addiction? Very simply, you watch for undisciplined compulsions. A student friend told me about one morning when he went out to get his newspaper and found it missing. He panicked, wondering how he could possibly start the day without the newspaper. Then he noticed a morning paper in his neighbour's yard, and he began to plot how he could sneak over and steal it. Immediately he realised that he was dealing with a genuine addiction. He rushed inside and called the newspaper office to cancel his subscription. The receptionist, obviously filling out a form, asked courteously, 'Why are you cancelling your subscription to the newspaper?' My friend blurted out, 'Because I'm addicted!' Undaunted, the receptionist replied, 'Would you like to cancel your entire subscription or would you like to keep the Sunday edition?' to which he exclaimed, 'No, I'm going cold turkey!' Now, obviously not everyone should cancel their subscription to the newspaper, but for this young man it was an important act.

Third, develop a habit of giving things away. If you find that you are becoming attached to some possession, consider giving it to someone who needs it. I still remember the Christmas I decided that rather than buying or even making an item, I would give away something that meant a lot to me. My motive was selfish: I wanted to know the liberation that comes from even this simple act of voluntary poverty. The gift was a ten-speed bike. As I went to the person's home to deliver the present, I remember singing with new meaning the worship chorus, 'Freely, freely you have received; freely, freely give.' When my son Nathan was six years old he heard of a classmate who needed a lunch box and asked me if he could give him his own lunch box. Hallelujah!

De-accumulate! Masses of things that are not needed complicate life. They must be sorted and stored and dusted and re-sorted and re-stored *ad nauseam*. Most of us could get rid of half our possessions without any serious sacrifice. We would do well to follow the counsel of Thoreau: 'Simplify, simplify.'

Fourth, refuse to be propagandised by the custodians of modern gadgetry. Timesaving devices almost never save time. Beware of the promise: 'It will pay for itself in six months.' Most gadgets are built to break down and wear out and so complicate our lives rather than enhance them. This problem is a plague in the toy industry. Children do not need to be entertained by dolls that cry, eat, wet, sweat, and spit. An old rag doll can be more enjoyable and more lasting. Often children find more joy in playing with old pots and pans than with the latest space set. Look for toys that are educational and durable. Make some yourself.

Usually gadgets are an unnecessary drain on the energy resources of the world. The United States has less than six percent of the world's population, but consumes about thirty-three percent of the world's energy. Air conditioners in the United States alone use the same amount of energy as does the entire country of China. Environmental responsibility alone should keep us from buying the majority of the gadgets produced today.

Propagandists try to convince us that because the newest model of this or that has a new feature (trinket?), we must sell the old one and buy the new one. Sewing machines have new stitches, stereos have new buttons, cars have new designs. Such media dogma needs to be carefully scrutinised. Often 'new' features seduce us into buying what we do not need. Probably that refrigerator will serve us quite well for the rest of our lives even without the automatic ice maker and the fancy exterior.

Fifth, learn to enjoy things without owning them. Owning things is an obsession in our culture. If we own it, we feel we can control it; and if we can control it, we feel it will give us more pleasure. The idea is an illusion. Many things in life can be enjoyed without possessing or controlling them. Share things. Enjoy the beach without feeling you have to buy a piece of it. Enjoy public parks and libraries.

Sixth, develop a deeper appreciation for the creation. Get close to the earth. Walk whenever you can. Listen to the birds. Enjoy the texture of grass and leaves. Smell the flowers. Marvel in the rich colours everywhere. Simplicity means to discover once again that 'the earth is the Lord's and the fullness thereof'. (Ps. 24:1).

Seventh, look with a healthy scepticism at all 'buy now, pay later' schemes. They are a trap and only deepen your bondage. Both Old and New Testaments condemn usury for good reasons. ('Usury' in the Bible is not used in the modern sense of exorbitant interest; it referred to any kind of interest at all.) Charging interest was viewed as an unbrotherly exploitation of another's misfortune, hence a denial of community. Jesus denounced usury as a sign of the old life and admonished his disciples to 'lend, expecting nothing in return.' (Luke 6:35)

These words of Scripture should not be elevated into some kind of universal law obligatory upon all cultures at all times. But neither should they be thought of as totally irrelevant to modern society. Behind these biblical injunctions stand centuries of accumulated wisdom (and perhaps some bitter experiences!). Certainly prudence, as well as simplicity, demands that we use extreme caution before incurring debt.

Eighth, obey Jesus' instructions about plain, honest speech. 'Let what you say be simply 'Yes' or 'No'; anything more than this comes from evil.' (Matt. 5:37) If you consent to do a task, do it. Avoid flattery and half-truths. Make honesty and integrity the distinguishing characteristics of your speech. Reject jargon and abstract speculation whose purpose is to obscure and impress rather than to illuminate and inform.

Plain speech is difficult because we so seldom live out of the divine Centre, so seldom respond only to heavenly promptings. Often fear of what others may think or a hundred other motives determine our 'yes' or 'no' rather than obedience to divine urgings. Then if a more attractive opportunity arises we quickly reverse our decision. But if our speech comes out of obedience to the divine Centre, we will find no reason to turn our 'yes' into 'no' and our 'no' into 'yes'. We will be living in simplicity of speech because our words will have only one Source. Søren Kierkegaard writes: 'If thou art absolutely obedient to God, then there is no ambiguity in thee and thou art mere simplicity before God ... One thing there is which all Satan's cunning and all the snares of temptation cannot take by surprise, and that is simplicity.' (Christian discourses, p.324)

Ninth, reject anything that breeds the oppression of others. Perhaps no person has more fully embodied this principle than the eighteenth century Quaker tailor John Woolman. His famous Journal is redolent with tender references to his desire to live so as not to oppress others.

> Here I was led into a close and laborious inquiry whether I kept clear from all things which tended to stir up or were connected with wars: my heart was deeply concerned that in [the] future I might in all things keep steadily to the pure truth, and live and walk in the plainness and simplicity of a sincere follower of Christ. And here luxury and covetousness, with the numerous oppressions and other evils attending them, appeared very afflicting to me.

This is one of the most difficult and sensitive issues for us to face, but face it we must. Do we sip our coffee and eat our bananas at the expense of exploiting Latin American peasants? In a world of limited resources, does our lust for wealth mean the poverty of others? Should we buy products that are made by forcing people into dull assembly-line jobs? Do we enjoy hierarchical relationships in the company or factory that keep others under us? Do we oppress our children or spouse because we feel certain tasks are beneath us?

Often our oppression is tinged with racism, sexism, and nationalism. The colour of the skin still affects one's position in the company. The sex of a job applicant still affects the salary. The national origin of a person still affects the way he or she is perceived. May God give us prophets today who, like John Woolman, will call us 'from the desire of wealth' so that we may be able to 'break the yoke of oppression'.

Tenth, shun anything that distracts you from seeking first the kingdom of God. It is so easy to lose focus in the pursuit of legitimate, even good things. Job, position, status, family, friends, security – these and many more can all too quickly become the centre of attention. George Fox warns:

> There is the danger and the temptation to you, of drawing your minds into your business, and clogging them with it; so

that ye can hardly do anything to the service of God and your minds will go into the things, and not over the things ... And then, if the Lord God cross you, and stop you by sea and land, and take [your] goods and customs from you, that your minds should not be cumbered, then that mind that is cumbered, will fret, being out of the power of God.

May God give you – and me – the courage, the wisdom, the strength always to hold the kingdom of God as the number-one priority of our lives. To do so is to live in simplicity.

Richard Foster 1978, *Celebration of discipline*, pp.108-115

Other pieces which examine the social testimony on simplicity are:

7. Creation   Some thoughts on juicy puritanism

4. Equality

Where are the poor Quakers?

Recently, my monthly meeting has had to consider a bequest from long ago. A piece of land was left for the benefit of poor Quakers.

I don't know what conditions were like then, but these days we don't see very many poor Quakers. There are some, of course, who are poor by circumstance or choice, but what most outsiders would see at any gathering of Friends, from meeting for worship to yearly meeting, is a group of people whose dress identifies them as comfortably off and whose manner of speech identifies them as middle class.

Quakers are very quick to proclaim their concern for the poor. Meeting houses are full of appeals, petitions and news of good deeds in 'deprived areas'. But while such Quaker actions may be socially useful, they also tend to establish Quakers on the comfortable side of a social divide. Quakers are identified with those who can give and help while the poor are seen as in need of kind, Quakerly attentions.

But it seems to me that as a Religious Society we stand in need of poor Quakers and that, without their presence as members and equals, our Society might be called a deprived area. We need to learn from poor Quakers, both spiritually and (if this is separate) in our social testimony.

Think what our meetings would be like if the poor were among us in the proportions in which they exist in the country as a whole. Suppose many Quakers in each meeting were struggling to live on state benefit. What would this teach us about Quaker simplicity? Suppose we didn't all have bank accounts, let alone investments. Would some of us have to question our unearned income? Suppose we couldn't assume that most Quakers owned cars. Would we begin to rearrange meetings for worship and business in accordance with public transport schedules and find ourselves caring more for the environment and the needs of others? Suppose a large percentage of the children in our meetings lived below the poverty line. Would our regular discussion of children move beyond the programme for children's meeting and the welfare of Quaker schools?

It's easy to multiply examples along these lines. But why are there so few poor Quakers? One reason must be that in outreach activities we tend to assume that new members of the Society will be people like ourselves. For instance, Quakers tend to advertise in broadsheet rather than tabloid newspapers. Quaker history doesn't help either. The rather sentimentalised (and inaccurate) picture we have of Quakers as philanthropic and reforming employers suggests a wealthy, upper middle-class sect that does not encourage poorer members.

And if poorer, working-class people do find and come to our meetings for worship, they tend to find a gathering of comfortably off, well-dressed people whose wealth, social class and assumptions about the poor quickly make them feel uncomfortable.

I squirm with embarrassment when Quakers who have never lived on a council estate make generalisations about them and their inhabitants. I am deeply unhappy and wonder if I'm in the right place when Friends generalise uncritically about the Society's middle-class identity or the presumed incomes of its members.

I have been a member of the Society for fourteen years and was an attender for ten years before that. It is a long time since I could have been called a 'poor Quaker' but I can't forget the way in which my poverty and class origins made me feel out of place in Quaker circles.

Once I thought this was my problem. Over the years, I have come to think it might be a problem for the Religious Society of Friends as a whole.

Kathleen Bell, *The Friend*, 16 October 1998

The institutional evil of homelessness

We need to see the problem of homelessness as only one end of a spectrum of evil that has the massive subsidies to owners at the other. It is a problem that will be as difficult and painful to solve as slavery. Slavery as an evil shared many of the qualities of the present housing situation – it benefited the wealthy, created an underclass and denied them human rights. The solution was painful, for abolition often required that slave owners abandon their investment with no recompense. To change our attitudes to housing will be no less of a challenge to us than slavery was for the reformers, not only because institutional evil is hard to recognise but also because so many of us benefit personally from the present situation.

We must first understand the present system and become clear about the extent of right and wrong that it contains. If we could achieve this, we could first work towards a consensus on goals and then, I hope with other churches, start on the secular arguments.

This is a challenge that the Society, and indeed other churches, must face. If we fail to address the roots of an issue in which most of us are unwittingly part of the problem, we will need to look very carefully at the claims we make about our contribution in the world.

Richard Hilken, 1992, 1993, *QFP* 23.23

'Be patterns, be examples...'

'We have heard the urgent summons to join in the building of the new city and to live by its values, even while we inhabit the old, with its too frequent denial of human dignity. To that end, we must inform ourselves, master our material and train our faculties for a lifelong commitment to service.' (London Yearly Meeting Epistle, 1972)

These words, which made me apply for membership of the Society of Friends after nine years as an attender, also express for me a Quaker approach to work. Our jobs are many but we have a common quest to make them serviceable for the building of the city of God, which takes little account of the world's preoccupation with pay and status. The Epistle signalled a readiness to address again class inequality and economic injustice; perhaps even to take up Jesus' challenge which has defeated so many since the rich young ruler turned away when he learned that to join in the building of the city he must share his wealth.

The vision of Yearly Meeting 1972 seemed to match that of early Friends and must have appealed to many who identified especially, as I did, with those of the Digger sort. Its aspirations seemed consistent with those which long ago had enabled us to rid our speech of the world's unfriendly language of class division.

In the course of the next few years, seeking new models of work which expressed the values of the Epistle, I discovered Friends working to make them a practical reality. Their work was celebrated and explained by the late E. J. F. Schumacher in his book, also published in 1972, *Small is beautiful: a study of economics as if people mattered*. His record of the conversion of the private company owned by the Bader family of Wellingborough Meeting into a common ownership co-operative, owned and democratically controlled by all who work there, created much interest – and still does. Visitors come to the Scott Bader Company and Commonwealth from all over the world. If it were not a common ownership, it would probably have been taken over by predators years ago and asset-stripped. As it is, it continues to be part of the community in the village of Wollaston, employing up to five hundred people, highly successful, very conscious of the responsibility to communicate and hand on the values and practices which have been inherited and maintained.

Grace Crookall-Greening, 'Be patterns, be examples', *Life and Work*, QSRE 1992

Real work and the imagination: leaps into the future

Unemployment that is involuntary destroys the soul. Denying young people the social affirmation of work undermines their fragile sense of emerging identity, so that discovering meaning and making purpose in life wither in the same snare. Then, social exclusion becomes the breeding ground for cynicism and crime. Lack of paid work is the greatest evil of our time.

LEAP, the Leaveners Experimental Arts Project, is a Quaker project which addresses this issue with young people in inner city London. Originating in training programmes in community theatre and group work, LEAP evolved into training courses in the creative use of conflict and supervised placements in voluntary agencies. Ten years of this work has enabled thousands of young adults to learn new skills, find new empowerment, make new friends and set out in new directions.

Creating a play together in a LEAP theatre workshop is a political metaphor. What didn't exist in week one is now a creation by week six, with everyone's involvement and a product to share with others. Performing a play depends on everyone's involvement; each member is needed and is making a contribution. Bringing their real life experience to the project means that the play is struggled over and passionately owned; then the work has a deep truth and a credibility. Out of the spark of inner group tensions and conflict will come the edge and originality of the piece. If relationships are too sweet, the work can become too bland.

Over these weeks, a personal change has been made possible; inner work and outer work have happened together, to give a taste of the Great Work that Matthew Fox writes about so persuasively in *The reinvention of work* (Harper, 1994). That Great Work is the investment of spirit into 'real work' so that the individual fully flourishes and fulfils the purpose of existence. LEAP can only give a taste of that Great Work because it is a training scheme and not paid employment. Even so, it reaffirms the values and practices that for participants have long been overwhelmed, and it opens doors onto new techniques and understandings, relations and opportunities. This frequently leads to part-time or full-time work, volunteering commitments and further education. Its record is impressive – the Joseph Rowntree Foundation's recent report 'Work out – or work in?' showed that mass unemployment is set to continue into the next century. Some of our young people will never know any paid work; never discover their identity, never feel fully valued in a society that only values money and materialism.

Unless. Unless we share out our existing work, so that all have some and no one is overworked and overstressed. Unless we all engage in committed volunteering to complement that paid work, creating a social ethos of volunteering and service. Unless more projects like LEAP give young people the chance to experience new learning and change direction.

Alec Davison, *QUNEC newsletter*, November 1996

Deaf hearing work
During a residential Yearly Meeting I became aware of a profoundly deaf child within Friends. Although he was not then old enough to join Quaker Youth Theatre he expressed an interest in joining in the future as he was involved with drama activities at his school for the deaf. Leaveners operate

an equal opportunities policy and in the past we had included a blind young person as well as one with speech problems.

The Quaker Youth Theatre encourages participants to bring to our projects their non-Quaker friends. This gives them the opportunity to share with them what living in a Quaker community means. Although this particular young person would not be eligible to join us for a few more years it was apparent from our previous experiences of trying to integrate young people with disabilities that we would need to do some careful preparation if we wanted to offer this deaf young man and his friends a positive and affirming experience.

The search started for an organisation which could help me gain experience of deaf people, either through training courses or volunteering. We organised our first deaf-hearing weekend workshop, using two volunteer deaf drama workers and two volunteer hearing workers. We arranged deaf awareness training prior to our Annual General Meeting and were pleased when Friends travelled to London especially for the workshop from as far as afield as the Wirral and Brighton.

We have struggled with overcoming stereotypes of all deaf people using sign language, and with their ability to be integrated into large and small groups. During busy summer projects we also struggled to give them an affirming experience without ghettoising them into a separate unit. We have had to manage the costly support necessary for a few members within a much larger company of youngsters, and were confronted by the hearing members who felt that there was too much emphasis on deaf members. In addition to communication issues two of our deaf members were our first Muslim members, and that presented new challenges to our pastoral team who endeavoured to explain our meetings for worship as well as having to explain our silent worship to youngsters for whom silence is not always welcome and can be seen as a barrier and isolating.

Although our deaf young Quaker has gone on to full time employment and is unable to join in many of our projects, other deaf members have continued their involvement with the youth theatre and we continue to work with our other deaf members and to offer projects which give opportunities best suited to their needs. This means seeking additional funding to buy in skills not available to us from Quaker volunteers. It means offering smaller projects with equal numbers of deaf and hearing participants in order that they are not always a small minority of the group We have sought to ensure that we find deaf workers to give them positive role models. During our projects it has required patience when they stay up late at night and are not aware of how noisy they can be. But for our hearing youth theatre members and adult helpers it has opened up new ways of communicating and made us more aware of our own limitations. It has also given us new opportunities to consider different types of silence and its meaning to us.

Tina Helfrich, December 1999

The amazing baby and her schooling

For me a recurring experience that sweeps all else away and leaves me overwhelmed with wonder is a seemingly simple one. It comes about through watching babies and young children as they grow and learn. The wonderful achievements they make as they master so much complex thought and behaviour are celebrated in the delight their parents and families show. The mastery of movement as they learn to walk, to run, perhaps to skip and jump is being matched by intellectual attainments as they try out their voices and learn to speak and so begin to develop ideas. Sometimes they amuse us with clever but not quite correct ones, such as the child who invited her parent to put her head on the pillow and watch the same dreams.

The list of accomplishments is endless though and, from my observation, achieved through great effort. Yet my earlier wonder at these babies' and young children's capacity for learning meets an almost terrifying stop when I contemplate our educational system. The very schools we set up to cater for all find remarkable differences between their pupils. Not the differences which make us wonderfully unique as persons but differences which order us.

I find myself profoundly unhappy with this outcome, feeling it represents a fragmentary and contrived view of the whole person. Who is allowed to learn in our educational institutions? The literature on the subject of educational achievement lists the variables with which I for one feel over-familiar: class, sex, geographic location, ethnic group and others appear time and time again. If I allow them to intrude into my thinking I find them burdensome. Too easily they can come between me and my friend, between teacher and pupil.

As a teacher I know I must be an interpreter, that I must try to bring about the conditions in which others can learn. If I can stand alongside the learner, if I can openly share all I possibly can, then I may be able to make some small contribution to her learning. To this end I must rid myself of negative pre-suppositions about the likely outcomes of her performance, I must find out how to interpret for and with her the learning tasks that society would impose as well as those she is setting for herself.

Each person, each pupil I encounter is that same amazing and wonderful baby who once delighted all round her with an innate potential for learning and for responding so similar to other human babies yet so unique as to make each one 'our kid'. I cannot believe that the differences our educational system finds are so great. Rather for me wholeness comes through the thought that although they may do them differently most people can do most things.

Marie Lasenby, *Learners all: Quaker experiences in education*, 1986

Focusing on the joy in diversity

Although I have met many Friends in Britain whose lives bear witness to Quaker ideals, there are many others whose actions and attitudes do not uphold these ideals in the context of racism and prejudice. So over the years, my idealistic view of Friends took a severe battering and was replaced by a more realistic view and attitude. Why should Friends be any different from people who make up the wider community? Why should they be any better or any worse than non-Friends generally? Why should they not be racist and prejudiced? The answer to all this is that in Britain Yearly Meeting there will always be actions and attitudes of racism and prejudice since we are, after all, influenced by the environment we live in. However, it is only by acknowledging these attitudes and facing up to our vulnerability, that we can make the necessary journey towards understanding and wholeness which will allow us to live out our Quaker testimonies in daily life, in the context of racism and prejudice.

Although there were times in my ministry when I felt angered and frustrated I was never disheartened. Nor was I tempted to give in or give up, because I feel very called to carry the work forward and find it both challenging and fulfilling. As I developed the work, experience taught me to distinguish between actions and words that were intentional and done to hurt or harm; those that were done because of white people's insecurity and the need to keep black people down; those that were done to maintain the status quo of the white power structure; and those that were unintentional and done out of ignorance, insensitivity or thoughtlessness. During the early part of the project, my idealism regarding Friends led me to believe that all such actions and words were unintentional and not intended to harm!

The diverse cultural traditions that make up British society today have a huge amount of richness and joy to offer. The tourist industry has made it easy for people to travel to 'exotic' places to try to experience the cultures of different races. And while we are doing that (and boring our family and friends with slides of our 'holiday'), the culture, spirituality and riches on our doorstep go unrecognised and unappreciated. I try to encourage Friends to join me in focusing on the joy in the diversity around us, adventure in the unfamiliar and love at the heart of all things.

Lilamini Woolrych, *Communicating across cultures*, 1998, pp.60-61

Epistle of Black, white, Asian and mixed-heritage Friends

Quakerism need not be defined exclusively as white, Christian and middle class, and such culture need not be adopted as the culture of those who are convinced. When this does happen the inequalities and unequal power dynamics of our Society are reflected in our meetings and in this way Black people are discouraged from fully participating in worship.

Our Society is often blind to the gifts and richness of other traditions and this cultural chauvinism impedes its development. Racism within the Society of Friends is perhaps more damaging because it is unconscious and springs from stereotyped assumptions: 'And no harm is meant by it. Harm may be done but it is never meant.'

We recognise and celebrate what we as Black, Asian and mixed-heritage Friends [in Britain] bring to the Society and with pride we affirm our rich positive contributions. However, we find spoken and unspoken assumptions that because we are Black people we are economically needy, socially deprived, culturally disinherited and spiritually in need of Quaker instruction. We experience isolation both physical and spiritual within our meetings. It is not just a matter of numbers but without the active commitment to promote diversity within the Society of Friends it will continue to be difficult to foster a true experience of a spiritual community.

As Black and white Friends we recognise the importance of our children's needs to know and value themselves and the world around them with the love and support of a settled and secure family environment. We must all strive to ensure that race is not a barrier to our children's success. We need to look honestly and openly at the structure of our meetings and seek to broaden our experience of other enriching forms of worship. Quakerism enables us to face both the glory and the seemingly unfaceable in ourselves. Let us do so now – together.

Epistle of Black, white, Asian and mixed-heritage Friends, 1991, quoted in *QFP* 10.13 & 29.15

Friends' racism

In 1984 I moved to London. I worked at Race Equality Councils in Lambeth and Bexley, and in 1988 had joined GLARE (Greater London Action for Racial Equality). I was by this time clerk of my meeting, having rejoined the Society in 1985. Perception of racism (or at least inaction over it) had been one feature of my formally leaving the Society in 1982.

I now came up against the same problem again, most clearly at the 1988 Woodbrooke Conference at which Friends' racism was an acknowledged theme, and where in fact *Quakers and Race* was launched. A Black Friend told us in a crisp phrase that Friends 'colluded with racism by their silence'.

This stung me personally, as it forced me to acknowledge I lived two distinct lives. One as a race professional with a radical programme based in constant closeness to the Black experience and perspective. Quite another with Friends. It was much more of a duty than a pleasure for me to strive not to collude with racism by *my* silence.

In those last six years I have had the unmistakeable and unforgettable experience of being blocked (usually but not always with silence) at every level in the Society. But our Friend's words were powerful enough to keep me on, as I knew they were true experimentally. Since then other Friends (mostly white, as Friends mostly are) have joined me, and I pay tribute to them.

James Gordon, *Quakers and race* No 14, Spring/summer 1994

How racist am I?

Though I was born in this country, my family moved to Tangier in North Africa when I was eighteen months old. I soon spoke French as my first language with my friends and at school, speaking my mother tongue, North American English, only at home. Like everyone in Tangier I had a street vocabulary of Arabic, English, French and Spanish. I read North American, British, French and Belgian books and comics. I grew up eating food bought in Spanish grocers and Moroccan markets and cooked by my Canadian mother. The richness of my childhood infected me for life.

We returned to the UK when I was nine and I went to a boarding school for the next three years. I thought I was coming home. My North American accent identified me as a foreigner, however, and I suffered until I was able to mimic the English of my contemporaries.

The pain and rejection I suffered when I came to this country has left me with some scars and a little wisdom. I am caught between two worlds.

One world is filled with the power and privilege I enjoy as a white, hetero-sexual man. The other world is that of being treated as a stranger in the land of my birth. It has given me a window, a glimpse of understanding into the lives of those who are marginalised by this society.

I have come to realise that racism is not simply another name for racial prejudice, it is racial prejudice re-enforced by power and privilege. Few people will comfortably admit to racism because it has become equated with fascism. Yet in truth racism encompasses a spectrum of behaviour that includes both thoughtless, uninformed white liberalism and the brutal horror of ethnic cleansing.

Racism is not a simple matter of either/or: it's not whether I'm a racist or not. I have grown up in societies and in a world where white people have most power. It would be naïve to suppose that I am exempt from the influences of the world. However much I aspire to be 'in the world but not of it', the world has touched and shaped me, just as my parents did. So the question is rather how racist am I?

Racism is a problem of white people suffered by black people. It is the actions of white people which cause pain, not the supposed woundedness or vulnerability of black people. Thus racism is a problem for white people to deal with.

Many Quakers have a problem with power; we like to be thought of as meek. But to avoid acknowledging powerfulness is to exert power without responsibility. In avoiding my own racism, I am aligning myself with power and privilege. Jesus did not align himself with power and privilege.

Ol, *Quakers and race*, reprinted in ROST *Responses & challenges*

Quakers and race

The report of the inquiry into the murder of Stephen Lawrence is a defining moment in our country. As Jack Straw has said, 'The very process has opened our eyes to what it is like to be black or Asian in Britain. I want this report to be a watershed in our attitudes to racism.'

The report comes a week after the most recent meeting of the working group on racism in Britain Yearly Meeting, held over two days at Jordans. This working group spent two full sessions trying to understand something of how institutional racism might be at work among Friends. We were helped by the report of Lilimani Woolrych's Joseph Rowntree Fellowship *Communicating across cultures* and by reports on the way the current Quaker video *Searching our own hearts* has been received in meetings.

The new definition of Institutional Racism offered by the Lawrence Report is:

The collective failure of an organisation to provide an appropriate and professional service to people because of their colour, culture or ethnic origin. It can be seen or detected in processes, attitudes and behaviour which amount to discrimination through unwitting ignorance, thoughtlessness and racist stereotyping which disadvantage minority ethnic people.

Quakers in Britain are obviously part of an organisation, and so it is likely that we have work to do. As well as seeking ways forward to extinguish any racism within our life (institutional as well as individual; unwitting, thoughtless or given to stereotyping), we have our part to play in helping our nation and our communities confront the issue.

Robin Bennett, *The Friend*, 12 March 1999

Listening to people with disabilities

Carol Gardiner has lived with multiple sclerosis for many years. In 1989 she wrote about her realisation that she did not have enough reserves of spiritual and physical energy at that time to go to a residential Yearly Meeting, and so it was not accessible to her.

Our Religious Society includes a considerable number of people who to some degree live with disabilities, and we generally present quite a good record of considering their needs and attempting to cater for them – a consideration born of our conviction that there is 'that of God' in every person. But we should ask ourselves continually if this consideration is being maintained and whether it goes far enough. If we really mean that there is that of God in everyone, then it behoves us to look with creative, loving imagination at the condition of every human being. This includes listening to what they say, and the words they choose to say it, and also listening for what they do not or cannot say. It does not mean listening to what someone else says supposedly on their behalf.

1989, *QFP* 23.38

Language and the balance between the sexes

The language in which we express what we ... say is of vital importance; it both shapes and reflects our values. One result of the emphasis on plain speech by early Friends was to challenge the class hierarchy of the day. The emphasis on non-sexist language by present-day feminists is likewise a challenge to hierarchy, in this case the sex hierarchy, which women have brought into the light by naming it – patriarchy. Our Quaker tradition enables us to recognise that our choice of language, and our reaction to the choice that others make, reveals values which may otherwise stay hidden.

Having in mind that much Christian teaching and language has been used to subordinate women to men, bear witness to our experience that we are all one in the Spirit and value the special characteristics of each individual. Remember that the Spirit of God includes and transcends our ideas of male and female, and that we should reflect this insight in our lives and through our ministry.

Are you working, in all aspects of your life, towards a better understanding of the need for a different balance between the sexes in their contribution to our society? Do you recognise the limitations which are placed on women and men by assigning roles to them according to gender, and do you attempt to respond instead to the needs and capacities of the individual? Do you recognise and encourage the many ways in which human love may be expressed?

Quaker Women's Group, 1982, 1986, *QFP* 23.44

Reluctance to live out gender equality

Despite its long reputation for treating the sexes equally, the Religious Society of Friends has not recorded and reproduced the journals and other writings of Quaker women with the same detail and depth that it has collected and made available the writings of Quaker men. Readily accessible resources about Quaker women of earlier periods have been lacking. Many Friends recall the reputation of the Society for equality between the sexes but are less familiar with the reluctance to live out gender equality in local communities or the yearly meeting structures.

Pam Lunn and Janey O'Shea, 'Our Quaker foremothers' in *Journal of Woodbrooke College*, issue 6, winter 1995-95

The challenge to learn gender equality

When I was twenty-two I married Emily and we went to live in St Andrews where I had a job lecturing in French. I joined the Fabian Society and the Labour Party. But it was university politics which brought out my dislike of unjustified authority. With others I campaigned for the democratisation of departmental government, bringing an end to the 'absolute' power of the Professorial Head of Department. However, that experience merely confirmed my beliefs; it did nothing to change me.

What really stretched me was my relationship with Emily. Her pain and low self-esteem (at times) very gradually linked itself to my treatment of her – for all our superficial equality about household chores, etc. It took years. In the end I was clear that I had been using my intellectual fire-power to downgrade her gifts and establish my dominance. This all widened out when St Andrews Meeting was joined by two wonderfully challenging attenders, Zoe White and Maureen Graham. Through their lesbian perspectives they were able to help me and the meeting to see that women were still being oppressed in the Society of Friends too. The concern went to monthly meeting and onwards, which is another story. I was left to work slowly on the changes I needed to make, first and foremost in my relationship with Emily.

Since then, I have felt that this was a key area of struggle – in terms of how to make equality more real. It still is for me.

Jonathan Dale, 1996

Sexual orientation and discrimination
All of us [Young Friends for Lesbian and Gay Concerns] have suffered discrimination or isolation because of our sexuality. We are all both angry and sad about the discrimination we face in everyday life, whether it consists of being unable to talk to work colleagues about a partner, or having to hide our sexuality in order to keep a job. The consequences of such necessary dishonesty can be very destructive both personally and for society.

Tessa Fairweather, 1993, *QFP* 23.45

Truth and spiritual experience
It is difficult for me to be quite sure when I first realised that I was homo-sexual. I was certainly not one of those fortunate enough to come to terms with their homosexuality during their adolescence. Indeed, it is only in the last few years, since the age of thirty, that I have attained complete self-acceptance and freedom from feelings of guilt. At the age of fourteen I became a Catholic, and at the time fully accepted the Church's teaching on homosexuality. I now realise that this coloured my attitude to my own awakening sexual feelings in a decisive and inhibiting way.

When I was thirty-two I started attending my local Quaker meeting, where I felt immediately at home. Imagine my joy at discovering, on reading *Towards a Quaker view of sex*, that, unlike the Catholic Church, the Society of Friends, with its faith in the validity of personal experience, could at least tolerate, if not always fully accept the likes of me. At a conference of Friends Homosexual Fellowship almost two years later, one of the speakers on the subject of 'coming out' so spoke to my condition that the burden of guilt and unhappiness that I had carried with me for so long completely fell away and has never returned.

I think I can truthfully say that this has been the crucial spiritual experience of my life and that I am still living under its influence. The purport of the speaker's message as it struck me was the primacy of love. Since that occasion I have learned by experience that within a loving partnership love and sex can confirm and strengthen each other in a wonderful and wholly beneficial way. I never cease to be thankful for the 'gift' of my gayness and the love that I am able to receive and, I hope, to give as a result of it.

Nick Chadwick, *Meeting gay Friends*, 1982

God's love has to include everybody

I was very aware of the problems of the total Christian commitment that I had made: my Christian witness and my feelings about women did not fit together. My religious hang-ups continued for quite some years ... I always wished and still do wish that the Churches would preach their Gospel in a more loving way and discover for themselves the liberating joy to be found in all the diversity of human experience.

I finally realised that I had to come to terms with my religious inhibitions and my gayness if I wanted to escape more years of dire misery. And I don't know whether the answer I found for myself is the answer or just an excuse; I just know that many other Christian gay men and women have come to the same conclusion. I decided that love did not mean just God, or me and man: it meant me and my fellow human beings, which included women, and this was the only way God's love could be for everybody. Also I realised that in every human relationship God is there in the midst of it.

Irene Jacoby, *Meeting gay Friends*, 1982

The legacy of John Bellers: pity with respect

In 1667 an outworking scheme was started by Friends in London and for four years from 1686 it was run by John Bellers. For the rest of his life John Bellers went on pleading for a society based upon sharing, with even the meanest of beggars cherished by the rest for what he might turn out to be.

Since all men were in the divine image, society dare not lose them. And since all were unique in their capacities, it followed that they had to be wanted for what they were and might be, not for what others would like them to become. Bellers produced many broadsheets and pamphlets on a range of themes: on the abolition of capital punishment, for example; on the need for a European federal system; on the possibility of a sort of national health service. But his constant enthusiasm was for social fairness, as a means of ensuring that each individual might live out his life in his own way. The following is from his *Epistle to Friends*, written in 1718:

> How many distressed souls and helpless orphans lie in our streets as the dry bones in the valley waiting to be gathered together by others' assistance before they can be united. And they must be united before sinews and flesh will come and skin cover them: and then may their labour make them happy in this world; and good instructions, through the blessing of God, may prepare them for the happiness of the next. The children of the Black Guard are a considerable part of these dry bones: they are our neighbours, our flesh and blood, our relations, our children, however mean and contemptible they may now appear. They are capable of being saints on earth, and as angels in heaven. How much is owing to birth and education that hath made the difference between them and us? Was it our virtue and their vice that made the difference? Had we any capacity before we were born?

What I find complete in John Bellers is his combining of pity with a respect for the right of the pitied one to live his life in his own way; and his sense of the inescapable oneness of human beings. Through all his writings there runs the conviction that even the poorest of fellows is *needed* for the well-being of the rest: he is its 'unworked mines of wealth'.

Michael Sorensen, *Working on self-respect*, pp.54-55

Other pieces which examine the social testimony on equality are:

5. Community   Gospel Order: God-centred community
                    Cultural homelessness
7. Creation   Living our social testimony

5. Community

Gospel Order: God-centred community

Early Christians and Friends, through their desire to return to the ways of early Christianity, are necessarily concerned with total social and personal transformation. Socially, this was expressed by George Fox through what he called the Gospel Order – a framework for the whole of society, as a God-centred community. It was an alternative society in the sense that the word alternative means 'of different birth' – with different origins. To George Fox the origin was clear; the Gospel and the light within. The creation of communities is a part of the building of the loving cells of an alternative society. However the Gospel Order is a consequence of faithfulness to God and not an attempt to identify a human-inspired creation with the Kingdom. George Fox made this clear in his Journal: 'For the authority of our meetings is the power of God, ... and so the order of the ... Gospel is not of man nor by man.' An alternative society does not mean removal from society around us even if that were possible; we must be in the world but not of the world. As the London Yearly Meeting Epistle of 1972 expressed it: 'We have heard the urgent summons to join in the building of the new city, and to live by its values, even while we inhabit the old with its all too frequent denial of human dignity.' The Gospel, the good news of the Kingdom for all people is social, is political – not by derivation or implication, but by nature and in essence.

Martin Jelfs, 'Quakers, community and social change'
in *Towards community*, 1980

How our meetings could be

A meeting ought to be a way of corporate living so creative, so liberating, so solidly joyous, so sustaining in disaster, that people who come within its radiance cannot help saying: 'This is the kind of life people are supposed to live. Let us in!'

The meeting ought to be ... a magnetic example of what the Kingdom of Heaven is like – here, now, available to people who will believe that it is just that – available.

Digging deeper, papers in preparation for the
FWCC Triennial Meeting in Mexico, 1985

Blessed community

There are different mystical experiences, and they may all have their own social effects ... [One] could be termed 'love mysticism', and ... most Western mystics are love mystics.

Thus George Fox writes, 'So here the God of love will in your hearts come to be shed abroad so that ye may come to know the saints' state, unto whom all things were become new.' (*No more but my love – the letters of George Fox*, p.35) And now, an appreciation of the social consequences of the experience: 'dwell in the love of God, for that will unite you together, and make you kind and gentle toward one another, and to seek one another's good and welfare.' (p.105)

The great thrust of this form of mystical experience is toward community. As Fox wrote, '[It] will unite you together.' So the mystic is committed to community, and, in consequence, he or she is opposed to whatever is destructive of community.

The most obvious social enterprise destructive of community is war. Hence George Fox's insistence that he and his followers live in a spirit which takes away the occasion of war. Warfare is the most obvious threat to community, but it is far from being the only one – entrenched social injustice is another. One classic form of this was slavery. John Woolman, a mystic of the same type as Fox, wrote that 'being inwardly united to the fountain of universal love and bliss enlarges the heart towards mankind universally'. (*The Journal of John Woolman and a plea for the poor*, p.235) It is the condition of the heart that contains the germ of the social philosophy, and being so affected himself, he travelled among slave-owning households, attempting to convince the owners to free their slaves, or at least to ameliorate their lot.

Of course, there are other threats to community, extremes of wealth and poverty, sectarian conflict, racial and national divisions, and so on. Anyone in Woolman's condition would seek to address them.

The ideal of community creates some uneasiness in that it may seem a threat to personal freedom. The orientation to community comes from the mystical experience itself. Other, non-mystical, aspects of experience may bring the mystic to other values. One such value may well be a regard for truth. It is well-known that a general respect for truth has implications for social freedom. For example, in order to ascertain the truth, we must be free to enquire, to obtain evidence, and if the truth is to be made available to all, freedom is needed to publish it, and as some truths are not of immediate interest but are nevertheless of long term importance, there should be freedom of association which enables people to support them.

There is a remarkable overlap between full social consequences of love mysticism and what Jesus' Messiah-ship was about ... The coincidence with the world Jesus was trying to bring about is no accident. What George Fox hoped for was a society held together by the shared experience of God's love. That is a form of blessed community, which is part, at least, of the Kingdom of God.

Reg Naulty, *The Friend*, 9 April 1999

Life in community – the final frontier for Friends?

It is now fourteen years since a resounding challenge to the Society from Ben Gosling appeared in the pages of *The Friend* of 23 August 1985. In an article entitled 'Quaker Kibbutz, Anyone?' Ben wrote,

> 'I think Friends should set up an intentional community, and others besides if this first one is successful. I think this mainly for two reasons: firstly because it seems that the identity of the Society is in danger of being watered down until it is unrecognisable, whereas a community could cure this by a fresh affirmation of a Quaker way of life; secondly because I

feel that society at large needs to find hope from a positive witness of this sort.

'We now live in a world which is desperate for a practical lifestyle based on a more caring and humane system than the one we have at present, that seems always to lead to war – trade, class, and inevitably military war.

'Would it not be useful were we to seek to revive our witness against "conformity with the World" in a way which is relevant to our times, to find a way of expressing our lives in which we will be seen to be trying to build the Kingdom, instead of always compromising and making the best of a bad job?

'Or shall we continue appearing as "nice" people, who can only practise our faith while still conforming to a system that survives by greed and waste, and that continually nurtures the worst side of people's natures?'

Going back to Ben Gosling's article today, the force of its message seems more irresistible than ever. So deeply did his words impress themselves on a number of people who read them at the time, that they formed a group which ultimately went on to establish the Quaker Community at Bamford.

Re-reading at a distance of fourteen years Ben's eloquent, passionate, and, I believe, truly prophetic call to Friends, fearlessly to embark on the adventure of life together in community, my pulse is once again set racing with the excitement and affirmative energy which led me then to become involved in helping to found the Bamford Community.

The hugely positive vision Ben set out in his article was nevertheless tempered by a sober awareness of the 'pessimistic prejudice attached to the idea of communes and communities generally: I can almost hear the groans going up,' he wrote, 'These things *always* fail' (italics mine).

How often in the embryonic stages of the project did the Quaker Community group encounter a similarly negative response, sometimes politely and obliquely expressed, on other occasions overtly and even patronisingly so? And yet things have turned out otherwise. For the past eleven years, the Bamford community has been providing a unique Quaker witness to the wider world, besides richly fulfilling its stated aim of helping those who live there to grow together spiritually in a caring environment, in a sense of shared adventure.

I would not have missed the eight and a half years my family were members of the Quaker Community for anything. Without a doubt, they will continue as years go by to seem the most influential and deeply satisfying chapter of my entire life, a fully committed attempt to live out, as Ben Gosling put it, 'the best Quaker life we can, and also to be an example to those who are seeking, so that they can see that there are other possibilities besides violence, exploitation and the gloom of inner cities.'

'As a long-term hope,' Ben wrote in 1985, 'a whole interdependent network of communities might be possible.' On the eve of a new century and a new Millennium, with Bamford now, after eleven years, beginning to reach maturity, Ben's resonant call to life in community still remains to be taken to heart by the Society at large.

'What about it, Friends?'

Andrew Greaves, 1999

Not the Damascus Road

This is one person's story of the discernment and slow development of a Christian community. It spans a period of twenty years. We call ourselves 'The Neighbours' and we live in five adjacent terrace houses in a tree-lined suburb of Northampton.

How did this come about? Susan and I with four young children came to live in Northampton in 1968. As regular attenders at our parish church we often heard those fine words about the early Christians in Jerusalem. 'They were one in mind and heart', they all 'shared with one another everything they had' and 'none of the members was in want'. Starting from that remarkable group the gospel was eventually carried to all parts of the world. So, we mused as we sat in the pew, was it something to do with this sharing which held them to Jesus' vision of the Kingdom and transformed their lives? And if so, what about us?

We shared very little outside our front door and we were under siege to share less. Night after night the TV advertisements in subtle ways planted in our minds the notion that our family was somehow inadequate if we did not have our own washing machine, our own tidy garden and our very own shiny car. We were encouraged to accept that it was not a question of sharing these things; it was a question of comparing our acquisitions with those of our neighbours over the fence, of competing with them in the prosperous years of the 1960s and holding tight to what we had got when a recession began to bite. This acquisitive society seemed totally at variance with what we heard on Sunday.

Four families and one single person in the parish began a small counter-culture by making an effort to share more, both our material possessions and our hopes and fears. [After some years] the way seemed clear to take a further step and a rump of four from the original nine began to look for a shared roof. By 1981 we had concluded that a more realistic way would be to buy adjacent terrace houses. It took us a year to find one which seemed to be right.

However, we were asking and seeking for three houses all a row, not just one like a normal house buyer, so the time had now come for knocking on doors to see if any would open. With Anne and Susan in support, Michael knocked on the next door, to ask if it was for sale. 'Strange you should ask', said the man who answered the door. 'I have just put this house on the market and it is advertised in tonight's paper.' Roger knocked on the other next door and rather than 'Mind your own business', the elderly owner said, 'Strange you should ask because I am going to live with my sister and we are intending to sell this house. Come in and look round.' We had knocked and, sure enough, doors had been opened to us, so we had no hesitation about making the major decision to move from separate roofs to a single roof. Within a week we had bought all three houses and set about an intricate plan of refurbishment. The mathematical odds against finding three adjacent houses for sale at the same time must be very large. Was it Archbishop Tutu who said, 'When I pray, coincidences happen'?

We moved in during 1983-84, each of three households with its own front door but also with three interconnecting internal doors and some shared areas, like a utility room with a washing machine, and a meeting room. We knocked down the garden fences without the help of the trumpets which Joshua employed to demolish the walls of Jericho, and made a square garden instead of three long thin ones: room for a pond and a shared compost heap.

Our new neighbour on one side was a wonderful elderly woman, a lifelong Baptist, who became a friend and supporter. Soon she said, 'I often thought of a shared house but now I need to move into a home for old people, so I hope you will buy my house and extend your project.' So we did and a newly married couple, Jayne and Richard, moved in and brought a Methodist perspective to what had been a Church of England initiative.

Now we have five front doors on to our suburban road, a garden big enough for trees to flourish and a lawn which keeps the communal mower in action for hours at a time. Some communities own substantial buildings in common, either by age-old endowments, like monasteries or convents, or by members pooling their own money to buy a larger shared house, perhaps by forming a housing association. We were willing to give up some of the so-called 'independence' of conventional house ownership to gain the 'interdependent' benefits of sharing occupation. The advantage of the terrace house concept is that it gives flexibility for the community to grow organically from one house to the next, without unduly large capital outlays. It also retains the patterns of separate legal ownership rather than the financial complexities of corporate ownership, a rock on which some Christian communities have foundered.

There are eleven people living in the houses at present, of whom seven are the core members of 'The Neighbours'. All these seven have jobs outside the house, full-time or part-time. Two are teachers, two work in co-operative businesses, one is an occupational therapist and two are probation officers. We have no formal rule, but we have agreed a statement of purpose to which we are committed and which other people living in the houses are invited to share: 'To develop a Christian community life which enables us to explore and share our faith and care for others according to the Gospel'.

We have developed a simple liturgy for morning prayers at 7.30 a.m. drawing from Iona responses and Taizé music. The worship is totally inter-denominational as we have Anglicans, Catholics and Quakers among the members and we are sometimes joined by people from other denominations.

On most evenings people will be sharing meals with each other somewhere along the five kitchens. We are committed to a 'Neighbour' evening every Thursday; after a meal together we have a meeting which rotates on a three weekly cycle between decision-making, bible study and a sharing of feelings and ideas about what we are doing, and where we are going. We have found it important to keep a written record and the minute books now run to hundreds of pages and are a frequent source of reference, precedent and guidance.

Sharing the same roof has its ups and downs. It demands a tolerance beyond that required by the nuclear family pattern, but it brings rewards of mutual support and energy saving. It gives greater freedom to be away from home without worrying about who will feed the cat and, for all concerned with spirituality, it supports a disciplined prayer life. It releases energy and money which would otherwise be spent on maintaining the independent household quite separate from the household next door.

Partly as a result of these savings, in 1986 we decided to offer some support to people recovering from mental illness, which is a major feature in this town as there are two large psychiatric hospitals. In due course, two such young people came to live with us and have stayed several years, one striving to live with schizophrenia and the other with anorexia. Both have been ill for ten years and their stories would fill a book. It has not been easy and we have been tested almost to the breaking point, but the reward has been to see them becoming less dependent, more interdependent and finding a better quality of life. None of our households, if they had been living in a conventional independent manner, could reasonably have undertaken this particular supporting role, but collectively among five households, it has been possible.

Our story over twenty years is not one of blinding flashes of inspiration nor sudden changes of lifestyle. Rather it is a series of somewhat hesitant moves towards our objective of a community life appropriate for lay Christians in the 1990s, and perhaps indicating a way of being the church in the next century.

Perhaps our most significant discovery is the bricks-and-mortar one of a community consisting of adjacent terrace houses, separately owned but with flexible shared facilities and shared access. This pattern could be repeated in many roads in most towns and from such bases there would arise opportunities for material and spiritual sharing and for caring for others in many different ways.

Roger Sawtell, *Journal of Woodbrooke College*, issue 2, winter 1992-93

Coming into community

Our vision of human beings living in harmony with the natural order on a restored planet is foreshadowed in a fellowship or 'church' that manages without a religious hierarchy and the kind of conventions and ritual practices that go with it. This produces a 'gospel order' that is not a constitution but an ongoing experiment in Christian discipleship. So the Society of Friends, like any genuine Christian church, has to be a rather particular kind of society that does not exist primarily for the benefit of its own members. The freedom Christ has given us is the glorious freedom to be brothers and sisters who serve one another and make sacrifices for one another. What we do for one another we must also do for and on behalf of all others.

So we are a community of servants and also a servant community. We must also accept that God is not going to do this work for us, but only with us. We must confront the conventional, distorted social values of the world and 'be valiant for the truth upon earth; tread and trample all that is contrary under' 'be patterns and examples' 'answering that of God in everyone; whereby in them you may be a blessing and make the witness of God in them to bless you' (George Fox, *Journal*. p.263). Within our own meetings the gospel can then empower us and offer us hope as we put our faith in the love of Christ in us.

In no way does this exclude finding ways of sharing and working with other faith communities, other 'people of prayer' who can demonstrate that they have the same vision. Then we can go by what other people are and do, 'treading down under our feet all reasoning about religion' as Howgill put it. This does not prevent fellowship with those who deny having any faith provided that they share the same personal and social values as we work together at a local level. Questions as to which, if any, faith has the ultimate truth in a philosophical sense are irrelevant: agreement at a deeper spiritual level will depend on the extent to which each community seeks to be true to its own deepest insights. That is why it is important for the Society of Friends to face up to the question as to who we are and what we are for.

Michael Langford, *Friends quarterly*, Vol. 31 No.2 April 1998

Social/community justice
These are examples of work with people who are excluded and in places where community is fractured.

Cultural homelessness
As Friends and attenders, many black people in Britain tend to find themselves isolated from their own cultures, friends and families. To those of us who come from traditions of 'extended families', this is a particularly painful experience, more so if friends and family from our own culture have no connections with the Religious Society of Friends.

Homelessness is a concern very dear to Quaker hearts. But have we given thought to the possibility that we may ourselves be causing people to be homeless? Home is not only a physical shelter. It is also people, family, faith, environment, a place where we *really* belong. And for most black people in our multicultural society, Britain is home. They have no safety net of another home overseas. If they are denied true acceptance in society, they are made emotionally homeless and rootless. This can be soul-destroying. And it is the everyday experience of most black people living in a predominantly white society.

I, like many black Friends, have often felt racially, culturally and spiritually homeless in the Religious Society of Friends in Britain. As Friends, we need to ensure practical action that demonstrates the Society's acceptance of people of all races and cultures. When human beings feel unwelcome, unloved and marginalised, they are forced to seek support and affirmation from their 'own people'. They then stand accused of creating 'ghettos'. This inevitably leads to polarisation and distancing. Communication becomes increasingly difficult, which in turn reinforces racism and prejudice.

Lilamini Woolrych, *Communicating across cultures*, 1998, pp.26-27

Restorative justice

The principles with which Quakers approach community justice are best seen at work in the growing practical implementation of an alternative approach to justice now referred to as Restorative Justice.

'Restorative Justice seeks to balance the concerns of the victim and the community with the need to reintegrate the offender into society. It seeks to assist the recovery of the victim and enable all parties with a stake in the justice process to participate fully in it.' (Manifesto of the Restorative Justice Consortium of which QSRE is a member)

Restorative justice aims to offer:

- compensation, healing, and a voice to victims
- a voice in setting priorities for criminal justice, resources and skills for preventing crime, and an understanding of why crime happens to communities
- a realisation of the consequences of their actions, a chance to make reparation and an avenue back into the community to offenders
- community support and confidence, partnerships with other agencies, and a new hope of being effective in resolving the harm of crime and reducing its likelihood in future.

These are hard aims to achieve, and they require all of us to participate actively in the process in whichever way is appropriate.

In order for us to make that contribution we need to begin by formulating our approach to crime and community justice in ways which will help us engage in the dialogue with our communities which is necessary. We may therefore want to begin by agreeing these principles:

- we recognise the widespread damage done by crime and disorder and are committed to work to reduce it

- we see crime and disorder as a breakdown in social relationships which should be dealt with as such wherever possible. We emphasise the needs of victims and do all we can to meet these
- we seek to confront offenders with the consequences of their behaviour, hold them to account and provide opportunities for them to make good the harm caused
- we take an inclusive view of society and recognise that membership of a community involves rights and responsibilities for everyone
- we encourage the families and friends of victims and offenders and the wider community to contribute actively to tackling crime and dealing constructively with offenders
- we acknowledge the role of imprisonment if it is limited to those who need to be held for the safety of the public
- we promote the use of positive community based penalties wherever appropriate and in particular those which include reparation
- we believe that tackling the causes of crime is better than dealing with its consequences and is ultimately a more effective approach.

In order for us to be effective and convincing in the contribution we wish to make, we also need to take action. This will depend on our role and our level of involvement, but is likely to include some or all of the following steps:
- we will be better informed and consider the latest research about effectiveness in community safety
- we will try to understand the complexity and the inter-relatedness of much community justice material
- we will form or join a community justice group, either one of Friends or of other groups locally
- we will learn about, understand and support the local crime and disorder unit based in the local authority as it works to implement recent legislation to develop strategies for a safer community, with an awareness of the limits and potential divisiveness of some of the measures
- we will participate in the local debate about the development of youth justice measures currently being addressed and involve ourselves with issues to do with education, health and employment which have a direct impact on community safety
- we will maintain our activity in traditional areas of direct involvement within the criminal justice agencies either as workers or supporters in

order to continue improve standards of care and challenge unacceptable developments.
'Towards a Quaker View of Crime & Community Justice', From QSRE *Crime and community justice resource pack*, 1999

What is AVP – Alternatives to Violence Project?

The Alternatives to Violence Project began in America in 1975, when a group of prisoners asked some visiting Quakers to help them find a way out of their cycle of violence. Since then the programme has spread to every continent (except Antarctica!) and similar workshops are enjoyed by people in prison and in the community. The common factor between both groups is a desire to resolve conflict and to look for a positive way of dealing with anger and violent behaviour.

The workshops last for three days, usually starting on a Friday evening and continuing over Saturday and Sunday. There are three or sometimes four facilitators, all volunteers, who take the group through exercises in both small and large groups, based on the participants' experience. There are also 'Light and Livelies' games, which help change the atmosphere, and get everyone up and moving about. There are no lectures, no note taking, and the work is all experience based (there may be one or two handouts).

The level one workshop builds on self esteem, communication (both listening to others and expressing how you feel), trust and co-operation within the group, and uses role play to explore conflict and conflict management. The level two workshop deals in more depth with a topic chosen by the group – it could be: anger, power, forgiveness, stereotyping. Again the workshop lasts for three consecutive days, and is run by voluntary facilitators. Groups range from a minimum of eight to a maximum of twenty participants. For those who would like to become facilitators there is training, also lasting three days. There is then a period of apprenticeship, working alongside more experienced facilitators in both level one and level two workshops.

The principles of AVP are that we all have experience of times we have not resorted to violence, that we are all equal and worthy of respect. Facilitators are there to learn, just as are the participants, who finally will get out of the workshop what has been put into it. The value of the workshops is that participants realise they all have a contribution to make, and that we can all change, through making different choices and through our own feeling of self worth.

The people who attend AVP workshops in the community come from different ethnic backgrounds, and are of varying age, sex and religion. Although AVP is non-denominational, it does have a spiritual basis, and promotes the making of positive choices in our lives.

I was drawn to AVP as a means of offering an alternative choice to the young men in Olney Young Offenders Institution. I have since facilitated workshops in India and Nigeria, and in the Balkans with Serbs, Croats, Bosnians and Albanians. I learn more about myself, the facilitators and group that I work alongside each time I do a workshop. It is sometimes tiring, but it is always stimulating and develops a sense of trust within the group that I have seldom found elsewhere. There is a special bond between those who have shared an AVP workshop together.

Karin Fry, 1999

Quaker therapeutic communities

Therapeutic communities and the practice within them is the subject of much discussion and scepticism by some. Over a couple of decades they have had a bad press and several have ceased to operate. Multiple environments have been and are being used as an alternative way of working with different groups – vulnerable children and young people needing residential care, children and adults with mentally ill health, offenders or others who require a healing environment. Key factors balance nurturing and care and, as necessary, challenges to inappropriate behaviour.

There are four cornerstones to therapeutic community practice:

- democracy – every member should share equally in the exercise of power in decision making about community affairs
- permissiveness – all members should tolerate from one another a wide degree of behaviour that might be distressing or seem deviant by ordinary standards
- communalism – there should be tight-knit, intimate sets of relationships, with sharing amenities and living, use of first name and open communication
- reality confrontation – residents should be continuously presented with interpretations of their behaviour as seen by others.

Friends are responsible for two pieces of work that operate in this way, besides individual Friends working professionally in other environments that use this practice. The following accounts look at one environment that has a thirty year history and another which has only just started to operate.

Friends Therapeutic Community Trust: Glebe House

Friends have often taken on inherited concerns as a matter of duty and out of respect for earlier Friends. This was so with the Therapeutic Community, Glebe House, Cambridgeshire. When I became involved a decade ago, Friends were in a dilemma. The buildings were run down, staff were worn out and demoralised, there were debts and the practice was being questioned by the Department of Health's inspectors.

What to do? It was a challenging situation but the outcome has been positive and timely. The work was under a concern but several Friends within the Responsible Body were questioning the appropriateness of the work continuing as a Quaker concern. Several separate but inter-connecting processes were applied:

- the concern was re-tested
- the Trust Deed was reviewed with a constitutional expert
- management and system of accountability were introduced
- better and more rigorous systems for monitoring practice were put in place
- training for trustees and staff has become an essential part of the experience
- a refurbishment programme was completed
- new leadership was introduced.

All of this took time, energy, hard work and faith by a dedicated group of paid and unpaid people. This exercise has taught us many lessons. Friends should be vigilant in ensuring that work undertaken in the Society's name must be properly managed and Friends must take trusteeship seriously. There is a need for appropriate professional advice, Friends must be more valuing and more rigorous in use of their business methods. It has been a salutary exercise to be at the receiving end of two ends of a spectrum. On the one hand experiencing insufficient diligence in recording and making and keeping minutes and then exemplary examples which have been the source of clarifying historic significant incidence.

Sufficient to finish by saying Friends Therapeutic Community Trust is in a sound state. It will always require extra resources in both monies and appropriate trustees to oversee the work, but it is under careful steward-ship, with management and accountability systems that should ensure a continuing non-punitive service for lads who need and value it.

Elizabeth Fry Young Offenders Trust: Acacia Hall

The challenge of a new concern brought different challenges from that of an inherited concern, but the need for a journey to both test the concern in the spiritual sense and to consider the feasibility of any practical outcome can be quite arduous. Sometimes Friends find the present laws restricting but even Friends need to know the law, to know why the statutory provisions have been put in place, and then to use the law to realise a solution.

The Children Act 1989 and subsequent guidance and regulation is a good piece of legislation. Those in the professional groups caring for children saw the bringing together of disparate pieces of the law and updating it as sensible and beneficial to children and their families. The maze of requirements is complex: building regulations, health and safety legislation, fire regulations, local planning laws, Children Act and registration requirements, charity law, and so on. In a local authority, a commissioning team would call on a range of expertise to advise and undertake work. Friends' resources were more limited: they had half time of one person over the critical period of refurbishment, commissioning and registering the facility in Lincolnshire.

Trustees of this piece of work wanted to intervene with a non-punitive approach and to stop the locking up of young offenders. It was with great rejoicing that the home was registered and the first four residents arrived in time for Christmas 1998.

Conclusion

A critical factor for any project whether within or outside the Society is the interface between those who are the responsible body – trustees, governors of school, non-executive members of health trusts, each of whom are responsible for the strategic framework and in ensuring the law is kept – and the professional staff who undertake the day-to-day operations. This interface is difficult but crucial. The balance between ensuring delegation and monitoring of operational matters and interfering is an area that is difficult to both understand and manage. A sound relationship between these two aspects of responsibility is crucial and needs constant vigilance.

Friends have been courageous in taking on work in this area and in a way that has few followers. Only a few benefit from these services, but by ensuring exemplary practice, it is possible to add to the body of evidence that shows an alternative way of working with those on the edge of society.

In these practical ways our social, peace and non-violence testimonies are constantly being tested.

Sheila J Gatiss, August 1999

Quaker Social Action (Bedford Institute Association)

Those pillars of the human spirit, the belief that you have a place in society, that you can influence your situation, that you are valued by others – these are undermined every day you are unable to play your part, every way you are made to feel powerless, each time you are excluded. When you are on the lowest incomes this is the daily fare and at times you will need support not to weaken.

Quaker Social Action upholds that strength in thousands of people each year through providing services and new opportunities. We seek that homeless people, unemployed people, refugees and those on low incomes look after themselves but get the extra help they need when they need it. What we learn we share through handbooks, advisory services and training with others fighting exclusion in other areas, sometimes leading to new work being established elsewhere.

Our practical 'sleeves rolled up' approach helps people in many ways. Geoff came to our community furniture store (HomeStore) after being housed following many years of street homelessness. Having no money at all he offered to earn the goods he needed by working on our vehicles. He liked the staff, he was cheerful and energetic and so stayed on as a volunteer. Some months on we moved to bigger premises and there we learned of his practical skills, that he loves restoring old furniture and when working in the Heron workshop has endless patience with the trainees with learning difficulties. Geoff says 'The challenges HomeStore presents keep me going. Without them I would probably have reverted to my previous lifestyle. What's more, I'm proud of my home which everyone says is so nice!'

The store has helped more than 25,000 people in ten years. A special recent moment was when for the first time a couple who had been HomeStore customers nine years ago called and offered to donate furniture now they were moving into a place of their own.

Dino Risvegli was a Somali refugee who we housed through our rent/guarantee (rent deposit) project, HomeLink. Single homeless people not eligible for public housing often need help with the advance rent and deposits private landlords demand and may need help with Housing Benefit forms, finding property and resettlement. Dino volunteered to help and eventually got a job with us and now helps around seventy people a year from the 'Horn of Africa' countries (mostly refugees) into accommodation. Other staff house a similar number and many of the trained and supervised resettlement volunteers go on to employment in this and related fields.

Quaker Social Action is currently the only independent provider of training for the rapidly expanding vending industry. As such we provide a ready source of basically trained recruits. Employers find it easier to come to us rather than advertise so in a sense we have 'captured' a supply of about fifty jobs a year. We recruit long term unemployed people like William Mapps, who came to us following a broken marriage and a period of homelessness. He started as an operator on £8,500 but only eight months later he is a supervisor earning £15,000. He got his own flat and now his daughter has come to live with him! QSA also has around seventy people a year gaining work experience in the various projects building that elusive vital ingredient – confidence.

QSA recently began to operate the Garrett Centre, a community centre in Bethnal Green, an echo of much of BIA's earlier work. Situated in one of the most deprived wards in the country it now provides a thriving Mother and Toddler group, indoor bowls for pensioners, tai chi and a women's development group. This is a twenty-strong mixed race group (unusual for this area) which is now forming its own management committee and setting its own agenda. Supported by our young Bangladeshi worker Reha, they recently fundraised £263 towards summer family outings by holding a 'cultural foods' lunch.

We are currently looking for funding for: loan finance for people without any collateral or guarantor but who want to start trading – this scheme will be called Street-Cred and follows the Grameen Bank example; a project to address the need for new Large Goods Vehicle drivers; and at the Garrett Centre community meals with nutrition advice, keep fit classes and new community enterprises.

1999 marks the 150th anniversary of the first Quaker work that gave rise to the Bedford Institute Association, our preceding organisation. As before it is driven by compassion and aims at releasing human potential. In 1999 QSA has eighteen employees, seventeen volunteers, a budget in excess of £600,000, twenty-five per cent of which comes from Quaker sources, and a wholly Quaker management council.

Mike Jenn, Director of QSA, 1999

Birth of the Leaveners

It is Pleasaunce Holtom who can be seen as the mother of the Leaveners. Her leading was to provide creative arts activities for young people at the new-style residential yearly meetings, in her hope that more families would then be encouraged to attend.

So when she was asked by Chris Lawson to host an extended Easter arts weekend for Young Friends at Woodbrooke in 1976, which Alec Davison was leading, she knew who to ask for lively support. Amongst her team came Jennifer Morris, a drama and dance therapist, and Tony Biggin, the young composer-teacher. There was more than serendipity in the coming together of this team at that moment of time. Each of them felt under a leading to hope to break the Quaker taboo against involvement in the performing arts and to yoke their Quakerism with what they knew from their daily professional work in education and therapy. For there they saw how deeply the inner spirit is nourished by a community working intensively together through creative expression.

It was no surprise, then, that the multi-media presentation to local Friends in the lounge on that last night was prophetically called *The new Quakers* and was enthusiastically received. Next day, after the evaluation-affirmations of participants and audience alike, the final meeting for worship was one of extraordinary depth with moving testimonies to the powerful experiences of the project. So much so, it was there and then decided to continue the work at the next residential Yearly Meeting two years hence at Lancaster. For Pleasaunce and Jennifer, Tony and Alec, a passion, a burning concern had been sparked that was to take fire in youth theatre, orchestra and chorus, a drama company for unemployed young adults and ultimately the work of Leap, the first conflict resolution training project in the British Youth Service. They and those who have continued to take on the torch have lived adventurously.

Time and again over succeeding years, following the opening-up experiences of increasingly dare-devil enterprises – white-water rafting the creative spirit – participants have known 'great, great meetings'. Each has richly validated this new form of outreach and symbolic witnessing to Friends' testimonies. For the greater the risk and the deeper the penetration into our universal story, the greater the bonding of the companies and deeper the inward life is known.

Alec Davison, 1999

Leap Confronting Conflict

In September 1999 *Leap* Confronting Conflict launched as an independent national voluntary youth agency offering specialist services to young people and adults involved in exploring the causes of and alternatives to conflict and violence in young people's lives. *Leap* was established by the Leaveners (Quaker Youth and Community Arts Charity) in 1986 taking forward the Leaveners' commitment to practical action to express both Friends' peace testimony, through developing interpersonal skills training in confronting conflict, and Friends' social testimony, through working with young unemployed adults in creative ways of addressing issues of social justice.

Leap has deep roots in educational drama. Educational drama in the 1980s was remarkably successful in exploring the causes and consequences of injustice and inequality, but *Leap's* founders were deeply concerned at how rarely young people were overtly learning the skills and strategies of empowerment to effect personal and social change themselves in reality. Educational drama seemed stuck with 'drama is conflict'. During the early 1990s *Leap* workers began exploring the claim that 'drama is conflict resolution', and that any education in drama is an education towards conflict resolution and the skills of communication and mediation.

This exploration was hugely aided by the publication in a *Leap*/National Youth Agency partnership of the youth service's first conflict resolution centred curriculum development materials, *Playing with fire*, a substantial training manual for those who work with young people and *Fireworks*, a handbook for use directly with the young people themselves. The sale of nearly 7,000 copies of the manuals in the UK and USA has shown the demand for materials exploring the creative uses of conflict; spilling over from young people's work in the youth and penal services into secondary and further education, youth work training and in-service teacher training.

Leap has continued to develop its enquiry into the potential of educational drama through the Theatre Workshop, which works with young unemployed adults (eighteen to twenty-five year olds) offering training in the creative use of conflict through community arts work.

Leap approaches violence as a lack of resources, both in personal and social terms. Young people need to be resourced when conflict has to be confronted and addressed. The skills of communication and assertiveness, and the techniques of dealing positively with anger and social injustice, need to be vigorously and non-violently rehearsed and owned. These alternatives need to be actively learned as integral to all social education, not as palliatives for social control, but as processes of empowerment for personal and social change. This approach puts *Leap* firmly in support of restorative justice approaches to young people who have committed crimes.

Leap has been running programmes for young men on remand in young offenders institutions in the South of England for five years. The initiative came from a pro-active funder who was moved by hearing of the suicides of four young men in custody within a six month period. Since then *Leap* teams have worked with many faces of victimisation – young men who have allegedly committed horrendous crimes, young men who have been accused of bullying and young men who have been bullied, young fathers who are separated from their vulnerable children, and young men who have suffered the bereavement or loss of a significant adult in their early lives. Naming your own experience and taking responsibility for your own actions remains at the heart of the three day intensive groupwork courses which *Leap* trainers run with young prisoners.

Wherever you stand in the debate on the causes of youth crimes, the rising numbers of young offenders and rapidly increasing numbers of juveniles on remand and in custody is a major cause for concern. Many of these young men spend short disrupted times on remand, without any careful needs analysis or after-care planning. *Leap's* programme can only make a tiny contribution in this context, but for many of the young men is the only opportunity they get to review in a structured and supported environment how they came to be where they are, and what choices they have about their future.

Offering young men in trouble the opportunity to take a 'leadership' course is intriguing enough to fill the workshops with volunteers. Over three days of structured groupwork the young men use enactive techniques to explore what it means to 'take a lead in your own life' and move on to 'taking a lead in your community'. The young men have a chance to reflect on their experience and put new skills into practice in follow-up groups run by *Leap* trainers.

The 'Does it work?' question is difficult to answer about this programme as we are able to work with young men for such a short period. However, psychometric testing of seventy young men before and after participating in the programme, by prison service psychologists, showed a significant shift in the young men's attitudes, a decrease in hostility, an increase in self esteem and a decrease in social avoidance and distress. Assessments of attitude shifts show a significant move in a pro-social direction; assessments of longer term behaviour change are much harder to make.

Conflict is an inevitable and normal part of young people's lives, so strategies for learning to limit, resolve or manage conflict should be an equally normal part of young people's personal and social education. We know that young people contain both the solution and the problem. Young people work as facilitators, mediators and creative problem solvers. *Leap* is committed to fanning the flames of positive attitudes, enabling and facilitating skills.

Leap has developed 'Quarrel Shop', a programme of training and placements for sixteen to nineteen year old young people which explores skills, approaches and work opportunities in mediation. The field of mediation is expanding dramatically with mediators working in criminal justice (victim-offender mediation), family/divorce, neighbourhood disputes, and in schools as part of behaviour management policies. 'Quarrel Shop' is the first peer-to-peer mediation service in the community, offering young people a chance to learn and practice the skills of mediation, and gain recognition from the Open College Network for doing so.

Adults who work with young people also need resourcing to work with conflict and violence. Exploring one's own responses to conflict is a first step in understanding the processes at work in young people's lives.

For the past eight years *Leap* has run training courses for adults exploring the *Playing with fire* materials and concepts working with hundreds of youth workers throughout the UK. In a structured and flexible series of drama exercises and activities which need experienced facilitation, youth workers are guided through the processes of conflict generation to mediation and reparation.

The style of the training is vital. Its key values are individual respect, a disposition towards non-violence, the experience of democratic processes, and an understanding of 'tough love' – being held accountable and responsible for choices and decisions we have made. The learning process of the course teases all theory out of practice through skilful questioning techniques; it recognises the supremacy of emotion and passion in most conflict; it allows time for reflection so that new understanding can grow before the next experiential input. It is profoundly personal, believing that creative movement in problem solving comes from our individual shift and change. It acknowledges that the most important aspect of the learning process is the integrity and humanity of the facilitators which is caught and not taught. The courses aim at whole self-knowledge, body and heart, feelings as well as new ideas, in exploring a shared humanity.

Helen Carmichael, *Leap* Confronting Conflict, September 1999

Law For All

In the mid 1980s a member of Ealing Meeting was studying at the London School of Economics. A Friend asked how things were going. 'Well,' she said, 'I've learnt that law has very little to do with justice.'

The student was Anna Barlow, who with her mother Ulla Barlow went on to start Law For All, registered as a charity in December 1993 and adopted by Ealing Meeting as a corporate concern, which opened its first Law Shop in Acton High Street early in 1994. Three more Law Shops, in Southall, Hanwell and Northolt – all less prosperous parts of the London Borough of Ealing – have followed and each services one or more local advice centres. More recently Partners in Community Law (PICL) has been set up as a separate charity, focusing on developing and implementing a model of good practice in realising the Community Legal Service proposed, alongside reforms to legal aid, by the Lord Chancellor's Department.

The two charities produced a joint report in July 1999, entitled: *Towards a Community Legal Service: two case studies*. Members of Ealing Meeting took copies of the report to the Summer Gathering at Canterbury. We are now posting three copies to every preparative meeting in England and Wales – one for the meeting, one for an MP and one for a local government official – with a covering letter explaining that this is a crucial period for influencing decisions about legal services for people least able to afford them.

Over the years members of the meeting have given and raised money, made interest-free loans (most recently to establish an Immigration Unit within Law For All), paid for advertisements in *The Friend*, given furniture for offices, cleaned and decorated each new premises in turn, leafleted potential clients in impoverished housing estates, hosted conferences in the meeting house, written to Friends in other parts of the country, produced a newsletter for a couple of years, organised displays at yearly meeting.

Last week the Ealing Meeting Law For All Committee heard a report from Ulla. Law For All has secured all the funding applied for under the new arrangements for legal aid in 2000, for both general and immigration work. A central office is to be rented, to take pressure off the Law Shop premises, all of which are full to overflowing. Ulla told us again that the practical, financial and spiritual support of the meeting had been essential during the critical early stages of the project, when everything was innovative and experimental and she and Anna had many sleepless nights, worrying about how to survive till the cheques from the Legal Aid Board came in, often several months after work had been completed. Now ways of working are set, a very high standard has been achieved (with the result that at a recent complete legal audit there was 'no non-compliance', a rare event) and funding is determined in advance by the Legal Services Commission.

'Law For All has now reached a stage where the continuing need is for spiritual rather than practical support', we minuted, 'and continuing to have a committee within the meeting would no longer be a right use of energy.'

'PICL, on the other hand,' our minute continued, 'is at a critical early stage. Many groups want to be involved but creating a suitable structure for this community-based enterprise is a challenging task ... Ealing Meeting could perhaps model setting up a service and seeking funding to develop it. Under a Community Legal Service regime there will be a growing need in every locality for volunteer input if poor and disadvantaged people are to be supported and helped. This is an area of traditional Quaker concern.'

Next month Ealing Preparative Meeting will re-consider, in this new phase, our corporate involvement with this work for social justice, at a time when new structures and systems are being developed by the Lord Chancellor's Department and informed comment may make a real difference. But it would not be in right ordering to pay lip service to PICL and claim the meeting's corporate concern for the work unless we can continue to be practically as well as spiritually supportive. Currently PICL in Ealing is struggling to get a form-filling service, staffed by trained volunteers, firmly established. Have we the energy to help on a very practical level?

Law For All is showing that law *can* have something to do with justice. PICL has the same concern, and challenges us to move forward in our thinking and support. As a meeting, we have experienced the wonder and excitement of innovative work developed in response to individual and corporate leadings. To the best of our ability we have been 'working to bring about a just and compassionate society which allows everyone to develop their capacities and fosters the desire to serve' (*Advices and queries* 33). It could be tempting for the committee to introduce the new work to preparative meeting in a way that assumes continuing corporate commitment. Yet we are also advised to 'try to discern the right time to undertake or relinquish responsibilities' (*A&Q* 28). Where is the Spirit leading us now?

Elizabeth Cave, December 1999

Trying to look after each other

We have worked with some pretty desperate characters over the past few years. Some of them were drug users, some alcoholics, some existing in a permanently damaged life, some ex-offenders, some of them 'family-less', all of them homeless even when housed and cared for. In short, they were convinced that they belong nowhere and those who tried to provide for them were misguided, could not be trusted, were 'on to something' or were just another kind of 'sad bastard' like themselves.

People ask us, 'How can you work with such people?' And our answer has always been something like 'because they are our brothers and sisters'. We believe that God created every one of us. Hebrew scripture requires us to love God, ourselves and our neighbour, which we interpret, very simply, to mean 'anyone who is not me', i.e. every one else in the world. Not to love another is to deny God's request. As a Quaker and an attender we believe that there really is 'that of God' in everyone and we seek not to find it but to be shown it by the other person. The way we do this is by revealing it, to the best of our ability, in our respect for the other person and treating them as Jesus might have done. Belief or even faith in God is not enough, we must let our lives speak. And that means action. Jesus the Jew did not say, 'I was homeless and you expressed concern, prayed for me and then refurbished your own homes to make them more comfortable for yourselves whilst I remained homeless.' He said, 'Sell all you have and give it to the poor like this widow has just done or at least give me a cloak to sleep under each night', reminding us that even the raw materials for the cloak came from God. If we love God we will try to look after each other in the way God expects us to.

Chris and Lyn Walker-Mollington, *This I affirm*, 1998 p.39

---

6. Peace and non-violence

Deeds not creeds

The peace testimony is about deeds not creeds; not a form of words but a way of living. It is the cumulative lived witness of generations of Quakers. The peace testimony is not about being nice to people and living so that everyone likes us. It will remain a stumbling block and will itself cause conflict and disagreement. The peace testimony is a tough demand that we should not automatically accept the categories, definitions and priorities of the world. We look to the Spirit, rather than to prescriptive hypothetical statements. The peace testimony, today, is seen in what we do, severally and together, with our lives. We pray for the involvement of the Spirit with us, that we may work for a more just world. We need to train to wage peace.

London Yearly Meeting, 1993, *QFP* 24.11

What the peace testimony means to me

The peace testimony has gained more meaning for me since I realised that it is not a verbal declaration against war, but a positive way of life, 'not a creed but an active witness, not an ideology, but an always imperfect and faltering attempt to live out a fundamental spiritual perception'. (Pam Lunn, *Deeds not creeds*) I had worried for some time about the negative character of our 'no to all war', and wondered if there was a positive 'yes' that we could put in its place. But 'yes' to what? Any answer to that question was likely to sound too idealistic and unworkable, and therefore not to be taken seriously. But that, I realised, was because it would be merely verbal, and theoretical. And verbal debate is the game of modern politics. To Quakers, the issue has always been deeper than that. The question is not whether war is a good policy for achieving our ends, but what we prize so much that we can think of taking a human life to achieve it. It is a spiritual question. And the answer to it that I see enshrined in our testimony is that nothing is worth that sacrifice. Not wealth, power or even political freedom. To believe anything is worth that sacrifice is to be deeply deceived about human life. Our testimony, then, as I see it, is both a no to deceit and a yes to reality, above all the reality of our common life as human beings. And we bear that testimony most effectively, I think, when we treat other human beings as they really are, free from the deceptions of our individual or national self-interest.

Rex Ambler, *The Friend,* 16 April 1997

The following is the testimony of a Friend who participated in the vigil, inspired and sustained by women, against the cruise missile base at Greenham Common in the 1980s.

Witness to peace

I stood at the fence one night in September, feet rooted to the muddy ground, hands deep in my pockets, watching through the wire that flat ravaged land that is now never dark, never quiet, imagining through the fence a field of bracken and scrub, a field of flowers, a field of corn, a field of children playing. Red police car, blue lights flashing, 'What are you doing, then, love? Not cutting the fence are you?' 'No, just praying at it.' A soldier with a dog walks up and down inside, suspicious, watching me watching him. 'Good evening.' 'Good evening.' I wait, not knowing what I'm waiting for. The kingdoms of the Lord? A hundred yards to my left, women cut the wire, roll away the stone, and walk through into the tomb. No angels greet them; no resurrection yet.

Yet still women witness to that possibility, the possibility that something may be accomplished which in our own strength we cannot do. Women waiting, watching, just being there, behaving as if peace were possible, living our dream of the future now. 'Why do you come here? Why do you keep coming?' – a soldier near Emerald camp on an earlier visit – 'It's no use, there's nothing you can do, what do you women think you can do by coming here? The missiles are here, you won't change anything, why do you come?' We come to watch, we come to witness, we come with our hands full of ribbon and wool, flowers and photos of loved ones, hands full of poems and statements and prayers, hands full of hope and the knowledge that such hope is impossible to rational minds. I come to be with the women who live here, the dykes, the dropouts, the mothers and grandmothers, angels with countenances like lightning, I come to talk with the police, the soldiers, men who might be gardeners standing by the tomb; I come to meet the Christ in them.

A member of the Quaker Women's Group, 1986, *QFP* 24.28

A defence of non-violent direct action

I do not wish to deny that on April 4th, the anniversary of the death of Martin Luther King, I was inside the Faslane Submarine Base, and that I was there as a deliberate act. However, I pled guilty to the charges because had I done otherwise I would have been guilty of far greater crimes against my conscience and against humanity.

If I may, I would like to outline very briefly the reasons for so acting, not so much as mitigation of guilt, but rather as a declaration of intent, for as long as those bases remain, I must continue to act as my conscience guides.

My charge is that I entered a protected area without authority or permission. My claim is that I had authority – the authority of my Christian conviction that a gospel of love cannot be defended by the threatened annihilation of millions of innocent people. It can never be morally right to use these ghastly weapons at any time, whether first, or as unthinkable retaliation after we ourselves are doomed.

I acted also with the authority of the nameless millions dying of starvation now because we choose to spend £11.5 billion on Trident whilst a child dies every fifteen seconds.

I am further authorised by my thirteen-year-old Vietnamese god-daughter whose guardian I am. She was adopted and brought to Scotland to take her away from the unspeakable horror of the Vietnam war. If all that I have done is to bring her closer to the nuclear holocaust, I stand convicted by her of the most cynical inhumanity.

I am charged under an Act giving control and disposal of land to the Queen, the Lords Spiritual and Temporal, the Commons assembled in Parliament and eventually the Secretary of State. I believe the world is God's creation. This beautiful, delicate world in all its infinite wonder is threatened with extinction. That to me is blasphemy.

And so, out of love, love of my god-daughter, love of my world, I had to act. If I see that base at Faslane as morally wrong and against my deepest convictions – as wrong as the gas chambers of Auschwitz, as wrong as the deliberate starvation of children – then by keeping silent, I condone what goes on there.

On April 4th, I made a choice. I chose to create the dream of another way. My only crime is not working hard enough, or long enough, or soon enough towards the fulfilment of the dream. If my actions were a crime, then I am guilty.

Helen Steven, 1984, *QFP* 24.27

A broad view of the peace testimony

Testimonies are about our practice of God's values, so that 'the kingdoms of this world may become the kingdoms of the Lord'. (1660 Declaration to Charles II) All the testimonies come from this call to transform the world as it is into something in accordance with the will of God as we experience it. They are not solely about changing ourselves, but require us to engage with the world as it is.

As testimonies are based on practice and experience rather than on a single form of words, they have developed and been restated over the centuries. This is particularly easy to trace in the case of the peace testimony. Our testimony against 'all outward wars and strife, and fightings with outward weapons' has been tested in times of crisis again and again, prompting reassessments of it.

These statements have not only called for an absence of war, but have also tried to look at what builds peace. The 1943 statement from London Yearly Meeting recognised that 'true peace cannot be dictated, it can only be built in co-operation between all peoples', and called for 'creative peace-making'.

The 1987 public statement from the Yearly Meeting of Aotearoa/New Zealand urges us all to practise the skills needed to resolve conflicts 'in our own homes, our personal relationships, our schools, our workplaces'.

'Peace work' is no longer just about international affairs, but also about us and our relationships with each other. This leads to the work of many Friends in community and victim/offender mediation schemes, work in schools against bullying, the Alternatives to Violence Project. This work is essentially 'social' work, but it aims to learn new ways of managing conflict.

Inequality is a cause of conflict. There is currently a massive imbalance of resources between the industrial northern states and the exploited countries of the two-thirds world. Where resources are scarce, conflict is likely, especially when fuelled by the arms trade plied by the industrialised north. It therefore has to be part of our peace testimony to implement our testimonies to truth and equality in our trading relations with these peoples.

The links between spending on arms and the under-funding of community necessities such as sustainable agriculture, health care and education are irrefutable. There is also a great deal of violence perpetrated because of the perceived inequality of those of another race, religion or gender. Thus the peace and equality testimonies are again seen together.

The phrase 'structural violence' is often used in reference to gross inequalities of status or wealth. However, it is just another way of saying structural injustice, an inequality built into the very fabric of society. Violence often occurs as a result. It is doing violence to the lives of those who have worse housing, less money and therefore, less access to resources and services. But it is the inequality and injustice that are the issues to be worked on, not the violence.

Whilst working for a community safety organisation in Sheffield, I found it alarming to see the differing views of what community safety was about. Some groups were concerned about getting greater security measures installed in their localities, such as CCTV, intercom systems for their blocks of flats, window locks, etc. They were desperately trying to protect themselves from members of their own community, building barricades. Other groups, typically the teenagers we worked with, felt shut out of everywhere, had nowhere safe to go together and frequently suffered verbal and physical abuse from the adults of their community, who evidently felt threatened.

The response of physical violence of a few young people to their perceived exclusion from society is matched by greater efforts to exclude them by the adult community. There is much violence inherent and contained within our societies. We can look at our social testimonies as forms of conflict prevention, intrinsically linked to ridding God's world of violence and allowing everyone to love and serve God to the best of their potential.

Many of us are involved in campaigns as part of our work of challenging social injustices and changing the world. We can write letters, lobby politicians; we can change the way we live, perhaps deciding to buy only fairly traded tea and coffee.

Some groups involved in trying to bring about positive social change use direct action as one of their campaigning tools. They are trying to use conflict creatively, sometimes trying to provoke a conflict in order to draw attention to an injustice. Many use their own bodies to try and prevent an action taking place, for example, to stop the deportation of a refugee. Acting non-violently is the key in these actions; the means of seeking justice has to be consistent with its ends.

The connection here is that our testimony against violence and our experience of non-violent change can be used to challenge the values of the world. It does not require passive acceptance of injustice, but can be a pro-active response to conflict, inequality and injustice. It can actually promote the right use of resources, creating an alternative model of community action. The peace testimony can be the tool we use to communicate with the world.

Peace is not the goal or the prize. I'm not sure what the 'Kingdom of God' looks like when you get there, but somewhere without violence is only part of the scheme, which also includes being somewhere where everyone can relate to the good, loving part of everyone else, somewhere where the good, loving parts of us all are able to develop uninhibited. Peace, non-violence, is part of the way to get there. We recognise that conflict occurs, but that it can be used to develop creatively new solutions and can teach us to love each other and live with each other in new ways.

And because the work we are called to do is to bring about the 'Kingdom of God' in this world, we have to relate to the world and not just to those who are Quakers. We are called to actively go out and change the world. But we must 'be patterns, be examples ... that your carriage and life may preach among all sorts of people'.

> The follower of Jesus is to discover and then promote the Kingdom of God. That Kingdom has two tenses: it is already here, in each one of us; and it is still to come, when God's goodness becomes a universal norm. We are to live now 'as if the Kingdom of God were already fulfilled. (Sydney Bailey, 1993, *QFP* 24.57)

Kiri Smith, 'Connected testimonies', *The Friend*, 19 June 1998

Using conflict positively

Conflict happens, and will continue to happen, even in the most peaceful of worlds. And that's good – a world where we all agreed with one another would be incredibly boring. Our differences help us to learn. Through conflict handled creatively we can change and grow; and I am not sure real change – either political or personal – can happen without it. We'll each handle conflict differently and find healing and reconciliation by different paths. I want nonetheless to offer three keys, three skills or qualities which I've found helpful from my own experience.

The first skill is *naming:* being clear and honest about the problem as I see it, stating what I see and how I feel about it. What is important about these statements is that I own them: 'I see', 'I feel' (not 'surely it is obvious that...', 'any right thinking person should'). This ability to name what seems to be going on, is crucial to getting the conflict out into the open, where we can begin to understand and try to deal with it.

Such a skill is dangerous. It can feel – indeed, it can be – confrontational. It feels like stirring up trouble where there wasn't any problem. It needs to be done carefully, caringly, with love, in language we hope others can hear. We need to seek tactfully the best time to do it. But it needs to be done.

The second skill is the skill of *listening:* listening not just to the words, but to the feelings and needs behind the words. It takes a great deal of time and energy to listen well. It's a kind of weaving: reflecting back, asking for clarification, asking for time in turn to be listened to, being truly open to what we're hearing (even if it hurts), being open to the possibility that we might ourselves be changed by what we hear.

The third skill is the skill of *letting go:* I don't mean that in the sense of giving up, lying down and inviting people to walk all over us, but acknowledging the possibility that there may be other solutions to this conflict than the ones we've thought of yet; letting the imagination in – making room for the Spirit. We need to let go of our own will – not so as to surrender to another's, but so as to look together for God's solution. It's a question of finding ways to let go of our commitment to opposition and separation, of letting ourselves be opened to our connectedness as human beings.

If we are to do any of these things well – naming, listening, letting go – we need to have learned to trust that of God in ourselves and that of God in those trapped on all sides of the conflict with us. And to do that well, I find I need to be centred, rooted, practised in waiting on God. That rootedness is both a gift and a discipline, something we can cultivate and build on by acknowledging it every day.

Mary Lou Leavitt, 1986, *QFP* 20.71

A Sunday morning in Derry

In Derry we have such a small Quaker meeting that we do not own our own meeting house. We hire a room. It was a bitter cold day in March, with temperatures below freezing. So I decided to go up very early and put the heaters on. I did so and arranged the chairs, and then I heard an odd noise coming from downstairs. I went quickly down to find two young men breaking in through a window. They had scarves wound round their faces, concealing all but their eyes.

They told me they were the Irish Republican Army. I simply did not believe them and ordered them out. I was sure I had caught two thieves in the very act of stealing. Just then a third man, who seemed much older, appeared at the window. He was wearing a hood and carried a gun. I knew at once that this was indeed the IRA. They had come to lay a bomb in the building in the hopes of killing some British soldiers if they were to pass by, as they usually did on Sunday mornings... They made me climb out of the window and led me about ten paces to a builder's shed, where they shut me in. They then checked the adjoining buildings and found several men who were painting or setting up an exhibition. They all looked so frightened as they were brought to join me in the shed.

As for me, the moment I realised I was in the hands of the gunmen I silently and urgently prayed. I asked God to help me not to show fear or aggression, and I handed over the situation to him. A wonderful thing happened. I was at peace and able to help the others in the shed. We had a long wait. At that stage I had no idea that a bomb was being planted. I imagined they were going to try to shoot a soldier from the window. I had no weapon in their sense of the word. But I had another one: prayer. Silently I prayed continuously. I prayed especially for the soldier who was to be their target.

The man who was guarding us kept asking for details of the Quaker group who would be coming. Then he told me to follow him back into the building and telephone our son to tell him the Quaker meeting would have to be held elsewhere. As I lifted the phone, he realised this would be too risky. After all, my voice might shake, and this would tell my son something was wrong. So he snatched the phone and told me to write a note cancelling the meeting, to go in the window.

I looked up at that moment and saw his eyes. I shall never forget them till I die. They were frightened and unhappy.

Suddenly everything seemed different. I realised that this man in front of me, my enemy, was just as much a victim of the Troubles as the soldier he was planning to kill. I thought if I could sit them both down in the same room together and let them talk, they would realise how much they had in common. If both their countries did not have unemployment, perhaps neither of them would have chosen to be in their armies. Both of them must feel they were fighting for their country.

Then I spoke to him. I said, 'I wish what you are planning to do would bring about what you want: a free, united country. But it won't, it will just be one more sadness to add to a long list.'

'That's your opinion', he said roughly. 'I know,' I went on, 'but I wanted to share it with you, and I want to say something else. I feel so sad that someone as young as you is caught up in all this.' He was embarrassed. It was not easy for him to cope with being cared about.

Back in the cold shed, the waiting continued. At last they came and told us they were going, but that if we wanted to be safe we had better stay in the shed. Minutes later the bomb went off. It was terrifyingly close. Later we learnt that no one had been killed. One soldier had a very small cut. That was all.

Diana Lampen, *Faith in action: encounters with Friends*, FWCC 1992, reprinted in *Spiritual basis of the peace testimony*

Curing the violence disease

It takes a lot of courage, confidence and indeed faith for a society to say of its most disruptive citizens that they need help not punishment. Suffering from severe internal terror, the last thing they need, or will respond to, is deterrence.

Symptoms of violence are rampant throughout our current society, from children's cartoons to video nasties. Violence sells. The reason why it sells so well can only be that the vast majority of us have been taught from an early age to glamorise violence. Thus we suffer, perhaps unknowingly, from the violence disease.

This viewpoint also adds a certain substance to the notion of 'defence'. Society must defend itself against barbarism, whether by street urchins or by misguided governments. Why not divert the spending of £1 billion from a Trident submarine to sorting out and curing those disaffected, mistrained members of society who daily assault our houses, cars and indeed our persons.

I speak from direct personal experience in Parkhurst Prison. The wider story has been well known to Friends since Meeting for Sufferings first met to relieve the sufferings of imprisoned Quakers in the seventeenth century.

The symptoms of violence now need to be tackled wherever they appear and more civilised alternatives suggested, or our civilisation, like the Roman empire before it, will assuredly perish from within. Could it be that Quakers will gird up their loins to tackle this social disease of violence as vigorously as they once tackled the social disease of slavery?

So here I am, a proud grandfather. I derive enormous satisfaction from my work; I am blessed with a blueprint for mental disorders which works every time – or nearly enough to justify my faith in it. What a contrast with my early student days: then, each mental patient was a different puzzle; now they all have a common link. I cannot always lay it bare, but I never doubt that it is there, hidden underneath.

So what is this link? And why do I hold my Quaker insights so dear? Because the two are one; violence evaporates when you make contact between two human souls; peace of mind blossoms of its own accord when you drain the hatred out of prejudice.

Not all Quakers will catch my drift, though enough will, to cheer me on. Even fewer psychiatrists will welcome my 'syntheses' – though the longer they delay, the further they will wander from practical policies for enhancing sanity.

Of course, for some the points I make are so obvious that they wonder why they need saying, the emotional 'figments' which so clutter emotional life are as clear to them as a withered arm or a hunched back. Indeed, having struggled so strenuously for so long, what do I discover when eventually I reach my sunny uplands?

I find that many have been there before me – philosophers, prophets, seers and, most of all for me, Quakers. I have re-cast in my own terms the human wisdom that we are all charged to rediscover during our passage through life – and now I wish to repay some of the debt for the unobvious treasures which so eased my passage.

Quakers acted for me like the monasteries of the Dark Ages. How many other groups were not only opposed to the First World War, but took decisive action which changed and sometimes risked their lives because they simply refused to accept that war could be a Good Thing? Indeed, they utterly denied it. I took these fragile insights in my philosophical knapsack, and I now see and apply their relevance to a far wider field. Quakerism is heroic on the grand scale.

I go further. Unless the new millennium vouchsafes the sanctity of every human being; unless we can learn to distil the human spirit from its verbal canisters and summon enough confidence to speak truth to power it will, without question, be the last.

What strikes me now is the almost miraculous relevance of early Quaker insights. The witness against force and violence, and to the God-given potential in all human beings, has profound practical value today. Prisoners are being treated like serfs, like naughty children – but their tantrums are those of adults, with potentially lethal consequences. Only an application of those basic Quaker principles could save the day.

Bob Johnson, *The Friend*, 26 August 1994; 3 January 1997; 9 February 1996

It never did me any harm

I first realised how I felt about corporal punishment in schools when talking to a complete stranger at a party – a teacher in a large, tough comprehensive school – who said that he had to send some boys for the cane because that was the only language they understood. I found myself suddenly in passionate opposition to him. If this was the only language they understood was he not ensuring that it was the only language they ever would understand? Was he not proving that Might was Right, that the only reason he was allowed to beat them and not they him was that he was bigger, that is in higher authority, than they were? Was he not putting the final nail in the coffin of their respect for him and all other authority they were likely to confront in the years ahead?

He reeled a bit at all this and so I admit did I. I took my rhetoric away to a safe place where I and it could calm down and I asked where it had come from. I remembered first my own experience of being hit. My mother on certain very rare occasions had felt that a certain misdeed, usually telling a lie, was so reprehensible as to admit of no other punishment. She then ceremoniously smacked us, kissed us to show that love was still there and left us alone. This may or may not have been sound psychologically or in any other way; I can only report that it left me trembling with outraged confusion.

I also remembered, sitting in that quiet recovery corner at the party, that on another occasion when I had as a young child been struck accidentally, I had experienced an overwhelming desire to hit back far more violently than I had been struck myself. I was too well brought up actually to do this but I remember my shock at the strength of my own feeling and the realisation even then of the consequence of violence.

Later as a teenager I had an even more shocking realisation. When grubby paperbacks about Nazi war crimes were passed around the school – a Methodist boarding school, founded for the daughters of ministers – I experienced to my horror a small version of the excitement that must have possessed the perpetrators of those crimes.

I knew from my own reactions that violence of necessity breeds violence. When I eventually became a member of the Society and learnt about its work not only to renounce war but to promote peace, I knew that peace had to start inside myself and with relationships between individuals: not by repression, by rules and by fear but by respect and understanding and even sometimes by the great release of fun and laugher.

Alison Sharman, *Learners all: Quaker experiences in education,* 1986

Creative conflict resolution in schools

Conflict is a part of life, a necessary result of the varying needs, aims and perspectives of individuals and communities. It is part of our daily experience, both directly and through television and other news media. The ethos of the home, school or workplace will provide some rules (spoken and unspoken) for handling conflict situations. However, these often contradict each other and the pressures from friends and peer groups can work against the 'official' ways of handling conflict. Society educates young people at best haphazardly and at worst quite destructively as far as conflict is concerned. From an early age, people are led to think that conflicts should be settled by someone in authority: the parent, the teacher, the headteacher, the gangleader, the policeman, the judge, the boss, the president. If there is nobody to arbitrate, then the 'stronger' will 'win' and the 'weaker' will 'lose'. Traditionally, little encouragement has been given to young people to take responsibility for resolving conflicts, to look for 'win-win' solutions. Yet the way in which young people learn to respond to conflict will have a pervasive effect both on the quality of their personal lives and on the prospects for society as a whole. Affirming the personal value of each individual, encouraging mutual respect and consciously developing the skills and attitudes involved in creative conflict resolution must be regarded as an important educational priority.

Sue Bowers and Tom Leimdorfer, 1990, *QFP* 24.54

Quakers, teachers and disruptive pupils

One of the most pressing social concerns today is the rapid increase in school exclusions. In 1990-91, about 3,000 pupils were permanently excluded. By 1993-94 over 10,000 were excluded, and numbers are still rising. Many thousands more pupils are temporarily or unofficially excluded and seen as disturbed and disturbing, disrupting their classes and frustrating their teachers. In many schools, there is a hopeless sense that the only solutions are negative ones: punishment and exclusions which are followed by a small chance of ever returning to ordinary school.

Each pupil tends to be seen as an individual, to be judged on his or her own behaviour, rather than also being seen as part of a huge group which is affected by great changes in society: in family structures; the education 'market'; the poverty in which one in three children now grow up and other major changes in national life.

Teachers who are also Quakers are perhaps among the most perturbed group of teachers. They long to be fair to individuals but also to whole classes; they want to see good in all pupils but feel too rushed and stressed to engage in the slow, complex task of establishing mutual trust with each pupil.

In the 1996 Swarthmore Lecture, Jonathan Dale noted the individualistic inward-looking bias of the second fifty years of Swarthmore Lectures, in contrast to the social outward-looking approach of the first fifty. He called on Quakers to return to more collective political awareness and action. This can be valuable in helping us to understand the social pressure on difficult pupils. Yet, as I heard the lecture, I wondered how many other Friends were as unsure as I felt about what a spiritual-political solidarity might mean in everyday practicality in the mid-1990s.

I was soon to learn what Quaker principles of justice and respect for everyone, of community effort and dramatic change through mediation, can mean in practice. After hearing a headteacher talk about her junior school on a deprived estate in Plymouth, I became writer in residence there and edited a book by the school (*Changing our school: promoting positive behaviour,* Highfield Junior School). The staff and pupils tell the story in their own words of the past five years. From violence and vandalism they moved into being a dynamic close community, all working for change.

Some of the techniques are used in many other schools – circle time, mediation, school council. Yet Highfield is unusual in combining a range of methods so that they reinforce one another. Personal work on self-awareness, emotions and behaviour enriches the circle time and conflict resolution work for which even the youngest children take responsibility. Individuals report their problems knowing that they will be heard with respect. The whole class discuss what action or changes are required to address the problems; if necessary the matter is taken to the school council to consider whole school changes. The council also meets as a circle time, issues are raised by the class representatives who report back to the class. 'Guardian angels' are among many ideas developed through the school – chosen peers fly to the aid of children who, for example, keep being bullied or keep bullying, in order to help them change their behaviour. Highfield is unusual in the explicit emphasis placed on democracy. The key to success is the way each person is held to be a responsible moral agent.

The current media debate about problems in schools is almost entirely concerned with naughty children and the need for firmer adult control and even greater exertion by teachers. Yet this can simply increase the original problem – pupil-teacher conflict and inordinate demands on teachers. The practical answer is for teachers to share control and responsibility with pupils, rather than trying to impose rules and enforce obedience. If someone misbehaves in the class or playground then everyone shares in helping to resolve the problem. Parents may be asked to work out solutions with the class circle time.

Does this take a lot of time? Yes, time has to be allowed for the new methods, but this prevents far more time being wasted on ineffective attempts to control misbehaviour. This is not a privileged school; over half the pupils have free school meals and identified special needs. If this school can succeed because the staff and pupils work in solidarity (it gained a glowing OFSTED report) then any school can succeed.

No one in the school mentioned being a Friend, although they used literature from Friends House and Kingston Meeting. However, I felt that the spiritual-political vision in the Swarthmore Lecture was becoming real in this school, and that its innovations could interest and help many other schools.

Priscilla Alderson, *The Friend*, 21 February 1997

A People of God
We are a people of God
That follow after those things
That make for peace, love and unity. (Margaret Fell, *QFP* 19.46)

Nation shall not lift up sword against nation,
neither shall they learn war any more. (*Isa.* 24, *Mic.* 4:3)

We are a people of God
That follow after those things
That make for peace, love and unity.

And the word of the Lord came unto me
and said, 'Put up thy sword into thy scabbard;
if my kingdom were of this world,
then would my children fight.' (William Dewsbury, *QFP* 19.45)

We are a people of God
That follow after those things
That make for peace, love and unity.

I told the Commonwealth Commissioners
I lived in the virtue of that life and power
that took away the occasion of all wars. (George Fox, 1651, *QFP* 24.01)

We are a people of God
That follow after those things
That make for peace, love and unity.

With military power we cannot protect our life
nor keep our human dignity.
My way of living or dying,
to point to the love of God shown by Jesus Christ,
will invite others to walk rightly
so that humankind may live together peacefully.
　　　(Susumi Ishitani, 1989, *QFP* 24.16)

We are a people of God, Amen.

This chant, in Taizé style, was composed and the texts chosen by John Sheldon. It was sung as part of a Sunday Half Hour on BBC Radio 2, broadcast on 2 November 1997, performed by the Quaker Festival Chorus with Helen Whittington as soloist.

Other pieces which examine the social testimony on peace and non-violence are:

5. Community　　　　　What is AVP – Alternatives to Violence Project?

7. Creation

Learning respect

Slowly, over the years, I am building a new motivation, learning to base my life on respect – respect for the animals who give their lives that I might eat and dress, respect for the trees and stones that give their lives that I might have shelter and warmth, respect for all those who labour to dig and grow and work around the world that I might live comfortably, a respect for each other as we labour to live in a confusing and noisy society.

The values and ethics upon which we are based are often not those that appear immediately on the surface. They have to be winkled out and considered; they are often long, not short, term and require both individual and community recognition. Progress is not a matter of absolute rights and wrongs, of building new rules and regulations. For me there are a string of key words such as *integrity* and *harmony* which express our inter-relationship with and dependence on all life, both seen and unseen. Dancing to that particular music has become an enormous and exciting challenge.

Jeni Edwards, 1992 *The Creation was open to me*, 1.14

Managing global resources

If only we could let go of the idea of 'the right of ownership' we might see more clearly how we all are part of the creative life of the Spirit; that our very existence depends upon the mystery of Creation, that every form of life is imbued with that spirit and that we, therefore, need to share the abundance of life as a whole. Once we do this we might begin to glimpse the potential creativity with which we are each blessed. We have so many gifts to offer, to give and to share. It is likely we shall not discover this if we grimly cling to 'ownership' as being a 'right'.

Stewardship is a different approach and is, in my view, far more appropriate to the good management of global resources than is private 'ownership'.

With stewardship we are entrusted with that good management, good nurturing, good husbandry, sensible forms of distribution and with an assumption that there will be a genuine service offered to each other, benefiting not only the human species, but all other forms of life which we are, at present, so bent on destroying.

Kenneth Hartford, 1993 *The Creation was open to me*, 2.05

A new compassionate consciousness

We were not sent into the world as despoilers and destroyers, and yet it is already too late to save much of beauty and glory which has already fallen to man's depredation, greed and thoughtlessness. Unless the new consciousness can overcome these propensities, this wonderful earth is doomed and the spirit of man with it.

All the great religions teach compassion, reverence, self-denial, humility as the qualities necessary for the regeneration which is now so sorely needed. But the conception of the oneness of life and the power of love to unite all living things has in the past been mainly felt by individual saints, philosophers and humanitarians. What is new about this consciousness is that it is now experienced by so many ordinary people the world over.

Is concentration on our own species hindering our spiritual development? It does seem that the spiritual as well as the physical health of mankind depends on the well-being of the whole natural world.

Joanne Bower 1986 *The Creation was open to me*, 1.06

The care of the earth

We seek to realise in practice the deep bond that we can dimly perceive holding us all together. In the new situation of environmental crisis we can surely perceive another bond between ourselves and the earth. The life of the earth, because it is now vulnerable to our power, is part of our life. Our life therefore can be realised and fulfilled only if we commit ourselves to the care of the earth. Making peace with the earth is now, or should be, part of our spirituality.

Rex Ambler, 1990

A testimony to all creation

Does what I do or refrain from doing help or hinder the global community? This is the question which I am now beginning to ask myself. I feel more and more clearly that we are all part of a network of relationships, between human beings, but also between humans and other species and even the inanimate world. We are all bound together in intricate and delicate relationships, interdependent upon one another, and somehow God is also involved as a spirit, the 'go-between God', continually creating and recreating the world.

I have come to this gradually over the years, and adjusting my lifestyle to my beliefs is a life-long process. It is, of course, almost impossible to avoid damaging other parts of the network. Everything we do has some effect, whether it is switching on a light, eating a banana, or going to a supermarket. Some actions, however, are less damaging than others, and some may even be beneficial, such as planting and maintaining trees, establishing a wildlife garden, and picking up litter. Every minute choices seem to come up, whether they relate to small matters such as what shall I eat, where shall I buy it, and how shall I travel, or to larger ones such as where shall I put my savings, where shall I go for a holiday (or should I have a holiday), and where shall I live.

I am much influenced by John Woolman, and would like to quote two sentences from his Journal. Firstly: 'So great is the hurry in the spirit of this world that in aiming to do business quickly and to gain wealth the creation at this day doth loudly groan.' One can almost feel creation groaning as the percentage of carbon dioxide increases, climate changes, and sea levels rise. Secondly: 'May we look at our treasures, the furniture of our houses and our garments and try whether the seeds of war have nourishment in these our possessions.' These are exactly the problems we face today. The natural world is exploited and its delicate balance upset, while the 'treasures' we demand are distributed unequally, causing poverty and often war.

Changing one's life style does not come easily. As George Fox said to William Penn about his sword, 'Wear it as long as thou canst'. For a long time I worried over the shared possession of a car, which I have now given up, thankfully. But with other matters I am dilatory. Luke Cock (*QFP* 20.22) was led on by his 'guide', and a similar process can go on in us. John Woolman provides a good example of the process. He was exceptionally sensitive to certain events and customs of his time, questioned them, was troubled by them, prayed about them, and finally acted. Even if others did not agree with him and he appeared to be 'singular', he quietly and patiently made his witness.

Radical changes in lifestyle require a new vision of how we can be in the world, which seems to need a paradigm shift in attitude. This shift is supported when we actually take on board the fact that we humans could not exist for a minute without the other living species which we tend to take for granted. Just one example is that the quality of our water, air and soil depend upon the myriad organisms working on them to recycle the pollution which we engender. In contrast, without *Homo sapiens* life would exist in abundance. So our consciousness needs to widen to include the whole community of the planet, not just our own species.

I find it disappointing that we have not yet got a written testimony to all creation, although there may be a case for saying that we do have one, which is not owned. I know many Friends who do their best to live lightly on the earth, but others who do not yet seem aware of their part. What perhaps is needed is a concerned group of Friends within each meeting to support one another and help to make our witness clearer, to Friends and non-Friends. As Quakers, we have a responsibility to own this testimony and to witness to it, as we have said from early times that the whole of life is sacramental.

Anne Adams, 1998

Some thoughts on juicy puritanism

> Be patterns, be examples in all countries, places, islands, nations, wherever you come, that your carriage and life may preach among all sorts of people, and to them; then you will come to walk cheerfully over the world, answering that of God in everyone. (George Fox, 1656)

We live in a culture where people have been cut off from the land and the changing seasons. We have been tied into a money system, and have become dependent on transport, electricity and a mechanised food-production system. Communities have been scattered, neighbourhoods are criss-crossed by roads, our social fabric is disintegrating. We have been indoctrinated into an ethos of unthinking consumerism and instant gratification. Trying to be 'green' within such a society is a journey that shakes us to the roots.

The structural violence of the whole set-up hit home to me several years ago when I wrote a book on climate change – the industrialised countries are the prime culprits in carbon emission, yet people living in vulnerable areas of the world like Bangladesh, the Sahel areas of northern Africa and the Caribbean and Pacific islands will be the first to suffer from floods, drought, increasing storm intensity, rising sea levels and food insecurity. The weather system has a 'delaying mechanism' of some thirty years so we are now experiencing the effects of the very much lower level of emissions in the 1960s. Stabilising carbon dioxide at today's levels would require emission cutbacks of roughly eighty-five per cent in the industrial world. At some stage during writing my book I began to read the statistics with my heart more than my head and went through a very dark night of the soul (in common, I imagine with most earthQuakers).

Of course it is just as possible to have the skin peeled off one's eyes by issues like the arms trade and weapons of mass destruction, hideous abuse of animals, extinctions, the military industrial complex, the cynicism of our foreign policy, multinationals, etc. The list is depressingly long. But there is one thing that marks out climate change from other issues – we have to take responsibility for our own involvement. We cannot pass the blame.

Since then I've made a modest start in reinventing the way I live. I try to keep my life as local as possible – travelling rarely and spending most of my time within a one-mile radius. I avoid the Sainsburys and Tescos of this world like the plague, trying instead to support small shops and local food producers. I have no insurance and don't lock my doors (yes I have been burgled but it seems a price worth paying). I've learned that life is better without a fridge (fewer snacks and 'factory food', more home-cooked meals). I have a (slowly realising) dream of making a sustainable living from local woodland. But... as I become more aware of my lifestyle and its impact I find that I have only just begun the journey. There is much further to go.

I might seem to be becoming a fully blown puritan. But puritanism can so easily degenerate into pious martyrdom, dry and humourless. This may have been a fault of early Friends. One particularly shocking passage in George Fox's journal tells of his meeting with 'the fattest, merriest man, the most cheerful and the most given to laughter that ever I met with' and of how he admonished [the man]. 'The power of the Lord so struck him that before he got home he was serious enough and had discontinued his laughing.' As someone once said, 'If I can't dance it it's not my revolution.'

So this year I've decided to embark on a creative adventure. My project will be to become more and more frugal *and* to have more and more fun. If I'm going to be a puritan I want to be a juicy one! I hope to minimise my dependence on the money system by cutting my necessities to the bone and relying on Calderdale's excellent LETS system for luxuries. Our recently formed credit union will provide a safety net for emergencies. I'm looking forward to more communal bulk-buying and more shared meals with my friends. I'm on the waiting list for an allotment and crossing my fingers that I'll get hold of one before planting time. I plan to home-brew for the major Celtic festivals – and to be more abstemious in my alcohol consumption the rest of the time. I want to spend my evenings making music, making things of beauty and making love!

I'm giving up my cleaning job which will give me time to devote to the things which are most important to me – developing our coppicing business, supporting Billy Frugal with *earthQuaker* and putting energy into various wacky projects. And finally I'm thinking of putting another book together with friends – it'll be a kind of Mrs Beeton for the millennium but the ingredients will include politics and religion and personal experiences. Above all it will make the point that we don't just live in households, we live in neighbourhoods and that our real wealth lies in our communities.

Penny Eastwood, *Quaker monthly*, April 1996, reprinted from *earthQuaker*, Issue 14 Spring 1996

Balancing the pollution

Living in the developed, minority world, I am forever conscious of how difficult it is to lead a life without plastic. It is so hard to live sustainably here. I know that every day my existence is having a negative effect on the planet, as I cause the consumption and waste of energy and resources. I am therefore committed to making up for this, and more. I am determined to ensure that my life will have as much of a positive outcome for the earth as possible. Just to balance out the pollution I shall cause in my lifetime (however much I try to reduce it) will be enough of a challenge. I believe many of the high hopes I have for my lifestyle stem from my upbringing as a Quaker. I am proud of the values my ancestors had and the lives they led, and I do not want my own life to be a comparative disappointment.

N12 in *Who do we think we are?* 1998

The major decisions

If we are looking at ways of reducing our consumption of energy and non-renewable resources, we need to start with the major decisions that we may take only infrequently. If we are choosing a house, will it be economical to heat, and is it near enough to work, schools, shops and friends to reduce or eliminate the use of a car? When buying a car, or a household appliance, is it the most long-lasting, and the most economical to run, that will meet our requirements? Finding the right answers to these major questions can make a huge difference to the amount of energy we consume, reducing the emission of carbon dioxide by several tons per household per year, as well as saving money to spend where it is needed.

Margaret Bodley, 1993 *The Creation was open to me*, 4.11

Discovering our social testimony and making changes

Before the Swarthmore Lecture 1996 I was relatively new to the Religious Society of Friends, having attended my first ever meeting for worship in October 1994, and having been admitted into membership in November 1995. I was trying to live ethically, through my work as a general practitioner and in my daily life. I had became vegetarian in 1986. I had been a member of Baby Milk Action for several years, and boycotted Nestlé products, and I subscribed to the *Ethical consumer* magazine.

A couple of Friends in my preparative meeting talked enthusiastically about the 1996 Swarthmore Lecture and I read a copy. I agreed with its message. Shortly afterwards, the Real World Coalition was launched and we got hold of copies of their book, *The politics of the real world*. We agreed on the seriousness of the problems and the coherence of the action programme proposed. A group of about eight of us, all Quakers, met together to set up a local Real World Group. We decided that we should have a public meeting and wrote to other groups, such as the Friends of the Earth, Oxfam, and the United Nations Association, inviting them to participate. We held our first coalition meeting in September 1996: approximately half the member organisations of the Real World Coalition were represented. We had already established that our Conservative MP and prospective parliamentary candidates from the Labour and Liberal Democratic parties were prepared to take part. We worked with the other organisations to produce a poster and to agree on questions, which spanned the whole Real World agenda. The public meeting, held in November 1996, was a success. Approximately one hundred people attended. We had a very good quality debate, and virtually everyone in the audience participated – the way we feel democracy should work.

The philosophy of ROST also affected the way I worked. The Health Authority had commissioned me to produce a Health Needs Assessment in a GP surgery. I approached this holistically, looking frankly at the link between health and poverty, and the causes of and appropriate responses to deprivation. I also researched the links between transport policy, pollution, and air quality. In October 1996 I realised that I could not continue the current use of my car. My initial reaction was: I can't do anything different. I am a single parent, my son Charles attends a school over two miles from home, and I need my car to get to work and to carry out home visits to patients.

I thought about what I most wanted to change. I didn't want to carry on contributing to traffic fumes or to the congestion on our roads. I wanted to reclaim the roads for bicycles, for my son and me as well as other people. I wanted to improve my abysmal level of physical fitness. It took me two months to come up with a solution: a tandem. We bought ours in January 1997. I knew from the start that what I really wanted was to give up my car completely, but I didn't know whether this would be possible. Initially I could only manage the round trip to school (four and a half miles) once a day, but as the weeks went by, I got fitter – and so did Charles. I was struck early on by how much less psychological stress I experienced on the bike compared with sitting in a car in the endless traffic jams round town. This tied in with the book I was reading at the time, *Free to be human*, by David Edwards. One of his messages is that sin is its own punishment and virtue is its own reward. I was cycling because of my concern for other road users, and I was reaping physical and psychological benefits.

Charles sees his father one weekend in three. Rather than drive to the halfway point, I decided to travel by train to the station near his father and my boyfriend, thereby saving nearly one thousand miles of driving, which would be clocked up by my ex-husband, my boyfriend and me. Again, I discovered that the car journey was inferior to travel by train, which gave Charles and me quality time together. For example, he played his first ever game of draughts on a rail journey – and many subsequently – and has become a good player. We can play other games, read together, and eat together.

The time for decision came – in September 1997. My sister got a job over a hundred miles from home and needed a second car for the use of her husband with their two young children. I offered to sell them my car, on three weeks' notice, with the proviso that I could reclaim it if I found I needed it. My mother, who lives near me, was extremely supportive and told me I could borrow her car if ever I needed it.

I was really frightened about the step I was about to take. However, I asked myself, 'What is the worst thing that could happen?' I might have to accept that I couldn't manage without a car. The only way to find out was to try it, so therefore this wasn't a wrong decision, but a necessary experiment.

A week before the day of the car sale, I bought a folding bicycle. Then, on September 18th, 1997, I drove the hundred and twenty miles to my sister's home, got out my folding bike, cycled to the railway station, and got a train home. I didn't feel elated, but I realised that I was embarking on a great adventure and I did feel hopeful. I am pleased that we have managed perfectly well up to now but I am not complacent.

When I turn up for work as a locum GP on my bicycle, the surgery staff are sometimes a bit surprised and puzzled, but they are happy as long as the work gets done. Of the patients requiring home visits, some either don't notice or don't comment, but many are very positive. A common comment is 'It's nice to see a doctor taking exercise, not just telling other people to.' One woman told me she thought what I was doing was wonderful: she is very concerned about her son's worsening asthma, is sure that increasing traffic pollution is to blame, and wishes more people would reduce their car usage.

A year later, I continue to act as the co-ordinator of the Plymouth Real World Group. We have meetings and a newsletter to inform ourselves of each other's campaigns and activities. Last month I represented the Real World on the panel of a public meeting entitled 'How far can ethics transform the market economy?'

At the moment the main concern of our Real World Coalition and of our preparative meeting is Jubilee 2000: we are taking part in local publicity events, and some of us will be going to Birmingham to help form a human chain round the G7 Conference on 16 May [1998].

My shopping has become more ethical. I spend more in Oxfam than in supermarkets. I buy fair-traded tea, coffee, sugar, muesli, and chocolate. I get a weekly delivery of local organic vegetables. When I shop – for clothes or camping equipment – I ask the shop assistant about the country of origin of the goods, and the workers' conditions. This has resulted in the assistant telephoning head office, raising awareness of the ethical issues amongst them both.

I make my holidays as ethical as possible. Last summer and this summer our main break will be the family week at the Centre for Alternative Technology in Machynlleth, giving us ideas about making our home more environmentally friendly and supporting the Centre, as well as being lots of fun.

I cycle between fifty and eighty miles per week, with most of the rest of our journeys being on foot or by train. I feel like I have a new heart and lungs; a glow to my skin; and iron in my muscles. These physical improvements contribute to my spiritual well-being, a feeling of being in harmony with the Tao, which is often nothing less than bliss.

I appreciate how lucky I am to have been able to make these changes in my life. However, there is plenty more to be done. One of my goals is to consume only fair-traded tea and coffee: I am working on my friends, relatives, the GP surgeries where I work, and public outlets. I would like to see far greater availability of information about the ethics of manufactured goods and food: including the workers' conditions, local environmental effects, and the real transport costs. I am sure that there is more work to be done with Jubilee 2000 and the Real World, and that other opportunities for expressing my social testimony will present themselves.

Clare Hamon, *The Friend*, 14 August 1998

[Since writing this article Clare has further increased her ways of expressing her social testimony.]

In June 1999, I sold my house for £145,000 and bought another for £65,000. This got rid of my mortgage, in keeping with my antagonism towards interest-charging, which transfers money from the less to the more affluent.

My new house was in a poor state, and required a lot of work, which I have carried out in the most environmentally friendly and ethical ways available to me. My main sources of information have been the *Ethical consumer, The whole house book: ecological building design and materials* by Borer and Harris (1998) and *Eco-renovation: the ecological home improvement guide* by Harland (1998).

The roof needed overhauling, and the most environmentally friendly option would have been secondhand Welsh slates, but I could not obtain these, so I bought new Welsh slates. At the same time I installed a Thermomax solar water-heating system. This has been researched and manufactured by a British company and is extremely efficient – and I have fitted radiator insulation panels behind my radiators to reduce the work of my gas central heating.

My rainwater harvesting system collects rainwater from the guttering downpipe and stores it in a tank in the cellar, to supply the water for flushing my toilets, the cold water in my washing machine, and a garden tap. I have 'Water Two' valves on the outflow to my bath and my kitchen sink, so that I can use the water on my garden. My washing machine is highly efficient in its use of electricity and water, and I use ceramic washballs instead of detergent in about half the loads, thereby reducing chemical pollution.

My kitchen units are secondhand, and were fitted by a good carpenter, with worktops made from antique pitched pine floorboards. I have a gas cooker, as this is more environmentally friendly than electricity, and foods which require chilling are stored in a coolbox – in most households, refrigerators consume more electricity than any other appliance, because they are switched on 24 hours a day. I do not own a freezer or dishwasher.

Most of my light bulbs are energy efficient, either fluorescent or halogen. The redecoration has used environmentally friendly paints and wood waxes, and I replaced rotten windows with timber framed ones.

I compost my kitchen waste, and our garden grows a wide range of fruit and vegetables. We choose organic and fair-traded foods whenever available.

We are still committed to environmentally friendly transport. Our day-to-day travel is on a tandem, although my son is gaining confidence on a single bicycle. For longer journeys we go by train. We used Eurostar to travel to the Jubilee 2000 demonstration in Cologne in June 1999.

Some of our ethical decisions cost more than the alternatives, but many are cheaper. We appreciate that we are lucky that the choices are available and that we can afford them.

Clare Hamon, January 2000

Doing the right thing

During the construction of a bypass around Newbury, there was a well-publicised protest against the environmental effects of the mass road-building programme of the early 1990s. Quakers were involved in similar protests at various road-building sites around the country.

Outside the compound at Newbury we talk to the security guards, their first words echoing those of the soldiers to the woman participating in the vigil against cruise missiles at Greenham (1995, *QFP* 24.28). And when, instead of shouting at them as they have come to expect, we listen to them, engage, and sympathise with them, we begin to talk together about life, poverty, hope, they agree with us that this destruction is awful, unnecessary ...

They are caged in, or so it looks to us, with the hundreds of police and their vicious dogs and their riot gear like servants of a fascist state, and the pile drivers, three stories high, banging, banging. And we agree with them, Ruth and I, that it isn't fair that they, as security guards, don't merit ear defenders because they're not important enough, though they are just as near as the construction workers themselves.

Some have already left, jumped over, joined the protesters, and this one says he would if it weren't for his kids and the mortgage he's got with his partner. He and his mate here tell us we seem like ordinary people. We laugh. We *are* ordinary people, just like them. I feel happy that I'm doing the right thing, I'm in the right place, I'm helping the world just as much as if I had been down the other side of the route earlier and got inside the compound to hold up the construction.

N19 in *Who do we think we are?*, 1998

Greening our hours

Our consumption patterns clearly have become more environmentally friendly, but this should not be viewed as an end in itself. Even if greener, our consumption may still represent unnecessary resource usage – scarce or otherwise – and unless goods consumed are totally biodegradable, will ultimately present an increasing disposal burden on our society's waste handling facilities.

To me a touchstone for assessing how green is a lifestyle, is to consider the nappy and the motor car. According to Penny Stanway in her book *Green babies*, three to four billion disposable nappies are annually used in the UK, accounting for four per cent of our household waste. Similarly Juliet Solomon in *Green parenting* comments on how unjustifiable is the habitual use of disposable nappies. She says it is 'unforgivable in a world which needs its trees' that they are being turned into throw-away nappies. Both authors recommend using terry towelling nappies, which are also available as seconds or secondhand.

Britain has one of the highest vehicle densities in the world. All of us car owners are probably only too embarrassingly familiar with the negative issues surrounding owning a car: the pollution created, the maiming and deaths caused to a wide range of living species, the non-renewable resources used in its manufacture, its considerable running costs. Yet we continue to opt for one – for its convenience, social status, and the freedom of movement it confers. For an increasing number of people living in rural areas, the car is the sole means of transport available as public transport facilities alarmingly continue to decrease.

Of course, the disposable nappy and the motor car are but two randomly chosen yardsticks of green living. Why I have singled them out, is that I suspect their main significance to us is the time we believe they save us. We would much rather do something else – probably something highly worthy – than wash and scrub nappies or catch two buses to the local supermarket or launderette.

But can we simultaneously truly claim that we are doing our personal best to live environmentally soundly? Or shall we acknowledge that we, Friends, like most of our fellow citizens in similar economic circumstances in the North, are still part of the problem and not the solution to the degradation of our deeply beloved planet?

Amber Carroll, *Quaker monthly*, June 1992

The social testimony discovery day: Leicester Meeting, September 1997

In children's meeting we were talking about ways we could make the world more clean and not so polluted. We stuck little 'Post-it' labels on a big bit of card about how we should travel. Then we talked about our ideas. A few weeks later we made a big poster (all together) to show things we shouldn't do to animals and the countryside.

Social testimony means being kind and caring and being fair to the animals and justice to people. But why do we do all this? Because God tells us to.

Susanna Mattingly (age 7), September 1997

Living our social testimony

I've chosen my title because it is the living, rather than the rediscovering of our social testimony that seems important to me. We need guiding principles but I expect I'm not the only one who finds that the hard bit is translating the inspiring words into lasting action. Persisting with the faithful performance of our seemingly insignificant contribution is a challenge and I hope the ROST process will re-energise us as we find that together our contributions could sow the seeds which will blossom in the future transformation of society.

I take our social testimony to mean that individually and corporately as Quakers we are concerned about other people and want everyone to have the chance to develop their gifts and talents and to live fulfilling lives. We therefore try to ensure that the way we live facilitates rather than hinders this and to use what influence we have to work for a society whose culture and institutions do the same. In fact, isn't the social testimony basically about living the second commandment to love our neighbour as ourselves, remembering that our neighbour is every other human being?

We affect other people directly and indirectly. Our direct impact, the way we relate to those we come into contact with, must be an important part of our social testimony and is probably more far reaching than we realise. But here I want to concentrate on our indirect impact which, I think, is becoming increasingly significant as the world's people become more and more intermeshed through the global economic system and the planet-scale effects of our treatment of our environment. Unless we wake up to this indirect route, we can be responsible for exploitation and oppression of other people without even being aware of it.

Once I realised I was partly responsible for the terrible suffering that is occurring in the poorest countries of the world, I determined to do all I could to put that right. It is hard to keep up the effort when you can't relate directly to the people you are affecting so I have to remind myself periodically that it is worthwhile. Also I don't often have a chance to explain myself and I know many people don't understand why I bother, so I welcome this opportunity to put my reasons down on paper.

The first thing I realised was how the way I spent my money affected other people, especially those in the poorest countries of the world. In the present economic set up, where these poorest countries have almost no 'power' in the free market, buying goods from them, unless they are fair-traded, is equivalent to owning slaves. So I now avoid unfair-traded Third World produce, though I make an exception for organically grown food and cotton for reasons I explain below. However I actively seek out fair-traded Third World goods (food, clothes and household products such as towels, cushions, bits of furniture) because I think these will help the people in those countries climb out of the impossible situation they are in regarding debt and lack of power over forces that affect them. Sadly, in the world as it is, money, not wisdom, brings power. If I can't buy fair-traded then I normally make do and mend, buy second-hand or buy British to cut down transport costs and encourage local work. However I only buy new after careful perusal of the *Ethical consumer* in order to pick the most enlightened manufacturer in terms of treatment of workers, care for the environment and non-involvement in arms, manufacture or exploitative practices in the Third World. This can make shopping a bit time-consuming but I feel I owe it to those people who are struggling to barely subsist, while I enjoy comforts and opportunities which they can only dream of.

My next concern is to encourage organic or vegan-organic agriculture and horticulture both in the UK and overseas, so I buy organically grown produce from the Third World, even if it's not marked as fair-traded, though fortunately the two principles often go together. My reason for this concern is twofold. Firstly, pesticides are causing widespread and long-lasting damage to people, either directly or indirectly through long-lasting pollution of the environment during use and manufacture. Secondly, fertile soil is full of living organisms which we destroy with all these biocidal chemicals at our peril, risking future generations being left with a lifeless earth. I've succeeded to the extent that it's rare for our family to eat anything which is not fair-traded or organically grown or both but we try not to impose on other people, who may have different priorities, and wouldn't dream of questioning the credentials of foods we eat as guests!

On the subject of food: I am vegan and my husband almost, because, in addition to according animals respect, vegans need less land than vegetarians, and much less than meat-eaters, to produce their food. I think the figure is vegans need 1/25th of the land area needed by the average meat eater. In a world of rapidly increasing population and decreasing fertile land, and where millions already go hungry, this seems to us a socially positive step and anyway a good vegan diet is healthy and tasty! Also the land released from agriculture could be used for growing trees, essential to the stability of the global climate which is, in turn, essential for the welfare of all people.

Another area is ethical investment. We don't simply avoid unethical investments but invest in 'positively' ethical places – for example Triodos Bank and Shared Interest – not to make a lot of interest but so that the money, while we don't need it, is used to help others and support positive environmental initiatives. Getting high interest rates from investments even in 'good' activities feels wrong to me in that it is earning money out of other people's efforts. It was the interest rate, and not the original loans, that caused the crippling burden of debt in the Third World.

I hope the above examples give some idea of how and why I try to 'live' the social testimony. There are other examples, particularly the way we try to limit our pollution of the environment, the campaigns and charities we support, and the number of letters we write to government departments, etc. I realise other Friends may have quite different priorities and put their efforts into other aspects of the social testimony. The important thing is that we each do our bit and together we'll work miracles.

As a Quaker, I value the support I get from the Society in my efforts to live out my spiritual insights in my life and I realise that most of those insights have come from those quiet 'promptings of love and truth' which creep up on one in meeting for worship! As we all listen to, and act on, these promptings, our social testimony will become a living witness.

Anne Brewer, *earthQuaker*, Yearly Meeting 1997/ROST edition

Potential work on the Earth and ecological problems: distinctive themes emerging in Joseph Rowntree Quaker Fellowship work

The concern that there will be no change in human behaviour towards the Earth, either in society at large, or amongst Ffriends, until we shift our values and beliefs, is by far the most powerful theme that emerges from discussions with meetings. It is evident that despite fine words from several yearly meetings, Friends feel that we ourselves have a long way to go to achieve the profound changes that are needful if our species is to live in harmony with other life forms and without destructive exploitation of the planet.

We do face a planetary crisis. It is fundamentally a spiritual crisis with practical consequences. Human society's beliefs created the exploitative behaviour which so threatens the stability of Earth's evolving life systems and climate at present. We Quakers stand in the heart of the culture whose global spread has caused much of the mess, and maybe that gives us a responsibility to search for the spiritual and ethical keys to change. Relationship with the Earth is the key to many 'peak' spiritual experiences. Yet we as a culture tend to isolate and romanticise these experiences, refusing them a social content, and not experiencing them as a spur to a radical questioning of our attitude and actions towards the natural world. If we look into ourselves more deeply, and relate more deeply to the Earth's sacredness, not denying the real teaching of our experience of the natural world, we may find as a Society a transformed and inspirational relationship with the Earth.

Quaker spirituality and mystical experience, from the seventeenth century on (when the relationship of early Friends to the natural world was as revolutionary as the peace testimony – 'God is the life of every creature, though few there be that know it' – James Nayler), has encouraged our Society towards social expression and critique. The respect for the land and kindliness of Quaker farmers was well known. Friends were amongst the first campaigners against cruelty to animals. If we have a unique contribution to make to the rising human ecological consciousness, it perhaps lies deep in the nature of Quaker experience. The openings of tenderness amongst us, and between us humans and the natural world, historically lead us not towards quietism and introspection, but to change our human ways. This gift the world much needs.

Quakers were in the forefront of radical concern for human social justice, from the early nineteenth century on, but a preoccupation with human issues has perhaps obscured our response to the growing ecological crisis. Had we acted as a Society thirty-five years ago, in the late 1960s when we were just beginning to realise the massively destructive impact humans could have on the earth by the year 2000, we would have been radicals in the seventeenth century mode. As it is, our spiritual and practical green awareness as a Society has lagged behind that of contemporary social radicalism, and we are responding late in the day to an already very serious situation, a crisis that many Friends are aware of in silent despair. We must bear in mind that at present no fewer than four species an hour are becoming extinct as a result of human activity, a collective responsibility we all share, and that global warming is already with us. We Quakers have much colluded with the ecological denial of our wider culture, and have taken a very long time to reawaken to William Penn's sense:

> It were happy if we studied nature more in natural things; and acted according to nature, whose rules are few, plain and most reasonable. Let us begin where she begins, go her pace, and close always where she ends. It would go a long way to caution and direct people in their use of the world, that they were better studied and knowing in the creation of it. For how could men find conscience to abuse it, while they should see the great Creator look them in the face, in all and every part thereof?

Meetings, and individuals within them, vary enormously, both in their general level of awareness and practical involvement in ecological matters. It is – sadly – generally true that hitherto Quakers have tended to assume greenness without taking it personally, a broad and uncurious sympathy that makes few, if any, personal demands. Complacency is unfortunately a word that springs to mind. Where the matter of the Earth has been taken to heart, and Friends have been involved in lifestyle groups, the action that results has tended hitherto to be limited to those involved with the group, though Hardshaw East Lifestyle Group is at present voicing its concern. Maybe it is high time we all asked ourselves the deep and searching questions nationally.

For children, planetary holocaust, already happening, is the reality they face and fear as they grow towards their adult lives. 'I worry that by the time I'm grown up, there won't be much left to save.' (Lucy Cowley, age 12, 1988) A rationalised response, sans feeling, without deep connection, is far easier for anyone encountering green ideas for the first time as an adult. I sense that part of our inertia is a tendency to put rationalisation first. Thereby we inadvertently teach the young not to risk carrying into adult life those deeper levels of spiritual openness and learning which lead to profound challenges to the status quo. It's a vicious circle. When change is overtaking us, if we adults do not engage our whole being, learning spiritually and emotionally as well as intellectually, responding as deeply and vividly as in childhood, communities may stagnate and fracture. Yet we can all change in deep awareness of truths new to us, old and young. In such change lies the becoming of freedom to act as a whole community, united across the generations. The spiritual growth of each of us gifts us all in some way with renewed vision.

Many Friends who are active in ecological concerns have expressed to me feelings of isolation and lack of concern and support within their meetings. Others who feel that their earth-focused spirituality is the cornerstone of their spiritual and active lives often feel unsupported to the point of leaving the Society, or distancing themselves to nominal involvement. I wonder just how many green Friends, potential Friends and disenchanted young Quakers have voted with their feet and left the Society in the last thirty years, not finding their spiritual experience and its leadings reflected in the central concerns and articulated beliefs of fellow Quakers. However, the experience of working with meetings indicates to me that shared concern may well be unexamined or unspoken, and therefore latent or unexpressed, rather than non-existent. Once Friends share their deeper feelings, their spiritual openings, the community of concern whose fruits are practical action begins to form. We cannot expect that Friends will change overnight. But there is a groundswell of change amongst Friends, which is giving new passion to our love for the Earth.

We must beware of addressing only the consequences of shifts in values and beliefs, and merely preaching practical action to the converted on areas which can easily be dismissed as 'just another issue which I'm too busy to deal with, and is already being dealt with by Friends of the Earth' by those whose spirituality has involved no deep questioning of belief. A strength-ened and renewed sense of the sacredness of the Earth and all life within our Quaker culture is the only authentic underpinning of our practical work. If that is the case, wherever we are working, as individuals or as meetings, or in co-operation with other groups, we will enable within that work the distinctive Quaker perspective that is genuine growth and outreach.

Potential work within the Yearly Meeting

Ecological audits and lifestyle groups:
A long-standing area for Quaker Green Concern, and as an expression of Quaker simplicity, many meetings are now interested in or are attempting ecological audits. Hardshaw East is bringing its concern to Yearly Meeting Agenda Committee. The witness of our meeting houses lies in what they are as well as in all that happens there: they are part of the 'pattern and example' we endeavour to become. As we work on the small realities of daily life, we wrestle with the greater problems of our society. Only by setting our own houses in right order, changing the reality of our own lives, can we live in 'the blessed Truth' and speak of our spiritual respect for the Earth without hypocrisy.

Transport:
Friends realise that meetings could form supportive communities and make it far easier to challenge the individualistic, selfish and destructive 'culture of the car' than it is alone. Campaigning for environmentally less damaging and socially more just transport systems would be part of that witness. Active non-violent protest may well play its part. Public education on the appalling costs of road and air transport to our atmosphere and to all species and their habitats, expressions at present of untrammelled greed, is maybe vital, and what more effective way than the witness of our lives? 'So great is the hurry in the spirit of this world, that in aiming to do business quickly and to gain wealth the creation at this day doth loudly groan' (John Woolman) is still true today: the Quaker past leads us to a new vision for the future.

The loss of indigenous species in Britain:
We are faced with an appalling and escalating holocaust of wildlife, plant and animal, in this country. This challenges us profoundly to bear witness to our society of the truth of 'God is the life of every creature', to take

action as meetings and within local groups working for change. Individual action to help save distant rainforests can only be symbolic, as in a gift of money or letters of protest. We can risk turning away from what is really happening on our doorsteps. Local practical work directly affects the environment positively, may lead us to wider social action, and grounds and inspires our prayers for the world.

Taking the organic gardening and farming message out into the community:

Within our own lives, many Friends support and practise organic methods of gardening and agriculture 'The key to the new Garden of Eden is working with nature rather than trying to confine, distort and enslave all life.' (Chris Marsh) This conviction has a profound spiritual basis, yet organic food is much the preserve of the middle classes. Our sense of social justice asks us to question that. Through effective study and networking, we can become more aware of the work of such organisations as Commonwork (a Quaker founded farm in Kent which teaches thousands of schoolchildren through its example), aware of opportunities to co-work imaginatively with organisations such as the Henry Doubleday Research Association, (who are trying to create programmes to work with socially disadvantaged people – especially the long term unemployed and those with disabilities), aware of all kinds of projects and opportunities. A wider vision can inspire us to work in wider society, and to move forward as Friends together rather than just digging our own backyards.

Developing Quaker thinking on genetically modified organisms:

Agricultural genetically modified organisms present a potential threat to all life's future and are an under-researched technology manipulating life itself to serve the drive for financial profit, not, as so often claimed, the best interests of the poor. The ethical and spiritual dimensions of the debate about genetically modified organisms are of particular concern to Friends. We need to be well informed, capable of asking the awkward questions, and campaigning as we feel led.

Suzanne Finch 1999

At a turning point

We seem to be at a turning point in human history. We can choose life or watch the planet become uninhabitable for our species. Somehow, I believe that we will pass through this dark night of our planetary soul to a new period of harmony with the God that is to be found within each of us, and that S/he will inspire renewed confidence in people everywhere, empowering us all to co-operate to use our skills, our wisdom, our creativity, our love, our faith – even our doubts and fears – to make peace with the planet. Strengthened by this fragile faith, empowered by the Spirit within, I dare to hope.

Pat Saunders, 1987, *QFP* 29.03

Other pieces which examine the social testimony on creation are:

2. Truth and integrity	Ethical investment and monthly meeting treasurers
8. Economic values	The real task of development
	Economics as if love were the guiding principle
Part IV	Witnessing corporately to our social testimony
	Hebden Bridge PM

8. Economic values

The testimony to economic values is not a traditional Quaker testimony but it is traditionally an area on which Friends have spoken over the centuries. It therefore seemed only right that it should be included in this examination of our Quaker social testimonies.

The centrality of economic affairs

It was once possible to argue that economic affairs might, like total abstinence, slavery or spiritual healing, be a field of particular interest to groups of Friends. We can now see that the economic order is not a peripheral concern, but central to the whole relationship between faith and practice.

This is not a claim that, say, the interest in peace and international relations ought now to take a secondary place in our thoughts and prayers. Still less is it a demand that the Society should cease to be first and foremost a religious body, or to say that it should in any way neglect its spiritual foundations in favour of more good citizenship. It is rather that economic affairs are now so central to our whole existence that no other aspect of personal relationships or individual life-styles can now be looked at without first understanding what it means in terms of our national wealth, incomes, and their distribution.

David Eversley, 1976, *QFP* 23.53

Bread for my neighbour

The study of Marxism taught me that even good people are helpless in the face of evil, unstoppable systems and that creative change is not possible without a common struggle. Life has taught me – and the gospel confirms it – that none of us are immune from the corruptions of power and that revolutionary justice without compassion is not always an improvement on the old oppression. All too often – for fear of something worse – Christians knowing this have stood in the way of radical change and safeguarded their vested interests instead of bringing to the revolution itself the humanity of Christ, with all the attendant risks.

[Although] those with easy ideological answers have been and remain the great deceivers of our century, that does not mean that piety is to be preferred to politics. It is to the affirmation of politics that my conversion to the world has led me. Not, of course, to the exclusion of God the Holy Spirit, but as the natural consequence of a spirituality based on the Incarnation, the affirmation that God is to be found not only in Jesus but (because of who Jesus was) in every human being.

When the Russian mystic and political philosopher Nicholas Berdyaev wrote, early in this century, that 'bread for myself is a material question but bread for my neighbour is a spiritual question' he was, in effect, saying that what is behind every economic policy is a prior spiritual decision about who is entitled to what.

Paul Oestreicher, *The double cross*, pp.34-5

Put money in its place

Poverty will persist and deepen while the present economic system continues, however much it is manipulated. Through the mechanisms of rent, dividend and interest, the work of the poor currently accumulates in the bank accounts of the rich – to the physical hurt of the poor, and the spiritual hurt of the wealthy. And, moreover, the present system keeps us all in insecurity.

The word economics derives from the Greek, *oikonomos*, for which the best translation seems 'care of the household', and this translation give us new light. A new economics based, not on these mechanisms of exploitation and violence, but on the collected values of friendship and love, would serve us all well – the currently rich and poor alike.

The time has come, Friends, when we must witness for money to be a public service rather than a public menace. It is time for us to speak out, in love, to put money in its proper place here in this part of God's house, this Earth.

John Courtneidge, *The Friend*, 11 November 1998

Joined up thinking: funding policy in a National Park Authority

One of the underlying causes of current environmental and social problems, I consider, is the compartmented way of thinking western societies have developed. Most of us live in urban areas, divorced from rain collection, ground water, food production, dealing with waste, generating energy. We are paid in money (wages, social security or pension) which bears no direct relation to the value or the consequence of the activities we engage in. Only the very poorest and most frugal of UK citizens is likely to consume at a level low enough to be 'sustainable' in the long term.

In an ideal world there would be no difference between the value of the activities we now describe as voluntary, housework, profession, caring. In an ideal world, all types of activity would be judged not on a monetary basis but on their social and environmental worth. And activities judged to be socially or environmentally damaging would have to be 'earned' by much compensating activity; or forbidden in a civil society by law. Scientists or financiers – or architects (my profession) would not be able to propose socially or environmentally damaging developments, because the cost would be outrageous. Indeed, such developments are outrageous now – but our money-only measure cannot recognise this yet.

I am a secretary-of-state nominated member of a National Park Authority. Two thirds of the members are elected county councillors, nominated to the Park by their authorities, and one third are nominated by the Secretary of State (soon the Welsh Assembly) to represent the wider public interest. Conservation is the Park's primary purpose; with access, enjoyment and understanding for visitors; and promotion of the cultural and economic life of the resident population, following closely behind. These purposes frequently clash, and the task is then to find a reasonable compromise. Very occasionally, one finds a solution that promotes all three purposes. But the Park has very limited powers or resources to initiate. One area of potential I see within the Park's control is its financial reserves. Local authorities and other public bodies hold accounts built up of a reserve for contingencies (e.g. natural disasters, public enquiries), and income not yet spent in on-going programmes. These sums are invested under strict treasury rules, usually through a bank in high-yield money-markets. The Park members agreed to ask the bank to screen the Park's investment, but the bank said it could not, even when the Park asked only that the UK top ten arms exporters be screened out.

I then proposed that we 'see what additional benefit we might gain from a positive selection of bank. If we were to deposit a part of our reserves or balances with a bank such as Triodos, we would have similar monetary returns as from Barclays. In addition, the bank offers preferential rates to organic farmers, community co-operatives and other such initiatives. The Park Authority could choose to earmark its funds to such groups. Thus we would be using the money twice, in the ordinary way by earning interest (as at present) but also by instructing the bank to screen the funds positively, directing them towards our own choice of economic activity.'

There is a limit to how much time in committee I can expect members to spend considering ethical investment, since this is not central to the Park's remit. However, when the county treasurer advised this proposal was not permitted under treasury rules, I tried another approach: could the Park set up a small ethically screened revolving fund targeted at projects within its area which promote its own purposes? The interest might be slightly lower, the risks might be slightly higher, but the money would be used specifically for proper purposes in this community, and not disappear into the bank's control to be used, unscreened. Even this, it seems, would not be permitted.

The underlying problems are manifold. Firstly, following scandals such as the collapse of BCCI, current treasury rules permit only a very limited range of banks to be used, thus perpetuating the status quo. Secondly, there is the culture of secrecy surrounding finances. Since the bodies involved are public sector, and the finance is public, it should be easy to find who invests what where; but the banks will not reveal this information. However, the greatest problem is attitude. Government finance officers are unused to thinking laterally in this way. Thinking about ethics would make their already complex tasks much more challenging. At present, local authorities lack guidance on an 'approved' way to evaluate social and environmental costs and benefits, as well as monetary ones. It takes an exceptional officer to 'trail-blaze' on an issue like this, and even then, the officer has to have instruction from the members to allocate staff time to it.

But I realise now after nearly seven years on the Park that legislative reform usually follows public action rather than leading it. So, we have to push from below if we want change.

I was not elected to the Authority, which may be held against me. But I have tried to think about the wider implications of decisions the Park makes, for the sake of the 'wider constituency' I am appointed to represent. I see my role as being a bit of a conscience, though I hope a kindly conscience and with practical suggestions to take forward. I try not to get put down by the worldly wise, who belittle my suggestions with 'You cannot change the world you know' and 'Politics is the Art of the Possible'. I remind them of the Park's purposes, which were well in advance of their time; and ask them to practise what they preach. That is all any of us can try to do. But we must keep trying; that is keeping faith with the future.

Frances Voelcker, 1999

A Friendly discourse on finance

A Yearly Meeting minute recorded our intention to keep the ethical nature of its investments under review. This article is a small contribution to what I hope will be an ongoing discussion.

I believe that all our financial decisions, including how we spend our money, should be made with respect for the integrity of creation. Money is a powerful 'out of sight, out of mind' mechanism. After the negative impacts of our financial choices have filtered down to the real, physical, world, they can either be spread diffusely, contributing to a general malaise (the rumbling of lorries and the fuming of the air), or else take place far from our gaze (the factory farm, the distant labourer's tired face, the poisoned stream). The first – and hardest – step is to bring uncomfortable things into the light. The second step, which is infinitely more joyful, is to realise that there are alternatives.

While I was musing for this article, I was able to get hold of a copy of *Ethical investment: a saver's guide*, by Peter Lang, which I wholeheartedly recommend to Friends, not least for its numerous useful address lists. One particular strength of the book is that it looks beyond the 'glass wall between financial advisers and the social economy'. In the past, most ethical investments have focused on the same base as conventional investments – the two thousand companies listed on the Stock Exchange – and have simply screened out those which offended against particular criteria. Lang casts his net wider to include non-listed businesses, and enterprises which have positive social and environmental effects – a category which includes co-operatives, community development associations, fair trade organisations and charitable groups. He contends that ethical investment will generally involve accepting lower rates of financial return – for example organic farming and social housing are not as 'profitable' as intensive agriculture and office blocks.

> In the short term, the more ethical you want to be with your savings, the lower will be the financial return, and the higher will be your contribution to improving the crazy world we all live in. In the longer term, the less ethical you are, the greater risk that the whole financial edifice will collapse; for the bottom line is that the economy rests on how well we look after the earth, the soil, the air and the water. (Lang, *Ethical investment*)

I hope that investing our money (and our lives!) in the social economy will be an important element of the Society of Friends' corporate witness, as a benchmark of our commitment to the Rediscovering our Social Testimony process. This would involve active participation by all levels of the Society.

Individual Quakers probably have stewardship of the largest 'block of money' within the yearly meeting – a huge resource, if channelled as far as possible into ethical consumerism and investment, and away from the black hole of corporate finance. At this point I'd like to put in a strong plug for some social investment pioneers – 'Shared Interest' who provide micro-credit for the working poor of the Two Thirds World; the newly established Aston Reinvestment Trust, lending seed corn capital to community projects and local small businesses in Birmingham; 'Radical Routes' and the Industrial Common Ownership Fund, which lend to co-operatives; and, of course our very own Quaker Social Housing Account, run through the Triodos Bank.

For Quaker charitable trusts, the idea of actively seeking out community investments may seem rather daunting, and much more complicated than the present system of 'screening out' particular stocks and shares using EIRIS (the Ethical Investment Research Service). Nonetheless, there are advantages – not least, in getting the maximum real value for money! I would recommend a pamphlet entitled *Lending money: the issues for grant-making trusts* by Julia Unwin (available from the Association of Charitable Foundations). Britain Yearly Meeting could also provide a resource for such trusts by joining (and actively participating in) the UK Social Investment Forum and the recently launched Rebuilding Society Network, then keeping all Quaker trustees up to date with developments. (Change is happening, quite fast!)

Any discussion of the yearly meeting's central funds takes place against the painful background of recent redundancies and cash shortfalls, which have caused hurt and insecurity to staff at Friends House. It does seem churlish, against such a background, to point out that the environmental standards of our investments do not yet match the generally high performance with respect to non-involvement in defence industries. However, I know I'm not the only Friend who is tormented by investments like Lloyds Bank (Third World debt), Prudential (major shareholder in Shell and Rio Tinto Zinc), British Airways and Enterprise Oil (climate change), Boots and Glaxo (animal experiments; unsustainable/unjust food distribution systems).

While I do not underestimate the difficulty of shifting the entire yearly meeting investment portfolio into environmentally acceptable investments, I am sure that it is possible, given time and effort. Tightening our EIRIS criteria would inevitably shrink the number of stock market listed investments available to us, but this could be compensated for by taking equity in non-listed businesses – for example, I note that Triodos Bank have introduced a scheme called 'Match' which links 'businesses which provide a social dividend' with potential investors.

Although some green investments will undoubtedly show good profits, in the narrow sense of the word (I am thinking here of things like renewable energy, and energy efficiency, which will surely be growth areas), we have to acknowledge that, overall, there would be a drop in income. I have been musing recently about ways around this problem, and one idea might be to establish a fund made up of money *saved* by individual members, preparative meetings and monthly meetings, committees and central departments as they engage in the ROST process. I am aware that there are some additional costs to be expected if the Society as a whole acts on ROST (e.g. fairly traded, locally purchased or organic products do tend to be more expensive, and there may be initial costs involved in energy conservation). However, overall, I would expect these costs to be more than outweighed by savings as people build unsustainable practices out of their lives (large or new cars, air travel, consumer baubles). This money could relieve the pressure on Friends in our finance department and committees, allowing us to put the yearly meeting's finances on a long-term sustainable footing.

Friends, let us put our core testimonies to the test in all our financial dealings. In the current climate (which could be described as 'the world' or 'mammon') this will require a deep level of commitment. If God wills it, our Society will flourish.

Penny Eastwood, *Quaker monthly*, December 1997

The extraordinary world of money

I have just sold 980 Norwich Union shares at £3.91 a share. Total proceeds: £3,774.32. Less £57.60 stockbroker's charges. Net proceeds £3,713.70.

Nothing extraordinary about that you might say.

But, wait a minute. How did I get the shares in the first place. Well, I once had a mortgage. But when we moved to a much cheaper house the mortgage was paid off, but the endowment policy continued; it was a very small one, just £7.10 a month. Anyway that 'entitled' me (so they say) to 300 shares, when Norwich Union demutualised. At that time they were priced at £2.65.

I decided to apply for as many additional shares as I could and was able to buy a fraction of what I applied for, an addition of 680 shares. I did so, because it was almost certain that someone was going to make an easy profit, and I wanted to keep as much as possible of that profit in the common domain – the voluntary and charitable sector at least.

It was, of course, very likely that the shares would rise. I didn't sell them straight away, partly because I was too busy; then because it was the day after the stockmarket crash in the Far East. But they recovered strongly and, in six months, they have appreciated by 47.5%. Yes, every one hundred of them is now worth £147.50.

Yes, I've done a few hours 'work', organising the purchase and the sale of them. Nothing more. Of the total proceeds of £3,774.32 I paid £1,802. Even if I allow the stockbroker's commission and a little lost interest I have gained £1,872. Of that, over £1,000 came from the sale of 'my' free shares.

Over £800 from my share purchase. In six months. Even if buying and selling is work, my profit, which is near enough a young person's income support for the year, has hardly been earned by the sweat of my brow.

How can I possible see this money as 'mine'? It represents the ability of those who have to gain increasing advantage, the power of capital to breed faster than wages, the shift of wealth and power towards those who already have. If I hold onto it for my own purposes, or my family's, I will become even more part of that cycle which I profess as contrary to my sense of God's loving concern for all equally. I have to return it to work for the community as a whole. Perhaps some of it through our Quaker work – for I must hope that what Friends are about is to do with witnessing to the channel for investing in justice, equality, simplicity, peace, truth and a sustainable world.

Is it? Are we?

Jonathan Dale, *Beyond the Spirit of the Age,* 1996

Changing for the better

The 'sciences' of economics and politics are often presented as being based upon laws which we human beings have no choice but to obey as best we may. Try to buck the market or to escape *de facto* oligarchic (democratic) rule, and chaos prevails. This is the fear, backed by plentiful examples.

For the laws of competition, profit-maximisation and minimal redistribution, and the political systems which go with them, are not only possible but necessary given one basic assumption: that we need not, and so will not, treat those we count as 'other' as we require to be treated ourselves. Once it is OK to treat other human beings – those not like us, or adequately distant from us – as expendable for the sake of a greater good, then it becomes a positive duty to maximise that greater good, be it economic profit or military power. The logic of the Nagasaki bomb was less to do with the necessities of war than of scientific experimentation.

But just as nuclear warfare is only possible once a certain moral boundary concerning the treatment of others is breached, so an economic system based on wage-slavery and destitution depends on the acceptability of such death-in-life. Shift that basic moral assumption, and what happens? If grinding poverty of body, mind and spirit, and corresponding indifference to the health of the ecosystem, are not acceptable prices to pay for an economic system, then one has to find alternative systems. The law of maximal returns is not written in the stars but in our hearts and minds; it can be unwritten, as other laws have been before it.

Such unwriting is difficult, because of the circularity of our assumptions. Having established a given level of exploitation, producing a given level of wealth, we who benefit become convinced that we cannot do without it. We become the prisoners of our own self-perception, allowing ourselves to be determined by the system which we ourselves created. And from day-to-day our desires and fears are confirmed by the adverts which we see and hear, our own creations, and our masters.

If it is not possible to accept the human and ecological costs of the current systems, then it becomes necessary to find other ways; and if less costly yet humanly satisfying ways can be found, then the apparent 'necessity' of paying such a price crumbles. Then we become free to understand the possibilities of our own cultures in a different way, just as modern Europeans did in relinquishing feudalism with its categories of villein, freeman and lord, or in recognising the political existence of women.

Change is not necessarily for the better; and human fear, desire and self-interested aggression will no doubt always be with us. Moreover, lasting change tends to be slow, and in a global economy it has to come in its own way from all corners of the globe.

But it is possible. We do not have to be imprisoned in our deadly circle of inevitability pursuing maximal personal, national or corporate self-interest at the cost of others' lives. In small ways, less abusive ways of living and working are being found to be viable, in human and economic terms. Hope can bear fruit in reality.

Deborah Padfield, *QUNEC Newsletter 16*, August 1998

An allegory on human society

Far off in the distant blue South Seas, a ship is being tossed in a terrible storm. Finally, the boat founders and is broken up, losing many souls in the deep. However, approximately one hundred remain on the surface, clinging to pieces of wreckage, flotsam and jetsam, exhausted by the ordeal. Gradually the seas grow calmer and it becomes clear that they are only about a mile away from a lush and inviting tropical island, which fact gives everyone cheer and hope of succour.

Almost immediately, seven of the fittest and strongest swimmers, all men, seize their chance and strike out for the shore. Those of the remaining party who are sufficiently able bodied direct their attentions to helping the sick, the elderly, the children and the handicapped also to reach the distant beach, and this is a slow, irksome and arduous process.

By the time the main party reaches the shore, eighty-four per cent of the land has already been staked out and laid claim to by the 'Dynamic Seven' who share many of the less savoury entrepreneurial characteristics, being ruthless, uncaring and highly competitive. The remaining land that is left for the rest is rocky or barren, and the ninety-three survivors huddle there, cut off from sources of food and water.

When they throw themselves on the mercy of the seven, it transpires that they are only prepared to offer them very meagre amounts of provisions from their own rich supplies in return for what turns out to be slave labour. They are to gather fruit and nuts for long hours, clear forestry for agriculture and plant seeds, build fine houses with stockades and guards round them for the sole use of what have now become the 'gentry'. And all this merely by virtue of the 'gentry' seizing an opportunity when no one else could.

A few of the 'peasants' get offered slightly better treatment when they agree to enlist in the private armies of one or other of the seven, when bitter feuding breaks out between them over land disputes. Some indeed get killed in the process. The 'gentry', whilst being supremely indifferent to the fates of the ninety-three 'peasants', are constantly vying with each other for supremacy, like a pack of dogs.

This picture could apply to almost any century, any country in the history of humanity, including now. When it was formed in the late 1970s, the 7:84 Theatre Company called itself by that name to draw attention to the Government Yearbook figure which stated that eighty-four per cent of the land in this country was owned by only seven per cent of the people. As far as I know, these figures have not changed much since then. The picture could also apply globally (for example the G8 countries vis-à-vis the third world).

Christopher Gibbs, *The Friend*, 31 July 1998

A reflection on ownership

We may say we are willing to pay more for social provision. But we need to go deeper. Do we set our lives against the possessive individualism which is at the heart of this failure to fund the welfare state. Possessive individualism says that what we earn is ours; and that the state is the instrument for confirming our absolute ownership of whatever we inherit or earn.

Are we closer to possessive individualism or to John Woolman? We pay a good deal of lip service to him these days. But have we really heard him? Take his allegory of the twenty Christians who settle on an uninhabited island. They share out the land equally and Woolman clearly believes they should continue to do so. But what if? Woolman imagines one of the original settlers following a whim to give most of 'his' land to just one of his offspring? This heir then becomes a landlord and forces the rest to work for his luxuries.

Woolman is absolutely clear that 'the landlord' has absolutely no right to his excessive share in the land: 'If we trace the ninth or tenth of these great landlords down to the first possessor and find the claim supported throughout by instruments strongly drawn and witnessed, after all we could not admit a belief into our hearts that he had a *right* to so great a portion of land, after such a numerous increase of inhabitants.' On the contrary it is those who have been squeezed out of equitable ownership who have the *right* to it. Every time we hear, 'Thus oppression in the extreme appears terrible, but oppression in more refined appearances remains to be oppression ...' we should remember that it concludes [this chapter] which so clearly distinguishes the gospel order of testimony from the positive rights of human contracts.

Jonathan Dale, 1990

Putney Debates 1997

On the 31 October and 1 November 1997, over 170 people gathered at St Mary's Church Putney, London, to mark the 350th anniversary of the Putney Debates in a series of dialogues organised by Quakers, in co-operation with the New Economics Foundation. Exploring the current challenges to government, business and civil society, we sought to set an agenda to build a politics and economics based on shared values of justice, accountability, openness and environmental sustainability. In the Quaker tradition, four minute-makers drafted the following statement over the two days to reflect back to those gathered points of agreement and challenge from the debates. This 'New Agreement of the People' was read to all present at the end of the event. We now offer it to all people everywhere who share our commitment to being part of shaping our politics and economics for the common good.

The New Agreement of the People

We are here as the inheritors of the Levellers' vision of 1647. We have, since then, come to know something of democracy in place of tyranny, liberty in religion, freedom of speech and equality before the law. But we are called, as the participants in the original Putney Debates were called, to challenge the distribution of wealth and power, to question the values of our age and to set out a radical agenda for change. We too are here to offer possibilities, to see the world as it could be.

We have been shown the impact of market globalisation: how it colonises food, land and the seeds of knowledge; divorces wealth creation from labour; divides common people; and takes away what little bit of the real world people have.

A search for our common future is a larger agenda, demanding commitment and ingenuity from social radicals across the world. Economics needs to return to its roots, where wealth is the embodiment of people's work and nature's work, and where the rules we apply are those of the household – so that the investor comes as a guest and behaves as a guest.

We have a deep yearning for a community in which we are more than compliant elements of a workforce or unwitting players in power struggles conducted in secret whose worst consequences are borne by the weakest among us. Our vision of community includes the earth we live on, which we can no longer treat as a commodity for plunder. If today we do not act collectively from obedience to a divine law mutually accepted, we have nonetheless discovered that nature's laws may also require obedience. We are not convinced that the earth's sustainability is safe in the hands of those whose primary motive is wealth creation and whose drive is towards growth at all costs.

We begin to see that as individuals we must choose to be less greedy, and to find ways to build inner reserves of spiritual energy, imagination and knowledge. Change begins with each of us. It empowers us to share and build with others at a local level, and at national level to act as informed citizens supporting and enabling politicians to make the right decisions.

Our government has received a mandate for change, and we wish to see deliberate moves to reduce inequality both of opportunity and income. The shift of taxation from labour to energy is one possible measure. Another is the exercise of control over the money markets and over the activities of major multi-national corporations. These too claim ethical and moral considerations and have individuals within them as anxious for clear consciences as the rest of us; but it is for the community as a whole, not the traders alone, to regulate the marketplace and find a place for the market.

What community do we seek to build, and with what values? It is a world of giving and sharing, of love and human appreciation. It works towards the reduction of poverty and the preservation of our planetary home. It is a community of purpose at street, parish, regional, national and

international levels. It may require us to forego some of the individualism
which we have come to accept over the past 350 years, and to acknowledge
that we cannot have complete economic freedom. It may no longer be
based on usury, or on an endemic demand for growth, though the systems
which will replace these are not yet clear to us because they will come from
a change in hearts, minds and spirits.

In *The little prince* (by Saint-Exupéry), the businessman tries to own the
stars – though he can't name them and he doesn't know anything about
them. The initiatives, ideas, dreams and visions we have named and taught
one another during our debates are our stars, and are not for owning but
for sharing.

Quaker economic witness in Europe

Friends from a number of yearly meetings gathered at the QCEA
Conference in March 1993 for a two day seminar on 'Violence and sharing
in the economy'. Agreeing on the inherently violent nature of the economy
and recognising and analysing the mechanisms by which the violence falls
on the poor and excluded of the world – that was the easy part. The difficult
question was what can be done about it, especially by Friends with their
testimony of non-violence.

One of the ideas underlying QCEA's purpose in holding the seminar
was that it might be desirable to draft a Quaker economic testimony to
accompany the peace testimony. The seminar concluded that an economic
testimony was not a promising objective at present. However, the seminar
felt moved to draft the epistle below, which captures the spirit which blew
among the participants.

Epistle from the Quaker Council for European Affairs seminar: violence and sharing in the economy

To Friends everywhere;

From our consideration, over two days, of violence and sharing in the
economy, we feel the need to express an urgent concern to Friends world-
wide, to share these considerations with us.

The Quaker testimonies against war have long been an important part
of our corporate witness. Our economic and social testimonies need to be
vitalised and re-stated for today. Those who have taken part in this seminar
believe that the same violence which expresses itself in war is also in the
workings of the economy. The violence is everywhere, hiding in the most

unexpected places – in our language, and therefore in our very thoughts. This was indeed stated in George Fox's formulation of the peace testimony: 'I lived in the virtue of that life and power that took away the occasion of all wars and I knew from whence all wars did rise, from the lust, according to James' doctrine.'

We have to see life as a whole, and not divide spirit and body. We should not exclude people from our society, neither should we exclude linkages and relationships in trying to understand our society.

We urge Friends to be open to the leadings of the Spirit in their behaviour and thinking with respect to all activities. We must ensure that the love of God has room to act in God's one and unique world. Specifically, we encourage QCEA in its efforts to bring Quaker witness to the European institutions.

Narrative by Edouard Dommen,
Printed in *Around Europe* No 154, April 1993

The real task of development

In reflecting on time spent working in Vietnam in the early 1970s, Helen Steven wrote:
Perhaps our most positive contribution to peace-making was to affirm and value Vietnamese culture in the face of the appalling destruction which we saw around us.

I believe that it is this fundamental respect for 'that of God' in everyone which is at the heart of all true development. On my return home I was horrified by our cultural, material and spiritual arrogance. I believe that it is profound arrogance which initiates aid programmes which force western methods of education, medicine or agriculture on people with traditions longer than our own; it is arrogance to assume that any political system or social or economic structure must be maintained and defended no matter how many people are bombed, napalmed or tortured in the process. Surely arrogance drives us to rape and destroy the earth's scarce resources to fuel and protect the needs of one generation in one corner of the globe. And supreme arrogance to believe that we have the monopoly of spiritual truth.

I came home from Vietnam convinced that the real task of development lies at home at our own door.

1987, QFP 29.06

Development, violence and sharing

'Development' has come to occupy a central place in the planning/public policy processes of government and other agencies. Development is a process of socio-economic change, and what is done in its name represents the priorities of society. Thus it is implicitly if not explicitly of interest to Friends for two reasons. Friends have always had concerns about the priorities, values and goals of a society. They have also had concerns about the right ways in which change takes place, namely peacefully and non-violently, and about what we ourselves are called to do about violence, change and the improvement of the human condition – all aspects of development.

Much of Friends' concerns about society have related to economics and worries about its central role. These economic concerns of Friends are part of our concerns about development. They cover at least the following two distinct (if causally inter-related) issues: quality of life issues involving the need for simplicity, and issues of social justice – poverty, inequality, economic exploitation, economic injustice within and between countries. More recently concern for the environment has been added as a dimension to our economic practices.

Our concerns show themselves in two ways: first, like the prophet Amos, we challenge and criticise what is happening in society today – materialism, injustice, exploitation, militarism, and so on. Many of the things which are wrong with society now and the kind of development pursued relate to issues of violence – apart from the violent, grasping actions of individuals, there is the structural and institutional violence of economic systems, the passive violence of indifference and omissions, the cultural violence of norms that legitimise these patterns of indifference and oppression. We may be angry, speak truth to power, and cry out against the processes of change around us which are called development but which project the wrong values and so obviously fail to achieve human well-being.

But at the same time many Friends have a vision of how a society might be – sharing, caring, with a proper balance between material and spiritual concerns – and this vision of the 'peaceable kingdom' may inform us in three ways – by providing a goal toward which we strive, by providing an orientation or guideline for assessing what happens now, and providing a personal standard by which we strive to live by example ourselves. Many Friends have this kind of vision. They may not call it their vision of 'true' or 'real' development, but that is what in effect it is.

What Quaker values are involved? Answering that of God is at the core of our relief of suffering and of the challenging of injustice, and for many Friends is seen as extending to reverence for all life and for Nature itself. Our vision of a really developed society would be one in which that of God is answered by everyone else in a harmonious chorus of mutual responses!

Simplicity of lifestyle has always been central, but for two quite different reasons. First, we need to be committed to this if we are to be liberated to care about suffering, injustice and so on. Second, a simple life style is essential as an expression of our spiritual nature, free from the encumbrance of over-commitment to materialist values.

The peace testimony informs our assessment of current development priorities and the dominance of economic values – by identifying the various forms of violence inherent in our way of life. (It also informs the way we advocate change and respond to violent change.)

All these Quaker values are highly relevant to development, for it tells us what our Quaker vision is of a society in right ordering – one in which poverty, injustice and environmental destruction are reduced or removed, one in which the primary measuring stick of progress is not material but spiritual, and one in which the way of non-violence should have priority. Just as Molière's character once discovered that he had been talking prose all his life, so in a sense Friends may come to realise that, with all their concerns about non-violence, poverty, injustice or the spiritual basis of the good life, they had been thinking about development all along! And this dawning is important if we are to engage as well as we might with the powers that be, who get away with their impoverished definitions of development if we avert our gaze from the issue.

Nigel Dower, 1995

Economics as if love were the guiding principle

In 1763 John Woolman wrote: 'So far as [the Creator's] love influences our minds ... we ... feel a desire ... to take hold of every opportunity to lessen the distresses of the afflicted and increase the happiness of the creation. Here we have the prospect of one common interest from which our own is inseparable, that to turn all the treasures we possess into the channel of universal love becomes the business of our lives.' John Woolman's use of the words 'treasure' and 'business' in the context of the practical expression of love makes, I feel, a good starting point for exploring the possible basis of a Quaker economics.

Much of our daily lives is taken up with economic activity. So unless we carry love through into that activity, love may not lead to anything at all! However, before considering how we might base something as mundane as economic activity on so high a form as love, it is important to note that the love of which John Woolman spoke was for the whole of creation, and not just for other human beings; and it seems to have been about sharing both Quaker spiritual treasures and our physical goods.

Economics should be about right relationships, a step which seems very Quakerly. It should aim to express a right relationship to ourselves, rightly seeking well-being, fulfilment and joy, provided these are sought without detriment to others, but being willing to forgo them for the benefit of others; and thus a right relationship to others and to the environment.

There seem to be two main ways in which people think about the way to better economic relationships. One begins – and often seems to end – with the personal: with how an individual can arrange his or her own life better. The other considers how people in general can be induced to conduct their economic dealings with greater consideration of one another and of the environment; and often fails to discuss the personal aspect. I find this a bit puzzling. For me both aspects seem vital.

Looking first at the way in which my personal economic decisions have been taken, I am struck by the fact that even when we try hard to get things right, we often lack vital information to be sure that we are doing so; and that at other times no fully satisfactory course seems to be open. We may wish, when acquiring the goods we need for an enjoyable life, to obtain them non-exploitatively, in a relationship of mutual trust and respect, from someone who feels that supplying them is the right sort of livelihood, and is as gentle as possible to the environment. But then we may find – as I did when trying to get a better wheelchair for our disabled son – that the only companies which make anything suitable are transnational corporations, and that no information at all about the way in which they treat their workers or the environment is available at the point of sale. My experience tells me that companies will actually be extremely reluctant to collate and supply such information, unless at least all their rivals are forced to do the same. This is partly because collecting the information will add to costs – so prices may have to go up, thus discouraging sales. It is also because, realistically, no-one will have a completely perfect story to tell, so all will fear losing custom to their rivals.

Nevertheless, a Quaker economics would, I feel, be constantly seeking better information and better means of evaluating how individual actions rate against the yard-sticks of justice, mercy, truth and all that flows from love. Being Quaker it would have sufficient realism not to hope for absolute perfection, but it would try to keep its standards high.

A Quaker economics might still find itself obliged to work with theories such as the existing ones on the relationship of supply, demand and price, because they seem, over the years, to have been approximately correct in predicting human behaviour. The distinguishing characteristic of a Quaker economics would be its purpose of restoring to economics a moral framework, based on the deepest truth.

Jim Challis, 1996, ROST *Responses & Challenges*

Other pieces which examine the social testimony on economic values are:

7. Creation   Living our social testimony

Part IV – Social testimony in our corporate Quaker life

ROST and Hartington Grove PM

Right, Hartington Grove
Right Hartington Grove
We've got a task to do.

We've got a real task to do –
They're all doing it
Yes, Central Committee at QSRE
started it
there are lots of Quaker groups
talking, reflecting
and Jonathan Dale gave the Swarthmore Lecture
and wrote the book.

Now,
it's up to us.
Yes, that day in September last,
six to eight chairs were all that
I thought was needed
Just a few would come
But the door kept opening
Twenty-four in all
Good job I'd done some reading, but – let's pause
Let's have some silence.

What a stimulating time together, five persons
volunteered to read from 'Responses and Challenges'
What a lot to absorb, to discuss, to share.
But – they want to meet again,
Again, but where and when –
'Just pick some dates, they'll self select!'
And so the house groups met.

Hm, silence, reading
and sharing – stories
Of lives long and rich.
Others rich but shorter.

But, let us remind ourselves
of the task,
Exploring our Social Testimony
What does that mean?
'Does that mean me? I am
fast winding down, my
doing days are passed.'
'I've only begun, I know
so little about Quakers.'
'I want some action, there
must be something beyond
the talking for me.'
'It's good to meet
I appreciate that
and I think we are coming
closer together
and, yes
opening up to one another
I like the small group.'

Yes, but remember
the world out there
Yes, yes, yes
The Real World Coalition –
Something must be done

politics is not my cup of tea
nor mine
but something must be done

Perhaps, there's something
for each of us to do and share.
There are different tasks, needing
different skills,
Different functions to make the
whole task easier to manage
Yes, we as individuals must
go through the rediscovering process
but then
come together, share and find our place
Individually we have much to give
and our needs are great.
Corporately we can only live and give
if we share and respect diversity.

What has the process been like?
Of course it's been painful for some, very
Pleasurable for others
But what for the whole
Has the life of the meeting benefited?
What about the world?

We have some new friendships that have formed
We have a greater knowledge of the richness
of lives within our PM.
We re-affirm the role and responsibilities
of those whose 'doing days' are gone
They are a source of wisdom and of prayer
They are a solid source of support
and sustenance for those who do.
A broad range of skills and ideals have emerged
Reviews and a condensed résumé
of *The Politics of the Real World* has meant
every member has access to

the basic information contained
in the book.
The Newsletter is recognised as
a valuable tool of communication accessible to all.
The Cambridgeshire Real World Coalition is
launched and working.
We have linked ROST
and Penal Affairs and the focus
brought by the Rowntree
Fellow gave new impetus to the
Penal Affairs group,
known as the
Community Justice Group.
Politics and political action is
acknowledged as having a role.
The Quaker Tapestry is seen
as providing lessons from the
past, for us to learn and honour
our tradition,
Our social testimony,
But,
it also gives us the tool for
future lessons,
lessons for today's children,
to open up their awareness
of crime, punishment and
forgiveness.

For Fry was one whose testimony
was a light, but each of us
can shine to make the
Light shine brighter from
Hartington Grove PM.

Sheila J. Gatiss, *Quaker monthly*, July 1998

Chain reaction

In March of this year Leicester meeting held a study day on world debt. Many members of the children's meeting were inspired and felt they would like to play an active role in the campaign to cancel the debt, so we asked other Quaker children throughout Britain, via a letter sent to children's meeting conveners, to help us by making a chain of paper links bearing messages about world debt. The messages on the links were addressed to world leaders meeting at the Cologne summit of 18-20 June 1999. Our focus was that debt by poor countries is overwhelming, unpayable and should be cancelled so that these countries can concentrate on providing education, health care, housing and work towards the elimination of poverty.

The reaction from children's meetings was astounding! Seventy-nine meetings responded sending 1028 links to our chain. Many were beautifully decorated and all had very clear and thoughtful messages on them. We had replies from meetings from all parts of Britain as far apart as Come-to-Good in Cornwall to St Andrews in Scotland and from Kent, Wales, Northern Ireland, and all areas between. Some meetings that had no children sent chains from the 'grown-up children of the meeting'. It was great seeing the envelopes arrive and what was really nice was that we received so many letters of encouragement and Friendship with our chain links. Several meetings told us what they had learned about World Debt when making their chains and how they had linked the chain-making to other projects they were doing at the time. We are making a scrapbook about the project and will put all the letters into it.

We all made the chain up during a children's meeting on 2 May, reading the messages as we stapled them together. We measured the finished chain and spread it over the meeting house lawn to show the adults in meeting. It was fifty-eight metres long. We decorated a very large cardboard box with figures of children from all over the world and then we packed the chain inside it to send to Jubilee 2000 London office. They had promised to take the chain on the barge that was taking petitions to the Cologne summit. We included a letter to Tony Blair explaining who had made the chain and why we wanted him to read the messages and pass them on to the other world leaders.

It didn't stop there. The links kept arriving so we decided to make a second chain and this soon grew to a further forty-eight metres, making over one hundred metres. We were too late to send the new piece on the barge and although we had Friends from Leicester going to the Cologne summit, we knew that security precautions in Cologne would not permit them to hand the chain over to world leaders there.

As a group of us and our families were already planning to go to the Jubilee 2000 event in London on 13 June, we decided to take the new chain with us and hand it to Tony Blair personally. It was the first time that any of us had been to 10 Downing Street and it felt very exciting to be escorted to the front door of Number 10 by a policeman. The person who we gave it to when we knocked on the door promised to hand it to Tony Blair personally. We hope he found time to read all the messages on the links.

After this we joined the rally in Trafalgar Square and joined hands with thousands of other people around the River Thames to shout for cancellation of world debt. The messages we heard all around us were that although the world leaders had already agreed to reduce the debt by fifty billion dollars the only way to affect the lives of people in indebted countries throughout the world was to cancel it altogether. As we learned in our debt study day, we are all indebted to others in some way or other and we need to free ourselves of thinking that helping others involves a repayment to the giver, especially when the giver has more than enough to spare.

We hope our messages were read and passed on to the world leaders. We don't think we have finished there and would like to go on working with other Quaker children to cancel world debt. If anyone has any ideas for what we can do next please write to us at Leicester Friends' Meeting House, Queens Road, Leicester.

Rowan Walker, 'Witnessing corporately to our social testimony'
The Friend, 2 July 1999

Hebden Bridge PM

'Seek to know one another in the things that are eternal.' It seems important to say that the more we listen to/share with/support each other the closer we grow and the easier it is as a preparative meeting to live out our testimonies more fully. Over the last year Hebden Bridge PM has:

- joined a LETS trading system and held a trading day
- started to use Fair Trade tea and coffee
- engaged in a ROST day where we minuted: 'We encourage the meeting, through the newsletter, and through further sessions like this, to develop the process of sharing individual concerns and actions. Such

sharing can develop our sense of togetherness, and may spark others to their own actions. It can foster corporate action, and support for individual prophetic action. We ask the meeting to encourage individuals, and groups of individuals, to bring forward to PM concerns with which we can grapple and identify. We need mutual spiritual as well as emotional support within the meeting, to sustain us in our work, unpaid and paid, in the local and global communities. We must value people for who they are, not just what they do. Meeting for worship sustains us in our actions; the Spirit works in the world through us.'

- supported Treesponsibility, a climate-change campaign working on two levels: planting trees as a response to the threat of a change in global weather patterns and actively seeking to change the climate of opinion and inform people of the options for living with respect for the earth.

As a follow-on to this we decided as a meeting to compensate for the pollution caused by our Sunday meeting for worship. We sent out forms to car users, calculated our share of the building's electricity and gas use, and added a small amount for paper consumption – and then worked out the meeting's carbon emission. For 1998 this amounted to seventeen trees. We based our calculations as follows: It is assumed that one tree will fix a tonne of carbon dioxide over its life. Each unit of electricity used $= 1$ kg of CO_2. Each unit of gas used $= 5.3$ kg of CO_2. Each litre of motor fuel $= 2.3$ kg of CO_2.

Looking to the future, we are starting a Lifestyles group where we can support each other to seek ways of living out our testimonies more fully in our lives. Sharing together will help us grow closer together as a faith community, as minuted at the ROST day, and encourage us to live out our testimonies more fully corporately.

Ruth Hustler, 1999

Winchmore Hill Preparative Meeting QSRE group

In Autumn 1997 five people were appointed by preparative meeting to form a QSRE group – the name kept the focus partly on education. Initial concern for the formation of the group came from study sessions held in Spring 1997 involving over twenty members and attenders of the meeting; the topic was 'Rediscovering our Social Testimony' and the material, Jonathan Dale's *Beyond the Spirit of The Age*, supported by ROST's *Responses and Challenges* (1996) and *Quaker faith and practice* (especially Chapters 19 and 23). We all felt challenged to change, to consider our comfortable feelings, to avoid secularisation and social pessimism, to challenge unjust systems, to consider how deeply we care. We developed a deep sense of shared values, rather than unity of belief, from the testimonies.

Since then we have been further influenced by Britain Yearly Meeting's corporate social testimony (1997) and by the sessions on homelessness and the ministry of money at Britain Yearly Meeting this year. We are also involved in the consultation day at Westminster Meeting House this November on 'Housing and Homelessness'.

We continue in our two broad aims which are to: a) receive and focus on QSRE social testimony information and to network with other groups, central and local – including the social testimony newsletter; b) provide opportunities for Friends and attenders to discuss and develop specific actions and responses relating to current social issues – especially locally.

The main focus of our group's work has been on homelessness, taking forward and widening action in which our meeting had already become involved and increasingly sees as a corporate concern. We have encouraged discussion of key issues in the tea run, especially co-ordination with other tea runs in London, as part of three special meetings on homelessness which we held after meeting for worship between autumn 1997 and summer 1998. We also began to look more locally at homelessness in Enfield and set out to research the scene, so that we could collaborate in local action, not act in isolation or re-invent the wheel. We have begun to monitor the progress of the meeting's homelessness fund to ensure that the money available is distributed regularly, not unintentionally hoarded.

We found serious and increasing homelessness in Enfield, made worse by extremely high rents in the private sector, a powerless rent guarantee scheme and the very difficult housing benefit restrictions. There had been no monitoring of rough sleepers, and a hardworking and committed council-run housing advice centre was increasingly subject to aggression and violence.

We also found positive growing points: the Single Homelessness Forum (a meeting point between Local Authority and voluntary groups); a recently opened Churches Housing Trust Hostel in Edmonton; 'Beck House' (for the homeless over forty, single and childless); plans for a Christian Action Foyer to open in 1999 for thirty-six young homeless; the CAB's commitment to advising increasing numbers of desperate people threatened with eviction and repossession of their homes. But we heard of the threat to the continuation of TAPP (Temporary Accommodated Play Group Project) which serves the deep need of many children and their families.

Now we are represented by members either of our QSRE group or of the rest of the meeting on the Single Homelessness Forum; on the new management group of TAPP; on the Friends of Beck House group, of which the meeting is now a corporate member; on the link group for the Foyer from which a Friends' group is likely to form (two of us were at the publicity launch earlier this year). Seven of our meeting took part in Enfield's first rough sleepers count one night last August, co-ordinated by the Local Authority (rough sleepers were found, dispelling assumptions that there would be none locally). Through the Homelessness Forum we are keeping ourselves informed on and asking questions about rough sleeping – as well as other issues – and at the least may be able to extend the meeting's tea run to local homeless people on the way into Central London.

We plan to mark Homelessness Sunday for the second time in January 1999, by a special collection, a talk by the manager of Beck House and by a children's activity, perhaps using the Friends' House resource pack 'Having a home is important'. We cannot afford to be complacent. The local press reports Enfield's growing homelessness crisis and refers to the quest for property as desperate. More *Big Issue* sellers are to be seen.

When we started out in 1997, we did not know our route, but we felt a sense of direction, of guidance from God. We move forward with our meeting.

Ruth Hanchett, Winchmore Hill QSRE group, 1998

Hardshaw East Monthly Meeting social justice group

We are not for names nor men nor titles of Government nor are we for this party nor against the other ... but we are for justice and mercy and truth and peace and true freedom that these may he exalted in our nation. (Edward Burrough 1659, *QFP* 23.11)

In the autumn of 1995 monthly meeting was considering laying down its Poverty Action Committee (PAC). The PAC had been set up to encourage Friends who had benefited from the tax cuts of the Thatcher years to put any undeserved gains back into the community. It distributed funds donated by local Friends to various organisations concerned with poverty issues. It had been effective but now was not functioning well. Monthly meeting appointed a search group to meet the PAC.

At that meeting a passionate conviction crystallised that the deepening injustice of British society was a spiritual matter, of the deepest concern to Friends. There was an urgent need to broaden the monthly meeting's involvement in thinking about and acting on social issues that went well beyond the remit of the PAC. The search group asked that the question of laying down the PAC be put on hold while MM explored how it could deepen its witness to social justice.

Work began in an exploratory way in the winter of 1995. There were open meetings for Friends and this was how the group, as it now is, was formed. Members were not appointed by the monthly meeting but joined it because of their interest and convictions. The work on Rediscovering our Social Testimonies (ROST) was an important influence here but the group also found within itself a deep dissatisfaction with the prevailing political climate. There was a spiritual imperative to speak the truth to the powerful and to express our profoundly felt dissent from what was happening to social values both in Britain and the world. We were helped greatly by the fact that at this time Jonathan Dale was preparing his Swarthmore Lecture and he shared his developing thoughts with us from time to time.

Two groups formed to think through some of the issues. One looked at how our own way of life impacted on society and evolved into what became known as the Lifestyle Group. The other group looked at social and political issues and evolved into the Social Justice Group. The two groups have an overlapping membership, so the relationship between them is subtle, hard to pin down into a neat structure. Several written contributions to the ROST book, *Responses and challenges*, were generated at this stage.

In early 1996 the Social Justice Group worked on four areas of concern: poverty and inequality; health; education; unemployment and economic change. The group ran a day conference for the monthly meeting in June 1996 to share its insights with Friends. Entitled 'Towards social justice' it included workshops on the four areas of concern and an address by Paul Goggins, who was then Co-ordinator of Church Action on Poverty. As a result of the conference a number of Friends joined the group and others expressed a willingness to help where they could.

At this time the Real World Coalition was starting to campaign in Greater Manchester and the Social Justice Group became actively involved. A Real World day conference at Mount Street Meeting House in November 1996 launched the Real World Campaign in Greater Manchester, and gave a presentation to Lancashire and Cheshire General Meeting in February

1997, with an address by Jonathan Dale and workshops run by group members.

At this stage it was clear that a general election was imminent and it was felt that a public assertion of proper social values was necessary. The group produced an election pack for local Friends setting out the policy issues and giving suggestions for possible action, which was distributed with the monthly meeting newsletter. There was also a carefully prepared and rather striking silent demonstration on the steps of Mount Street Meeting House in April 1997.

Since the general election the work of the Social Justice Group has been less public. But the burning conviction that the spirit of the age is one of injustice remains and the campaign to confront this continues. We feel very strongly that social justice is a spiritual issue and therefore the responsibility of the whole monthly meeting. We are glad to say that we have been supported in our concerns by monthly meeting. In particular, a sum of £2,000 per year for at least three years has been made available to spend on social justice projects. This has been a spur to action.

We have four strands of work:

- a campaigning role in which we help Friends throughout the MM to work on a current issue
- working with local meetings to develop our thinking on social testimony issues; we have spoken to preparative meetings and the Lifestyle Group recently led a general meeting
- subgroups involved in specialist work: one runs the PAC, now active again, which is supporting Manchester-based groups with a concern for the poor of the city; we also have working groups on excluded pupils and the support of immigration detainees in Manchester
- responsibility for suggesting uses for the funding; the first £2000 has been spent on a feasibility study examining what Quakers in Manchester can do to help with the problem of pupils excluded from school; future spending will be for a part time Campaign Co-ordinator to help Friends campaign more effectively on social issues and we have now set up a group to manage this project.

It is a challenging time as we are moving into the unknown. We go forward in faith.

Enid Pinch, Third Month 1999

The Quaker Lifestyle Group (Manchester)

The Lifestyle Group started at Mount Street, Manchester in the autumn of 1997. It stemmed from a group that had met in the spring looking at Rediscovering our Social Testimonies. This group had looked at our traditional testimonies (e.g. not swearing oaths), and questioned whether there were new testimonies that were emerging in our attempts to live our Quaker faith at the end of the twentieth century. Creating a Lifestyle Group seemed a natural progression: sharing our understanding of what living our lives as Quakers meant to us. We wanted a place not for intellectual discussions (though we had those as well), but for reflection, questioning and support.

We started by brainstorming the issues we wanted to work on together and laying down ground rules. We agreed to meet once a month, for each of us to take responsibility for leading a session, and for someone to act as note-taker to make a brief record of what we talked about. Initially there were twelve of us, after a while this had reduced to a core group of around eight people.

At first our plan had been to take a different topic every session. How naïve we were! We started with money and were still considering this issue four months later. We talked about what money meant to us, about the money we gave to charity, and how we made decisions about our giving. We also questioned our altruism. If we gave presents to our friends or family in the knowledge of getting something in return was this altruistic? If we financially planned for the future were we really hoarding our money rather than using it for good purposes? Later we talked about issues such as transport, holidays, simplicity and food. We tried to incorporate some of our thinking into the life of the meeting. For example, we liaised with the teenage group, who produced a map indicating where members and attenders lived, and offered to provide information about car-sharing and public transport on 'No Car Day'.

We often felt torn and divided about our actions, uncertain about how 'Quakerly' they were. People felt tensions between their own beliefs and their obligations to their family (especially if they were not Quakers). Age created differences; older members were perhaps more willing to live simply, whilst younger members were often still at a stage in their lives of accumulating life experience and possessions. It became clear that there could not be a simple rule or formula that we could follow to be 'good Quakers'. In different ways I think we decided that life was messy, and full of challenges to our aspirations of leading a Quaker lifestyle. However, in coming together we were able to face the questions we needed to ask if we were really to lead lives that were an expression – for example, when buying a car – now we had to consider social, spiritual, ethical and ecological dimensions.

On a personal level, the Lifestyle group was a way of getting closer to people at meeting, and hearing about their spiritual journeys. It made me more aware of the choices that I make every day and what assumptions lie behind my actions (not all of which are very Quakerly). I have made some changes to my life but I haven't, for example, got rid of my mobile phone. I haven't turned into an ascetic, nor do I think that this would be right for me. I've begun to realise, if only in a small way, the truth that the whole of our life is sacramental. Perhaps especially the boring, everyday bits (what we do with our rubbish, how we get to work, what we eat for our lunch).

The last few months of our meetings were spent planning a presentation to Lancashire and Cheshire General Meeting in February 1999. This was a nice way of bringing to an end the life of the group: by explaining to others what we had done and hoping to encourage them to start up their own groups. This is also the purpose of writing this piece: the feeling that we had an experience of deepening our faith, and a desire that we might help others do the same.

Antony Froggett, May 1999

Many meetings had experiences like the one described here:

Moving forward

We found putting the testimonies into words as they applied to our personal lives difficult; several of us wrote out a personal testimony, but some could not or did not want to, and all found it hard to get it 'right' or feel it to be authentic. The problems experienced had to do with making our particular actions truthful, simple, just, peaceful, or egalitarian – i.e. with moving from statements of beliefs to action in our lives. These problems arose from the complexity of living in modern society, from conflicts between prevailing values in society and our testimonies, and sometimes from different testimonies suggesting different actions. For instance protest in a just cause might not always be peaceful, cutting down expenditure in the interests of living simply might reduce others' chances of employment, or conflict with a desire to support fairer or greener kinds of production.

By facing these difficulties over several meetings, we were helped to see and say why writing or living our testimony was difficult, and what blocked individual and corporate action. We came to feel less isolated, less guilty and less daunted by the enormity of the task. The relevance of the testimonies to our ordinary lives became more evident, and the possibility of living them in our ordinary lives became more real. We saw also that in our meetings for worship and for church affairs we had a vital resource for helping us to discern the way forward on our social testimony in general, and in specific concerns.

We moved during the months, through the course of our meetings, towards a pragmatic but spiritually based position which does appear to free us for action. We saw more surely the importance and the possibility of living our testimony, without the need for a final statement or programme. We became clearer on the need to speak out and act, and felt especially the need to act locally, to act with integrity, to build networks among Quaker and non-Quaker active groups, and to develop our information resources and our outreach.

Redland PM – Sharing groups on *Rediscovering our Social Testimony*, statement from concluding plenary sessions, 4 and 18 June 1997

Public Statements Group, Bristol and Frenchay Monthly Meeting

The Bristol and Frenchay Public Statements Group arose from a concern in the monthly meeting to help Friends in local meetings articulate their concerns in a manner suitable for release to the news media. Our desire in setting up the group was to establish a procedure for issuing public statements which would be timely, succinct, well informed and spiritually grounded. We have issued few statements, and these have generally been on peace issues. The group responds to movements of opinion from within monthly meeting (especially from preparative meetings) rather than issuing statements of its own accord. To my mind, the Public Statements Group and the ROST exercise have in common a striving to make a relevant and authentic Quaker witness in the modern world.   Ian Beeson, 1999

Description of key working points:

The first action of the group was to draw up, and get agreement to, a working arrangement. The object of this arrangement was to make clear the procedures to be issued. This working arrangements paper has had wide circulation within the MM through preparative meetings as well as through the monthly meeting newsletter. Adhering to the working arrangement has been pivotal to the success of the process.

The Group itself is guided by a number of general principles:

- Insisting on a draft statement from the proposer (as set out in the working arrangements paper) helps to ensure that there is a general and strong support for the concern from the grass roots. It also helps to clarify the issue.
- Statements should not be too frequent. They are only made on major topics where a statement by monthly meeting is thought to be necessary to add weight to statements by individuals. It is *not* intended to be a substitute for individual statements or statements by preparative meetings.
- Statements should be short and simply worded.
- Statements should be clearly seen to be even handed. This principle applies to a wide range of circumstance; from terrorist/government conflicts to moral issues which are seldom clear cut.
- The religious basis of the statement should be made plain.
- It is not the job of the group to promote or advertise, nor to act in place of monthly meeting if there is time for a statement to go through MM.
- The MM Clerk sends the statement to an agreed but limited number of people or bodies. The proposers are expected to use the statement to promote it to a wider audience such as Members of Parliament. Individuals acting in this way will have a much greater impact than just one formal statement being circulated by the MM Clerk. Also, suggesting that individuals write themselves encourages monthly meeting members to take action rather than think others have done the task for them.
- The Group should not be making statements on subjects about which they have little knowledge, e.g. technical aspects of genetic engineering.
- The statements should make it clear that monthly meeting is only speaking for local Quakers. The issues covered will normally be associated with local affairs and how they impact on the locality.

Ben Barman, Convenor to the group, October 1998

Reflections & recommendation for Hampstead Monthly Meeting

Friends of Muswell Hill Preparative Meeting have been moved to consider our faithfulness in witnessing to those in need in our Society. For nearly a year at our monthly Sunday bring and share lunches we have reflected together upon Jonathan Dale's 1996 Swarthmore Lecture *Beyond the Spirit of the Age, Responses and Challenges* from the QSRE ROST group and our own members' concerns in local prison work, Quaker Social Action, supporting refugees, paid work and unemployment, social inequality and health, homelessness and social transformation both here and in South Africa. We also attempted to raise consciousness amongst Friends about the importance of the recent general election.

Believing as we all do that there is 'that of God in everyone' we have no hesitation in being fully committed to political and social change. Universal human rights and equal opportunity policies we feel are the secular expressions of our spiritual understandings. So the growing poverty gap in Britain and throughout most of the world, where the rich get richer and the poor become more marginalised and invisible, is obscene to us. We deplore the ethos of a society based principally on monetary values, competition and beggaring our neighbours. We recognise that no genuine feel-good factor can ever come from that. Social division, political extremism and the potential for the growth of fascism are more likely outcomes.

Our alternative values lie in

* sustainability, both environmentally and socially, through simpler lifestyles
* community, by networking, grassroots action, interconnections and celebration
* equality, rights and responsibilities politically and legally for all citizens.

We see good work for all people as the central part of the great purpose of humanity but we would wish to see the concept of work enlarged to include caring, domestic and voluntary work intertwined with paid employment. We see taxes as a privilege to pay – being the membership fee of a civilised and humane society that cares for others less fortunate than ourselves. A radical change in social attitudes is needed here, especially in pollution taxes. After the basic human needs of housing, income and work [are secured], the opportunities for lifelong education in formal, informal and youth-service modes are vital in our global society of increasing knowledge, discovery and change.

Muswell Hill Friends are personally involved in a wide range of national charities. Many of us in work are already engaged in social change through our employment. Some of us are involved in local politics and most of us make a strong commitment to the Society of Friends. We have not been led to undertake any major new projects together, although we respond as a meeting to the needs of the time and currently have an involvement in supporting local refugees and asylum seekers.

However, we are concerned that the Society is not currently structured so that Friends are able to give vigorous corporate public voice to our social testimony. We feel the need both to witness and for that witness to be known – not out of pride but so that the poor and oppressed will know that others stand along side them. As we have seen from the phenomenon of the death of Princess Diana there is an infectiousness about speaking to the good in others through a witnessed caring. Friends' processes are slow and cumbersome and not addressed to the needs of twenty-first century communication. We feel that this is a mutual loss to the witnessing of our social testimony and so to those who may be enheartened and empowered by it, as well as to the growth, outreach and development of the Society of Friends.

Proposal: our proposal is that Hampstead Monthly Meeting urges Meeting for Sufferings to liberate the Society's Communication Department to be more robust, imaginative and prophetic in using the rich human resources within the Society to evolve new ways of speaking to the press, media and public that will fit the twenty-first century. We call upon the resources of the Society's central work to be enabled to speak publicly with a bold and clear voice.

Muswell Hill Preparative Meeting, 13 November 1997

Action must be adapted to meet all situations

Current forms of action – demonstrating, writing letters to MPs, belonging to single issue campaigns – are certain to remain important while the political culture changes. But what I would like Friends to consider also is taking other forms of action which consciously seek to find common ground between different groups in society, particularly groups which feel they have little in common with or much to fear from each other.

This may mean simply seeking out those single issue campaigns which attempt to take into account the impact of their campaign on sections of the population other than the intended beneficiaries – e.g. supporting arms diversification rather than just the ending of the arms trade (which will clearly affect those people working in the arms trade).

At the local level – where much of the most effective political action takes place – it may mean working in coalition with people with whom you have little sympathy. Many Friends, for instance, are suspicious of people in other churches and particularly of evangelical Christians; yet overcoming this distrust and working together on social justice issues may be one of the most effective ways Christians, and other people of faith, have of showing God's presence in the world.

This will not be easy. Nor do I have clear prescriptions for action. We live in a time of such fluidity that all forms of action must be constantly adapted to meet new situations. But I am convinced that a new kind of politics is necessary (and not just 'new' Labour or proportional representation).

The nightmare vision of hell (or separation from God) with which society confronts us now can be averted – but only by ensuring that the needs of all groups in society are recognised and respected, and not at the expense of each other.

Christine Crosbie, *Quaker monthly*, April 1996

Working for political change

John Bright, the nineteenth century Quaker MP, clearly expressed his motivation: 'The moral law is intended not for individual life only, but for the life and practice of states and their dealings with one another.' *Quaker Faith & Practice* remembers him as someone who 'believed and therefore he spoke'. He withdrew his support from the government in 1882 over the bombing of Alexandria but this was in the context of forty years' political loyalty and in carefully calibrated terms: 'I think that in the present case there has been a manifest violation of international law and moral law and therefore it is impossible for me to give my support to it.'

Jim Challis (a former civil servant and warden of Canterbury meeting) in his involvement in planning and setting up the post of parliamentary liaison secretary, saw this role as 'expressing our spiritual insight in the context of political discussion'. I find it hard to give reasons for Quaker involvement in politics except to turn the question around and wonder how anyone who cares about the world can *not* be involved in politics.

It will be possible to develop a political expression of our values only if those of us who work centrally are committed to the process of corporate discernment and decision making in the Yearly Meeting. Any expression of policy has to be rooted in consultation, discussing concerns nationally and making the link between local and national work. The parliamentary liaison secretary works both by informing Friends of what is happening politically and also in a more active role of advocacy, pursuing concerns politically. These two aspects of my work are two sides of the same coin. One of the most challenging injunctions in the gospel is to be 'as innocent as doves and as wise as serpents'. That is a recognition of realism which understands the ways of the world without being overwhelmed by them. We need to carry both these principles side by side if we are to be effective and effective in the right cause.

Any influence that we have nationally as Friends depends on the strength and quality of local contacts. Our countrywide network of parliamentary links is the life blood of any political influence that we have. So here are a few guidelines on sharing your concerns with your MPs.

The first golden rule that we have to remember is we have no power except that which we share and derive from consent. All we can seek to do is to persuade. Failure to recognise this and some misperception as to the extent of our national authority, or a sense that the government is just waiting to listen to what the Quakers have to say, is the source of much miscommunication with government. If we are seeking to change opinions we have to give people reasons. We have to root our concerns in experience and truth. Experience here is best when real and immediate. As Basil Hume put it, 'Sincerity is the heart of oratory.' And here truth means objective fact. So clearly someone who has had experience of prison can speak best of the need for penal reform, and someone who has had experience of the army can talk of the danger of the recruitment of under eighteen-year-olds into the forces.

To achieve change we have to appeal to both enlightened self-interest and altruism. To give one practical example here – telling an MP with a slim majority, in an area of arms manufacturing, that we think the arms trade is morally wrong is going to be less effective than proposing a technology applications agency which would help to find civilian uses for military technology. We have nothing to fear from appropriately directed self-interest. William Temple (bishop and socialist) describes politics as 'the art of so ordering society that self-interest prompts what justice requires'. Any society that fails to take account of self-interest will be inherently unstable. As a friend and colleague of mine put it, 'I would be rather suspicious of someone who thought they did things only for the highest motives: they would probably lack self-knowledge.'

A second key to success is to make common cause. Find out your MP's interests, do some research, give them all the information they need to allow them to make up their mind. There is no better argument than the facts. Are we really respecting the conscience of another if we tell them what they ought to think? The best form of advocacy is almost always the gentlest. The most effective tone is perhaps quiet confidence, remembering that governments need to be lobbied. They need input from organisations in order both to test the waters and to fine tune policies.

Thirdly suit your argument to your person. To take the example of crime: simply saying we ought to be more compassionate to criminals isn't going to get us anywhere if we are talking to an MP in a constituency where concern over crime is the number one issue. But emphasising the cost and ineffectiveness of an undue reliance on prison and looking at re-offending rates might have more chance of success. The crucial point still is to appeal to, and in the deepest sense recognise and respect, the person that you are speaking to.

So if your burning interest is disarmament and you have a Conservative MP, far better than speaking of the evils of imperialism might be to talk with genuine respect about the achievements of previous governments in bloodlessly giving up empire. To recognise the skill of Lord Carrington in mediating over the independence of Zimbabwe and then to show how nuclear disarmament could be the most powerful and patriotic lead that Britain could give – not giving up power but gaining influence through courageous diplomatic initiative – might be a more appropriate way of approaching the issue than bold statements from an imaginary moral high ground.

A fourth guideline is to look to solutions rather than emphasise problems. This may be harder but it is more useful. With few exceptions, an MP will probably be more aware of most problems in the constituency than we are. What you can do is provide the solutions. For example, in the case of homelessness, the kind of programmes that are going to be most effective in combating it are practical and to the point, like the Quaker Housing Association rent guarantee scheme. We all know that there are young people who cannot afford to get into rented property because they can't afford the deposit. Working to provide a guarantee and then from that perspective being able to talk with authority will carry more weight than simply expounding the problem.

This is as true internationally as at home. Andrew Clark (former General Secretary of Quaker Peace and Service) describes diplomacy as the art of giving people ladders to climb down. We all need this from time to time and none more than the politicians. Informed advocacy in favour of a just and compassionate common European foreign policy may have more effect than bald condemnation of the use of sanctions and bombing of Iraq.

Fifthly and crucially, find out who your allies are. On freedom of information, for example, work with the Freedom of Information Campaign. On the problems of indebtedness go both for information and as local allies to the World Development Movement and Jubilee 2000. But don't stop there: think of the connections with Human Rights (Amnesty International) and the arms trade (Campaign Against the Arms Trade), and recognise the global reach of the problem (United Nations Association) as well as environmental implications (Greenpeace). Remember, too, the importance of working ecumenically.

Finally, work as a local meeting. There is all the difference between approaching an MP as an individual and as a meeting. One of the most creative ideas that some meetings have been involved with is asking an MP to come and meet you as a meeting. This establishes a natural constituency link and helps inform your MP about local concerns. Such a meeting works on several levels. Firstly it gives the MP the opportunity to understand what we as Quakers are about. It is a way of showing that we are concerned with them as an individual and not a slot machine for political manipulation. You may even – if done after a monthly meeting, for example – be able to ground your meeting in worship. The silence and worshipful reflection are as valuable as your views. You can make the connection between faith and work.

Perhaps at the heart of all work with MPs is the need to remember that, as God is in us, He or She is as surely in those with whom we meet and speak. Or to put it another way – we all share a common humanity. Human rights in the twentieth century is the secular counterpart of the seventeenth century insight that there is that of God in everyone. That presence is no less true of those who feel uncomfortable about using the language of God. The testimony to equality is not a uniquely Quaker concept. One of the most poignant moments in the gospel is when Christ turns to the disciples and expresses that equality: 'I no longer call you servants but friends for I have revealed to you all that I know.'

Just like us, anyone we meet will respond most effectively to support, empathy and encouragement when we feel that they have done something positive. Courtesy (hard as it may be) is the hallmark of good communication. Our relationship with an MP is one of constituent to representative; clear and balanced opinions courteously voiced should never be a problem but part of the support we can give to enable them to represent the view of their constituents in the forum to which they have been elected.

What George Herbert wrote three hundred years ago is as true today as it was then:

> Be calm in arguing; for fierceness makes
> Error a fault, and truth discourtesy.
> Why should I feel another man's mistakes
> More than his sickness or his poverty?
> In love I should: but anger is not love,
> Nor wisdom neither: therefore gently move.

Adapted from a talk given to Derbyshire, Nottinghamshire & Lincolnshire General Meeting and Staffordshire Monthly Meeting by Michael Bartlet, Parliamentary Liaison Secretary to Britain Yearly Meeting and a member of Westminster Monthly Meeting, and printed in *Quaker monthly*, May 1999

Testing a concern

In order to work in the Cabinet Office at all, one has to be positively vetted, which means that the Security Service look into your background, including relationships, finance and political affiliations. They knew all about me being a Quaker, and asked me if I would fight for my country – my answer of 'no' was not a shock, or unacceptable – and it is maybe surprising that I was still put onto the JIC (Joint Intelligence Committee).

What changed my views from actively enjoying the secrecy to finding it disturbing? I can only say that, fundamentally, my whole world-view was shifting as a result of my spiritual experience. The concern that I took to Dover Preparative Meeting in 1988 was about the morality of spying. It troubled me that, as I was seeing news reports of Thatcher and Gorbachev meeting and having what seemed to be constructive conversations, I was seeing reports at work of KGB involvement in the UK, and also MI6 agent reports coming back from what was then still the 'Eastern bloc', and from other parts of the world. The difference between the reality and the images that we were seeing on our television screens was startling. In quite a naïve way I felt this was wrong and potentially dangerous. How could spying and dishonesty assist peace-making.

It was this that eventually went to East Kent Monthly Meeting, and, when I moved to Brighton, to Chichester Monthly Meeting, and on to Meeting for Sufferings. One of the most important parts of the whole experience was the totally unexpected and wonderful joining together with Warwickshire Friends, who had taken a very similar concern to their Warwickshire Monthly Meeting. For all of us, this felt like the Spirit moving us forward.

Taking a concern to a monthly meeting I have found to be daunting, but also a very supportive and deep experience. It strengthened my faith in our business meetings, not just because Friends happened to unite with the concern, but because there seemed to be such a genuine seeking after the right way forward, and for what God was wanting us to do in this matter. It may sound disingenuous, but I can honestly say that I would have accepted the judgement of monthly meeting, Meeting for Sufferings or Yearly Meeting if they had said they could not unite with the concern. That does not mean that the concern would have gone away, rather it could have changed considerably, taken much longer, and maybe the Spirit would have moved Friends differently.

In a more practical sense, Warwickshire Friends brought a great deal of strength and hard work already done; we all shared our strengths and, when the national ad hoc group was formed out of a conference on the concern, different perspectives were found from Friends from all over the country.

Robin Robison, *Questions of integrity*, pp.8-9, 1993, originally published as 'Introduction: a personal view of a concern' in *Journal of Woodbrooke College*, issue no 1, summer 1992

Quaker community

The social testimony may not have been uppermost in my mind when the seeds of communal living germinated in my consciousness in the early 1980s, but the prospect of sharing possessions that it was not necessary to own individually seemed a logical extension of conserving non-renewable resources. So did the concept of not occupying more space than is necessary for reasonable comfort and only owning things that I use regularly. I recoil from using the phrase 'simple living' because compared with many people in the world I live in the lap of luxury.

Besides the advantage of being able to try and live the social testimony – and example is the best proof that it works – is the bonus of living close to like-minded Ffriends who are available for a chat or deeper conversation without having to make arrangements to meet or formally organise to entertain them (I hate cooking!). As it happened, when I was at a time in my life free to move into a community, I had a double bonus because there was at Bamford a Quaker Community whose members were willing for me to join them so that I could live among like-spiritual as well as like-minded Ffriends.

Angela Ayres, 1999

Our housing concern: a statement for Britain Yearly Meeting Friends

Yearly Meeting in Warwick 1993 asked for a Statement to be produced for Friends, expressing the basis on which its explicitly adopted concern for housing injustice ultimately rests. In December 1993 Meeting for Sufferings agreed that this Statement should be sent to meetings for their use. Such a Statement, whilst focused on housing, is necessarily relevant to all the issues which arouse our concern, because it is looking at the spiritual basis which is common to all our work.

The spiritual basis

Someone at Yearly Meeting in Warwick said that she had come because she was attracted by the themes of 'God in the silence', 'peace' and 'simplicity' for 'these are what Quakerism stands for'. We do 'stand for' these, but not for these alone. We also stand for social justice for all people and, in this context, housing justice for everyone. This is not an optional extra in our spirituality, it is an essential part of it.

We believe that the whole of life is sacramental. This means that there is no separation between the spiritual realm and other areas of our lives – or rather that the spiritual dimension is in everything, including social and political affairs. It follows that the housing conditions of other people – and our own – are inseparably spiritual, practical and political issues for us.

One of our least questioned beliefs is that 'there is that of God in everyone'. This means that there is a sense in which that of God suffers with those who suffer and with those who cause the suffering too. When our housing system denies someone a home or condemns them to a damp, insecure travesty of a home, what is being done is being done to God. Our response is that suffering lies at the heart of our faith. Our concern for justice is all bound up with this sense of the divine nature inherent in each one of us.

Within the early Christian and the Quaker traditions there is a belief in 'stewardship'. Everything is ultimately God's, so that we have no absolute right to what is in our possession. In this tradition the claims of justice may outweigh those of ownership. Those in housing need may thus have a right to some real response from those of us who are in housing affluence. In the face of need and the demands of justice or through the call to simplicity we have to look for the causes of housing poverty. As Friends it is our conviction that this will lead us to both examine our own lives and seek to influence public policy.

To see the suffering caused by the injustice of homelessness and grossly inadequate housing is to face a spiritual imperative to do whatever we can, however little or much this may sometimes be. To ignore it would be to harm those suffering the injustice, but also to harm ourselves – spiritually.

Our witness: what do our lives say?

The present system of home ownership in this country creates not only wealth and much very comfortable housing, but also poverty, homelessness and degrading housing conditions. This evil is intolerable and yet deeply entrenched in our lives.

How can we speak of 'that of God in everyone' unless our concern to overcome this social evil is manifest in our political lives and embodied in our own way of living? We need to find ways of working out more fully the meaning of the phrases we sometimes say too easily. The challenge of our housing concern is also a challenge to the depth of our spirituality; it asks questions like:

- does our housing encourage or prevent that true freedom which comes from finding one's security in God alone?
- what does my housing choice, my housing concern, my action on housing, proclaim about my faith?
- what is my fair share of this world's wealth and resources, including housing resources?
- do I consider that if I take more than my fair share others will have to manage on less?

We must examine our lives and the structure of society to discover what we must change in ourselves and what we must work to change in society. The search may be as painful and difficult as the actions. We must pray for the strength and wisdom to carry them through.

The first followers of George Fox found that the many forms of social injustice around them 'struck at their life' and could no longer be tolerated. That is the basis for our housing concern: it is also a challenge facing each one of us.

Our spiritual concern for housing

Like others, we believe that a secure home with adequate space and amenities is an essential foundation upon which individuals and households may base their lives. We know that housing is an essential part of making a community, and must not become a means to separate and isolate ourselves, excluding others from what we have. We know the problems are many and varied and complicated. In 1993, considering this matter of continued bad housing and homelessness within society and expressing our desire to change this for the better, Yearly Meeting said: 'We are well aware that whatever we do, this issue, one of the great issues of our times, will not be adequately addressed quickly. We are engaging in a process which will challenge our own values, and will involve our prayer and effort over many years; it may also require sacrifice by us.'

The major task now for Friends, as minuted by Yearly Meeting 1998 is 'not just about the provision of homes for those who are homeless or ill-housed' but also 'to challenge the heartlessness and hypocrisy of a society which denies fit housing and many other aspects of society for the vulnerable – especially the young'. A tall order indeed. During the 1998 sessions on Our spiritual concern for housing, Friends offered many solutions to the many problems.

The solution is economic: greater financial investment in housing; cheaper land for house building; more and cheaper rented housing; interest-free money for housing; more government spending; better use of our own, personal and corporate, assets.

The solution is political: campaigning to influence policy makers; putting housing high on the political agenda; strengthening the role of Churches National Housing Coalition, Scottish Churches Housing Agency, Shelter, and all our other partners.

The solution is practical: high housing standards for all and adaptable designs; sufficient variety of provision to meet all housing needs; repairing and maintaining the existing housing stock; sensible planning about what to build and where.

The solution is social: responding to the heartlessness of a society which excludes vulnerable people; helping people understand how to live in love; readjusting expectations (our own and other people's) to what kind of housing provision is realistic, feasible, sustainable, and fair – not necessarily lower expectations, but different; recognising the reciprocal relationship between housing and 'community'; making freedom of choice about one's housing independent of one's income.

The solution is with us who 'have': sharing our own space with other people; giving up some of what we have to those who 'have not'; leading by example.

The solution is held by those who 'have not': utilising the knowledge of people who have had, are experiencing, the problems of homelessness; learning from those who are excluded and denied access.

The solution is spiritual: believing in the spirit of those living on the streets; truly accepting the right of everyone to be included if they want to be; finding and articulating our own, Quaker, vision of what constitutes a 'just' housing policy; changing hearts; meeting the challenge of resolving conflicting priorities; making the hard decisions.

The answer, of course, is all of this and more. In 1996, considering the matter of social testimonies and faith into action, Yearly Meeting said: 'We have learnt that we can resurrect the world by facing the brokenness, the suffering, the pain and violence, for in that facing we find life and salvage the sacred. We have hope and can, as we return home, ask ourselves what is ordained.' The answer always was, and always will be – living our testimonies.

Paula Harvey, staff member responsible for housing issues in QSRE and
for the Quaker Housing Trust, *Quaker monthly*, Yearly Meeting issue, 1998

Public statement on the National Lottery: Quaker position on state-sponsored gambling

The Religious Society of Friends (Quakers) in Britain has today strongly affirmed its 350-year stand against games of chance and adopted this statement on the National Lottery and Public Life. It is the outcome of a widespread consultation amongst members which was set in motion nine months after the launch of the National Lottery.

Reasons for opposition:

Quakers are totally opposed to the promotion of a large-scale lottery by government for the following reasons:

- it fosters the attitude that it is right to hope for something for nothing
- it is a misuse of resources when many basic human needs are not fully met
- it promotes an addiction to gambling, exacerbated by the addition of Instant Game Scratchcards to the Scheme
- it increases the gross inequality between the majority of people and a small number of multimillionaires
- it encourages the belief that fulfilment and happiness depend upon riches.

Quaker action:
- Quakers will continue to press the Government to fulfil its responsibilities for social and economic welfare through normal public institutions
- the Religious Society of Friends will not itself seek any grants from the National Lottery
- The Society is divesting itself of shares held in the member companies of Camelot.

The following statements come from Quaker Meetings in Britain:

The National Lottery offends our spiritual life and beliefs about loving our neighbours and sharing resources. Gambling disregards our belief that our possessions are a trust.

Lancaster Meeting

People can be motivated by care and compassion and love and justice. We believe God's light shines in everyone and that it is evil to encourage greed and suppress this light. Everyone should contribute to society with the gifts and skills and money they possess to provide everyone with good healthcare, education, basic services and a sense of belonging. Seen in this light the payment of taxes is a privilege and not an imposition. We are called to live simply so that others may simply live.

South East Scotland Meeting

The National Lottery disregards our belief that possessions are a trust. The persistent appeal to covetousness is fundamentally opposed to the unselfishness which was taught by Jesus Christ and by the New Testament as a whole. The glorification of large winnings in the National Lottery, or any other form of gambling, is at the inevitable loss and possible suffering of others. It is the antithesis of the love of our neighbours on which Jesus insisted.

We affirm that taxation is the cost of a just and civilised society.

Two meetings in North London

It is clear that the 'success' of the National Lottery is an expression of the 'feel-bad' factor felt by so much of the population. People will do anything to alleviate the misery in their lives. The steady growth in unemployment, the decimation of industry, the impact of negative equity in the housing market, the huge rise in the numbers of self-employed and short-term contracts of employment, and other changes in the security of the lives of so many, mean that a large sector of society is now living in fear. There is a desperate need to eliminate the roots of fear and provide opportunities for all to rise above this fear.

Though we are a religious society, we nevertheless have the duty to make a clear political statement that we need to change the direction of government.

Hexham Meeting

At a time of widespread and growing public doubt about the rightness of Western lifestyle, Friends see the National Lottery as an officially-sanctioned action which is not in accord with honourable conduct. Poverty and lack of opportunity for many in society co-exists with inordinate wealth for a few; a true desire for greater equality needs to be sought by way of changed national policies, and not by exploiting the baser human instincts of competitiveness and gambling.

Dereham Meeting

Statement on alcohol and drug abuse

The QSRE group has considered possible ways forward to address the problems presented by alcohol and drug abuse in society, in the Religious Society of Friends and within our meeting. The following statement has been agreed by preparative meeting and is now passed to monthly meeting for consideration.

Recurring violence and abuse, illness and premature death underline the extent to which alcohol is blighting the lives of adults and children today. There are Friends in our own meeting who have been affected, directly and indirectly. The prevalence of underage drinking and drug-taking highlights the need for urgent action.

We wish to affirm that alcohol abuse represents a social problem of importance to us all. We are mindful that Friends could do more to bear witness to our historic testimony on alcohol. Friends can act by acknowledging the scale of the problem, in society at large and in our Society, by joining relevant organisations to lobby for more education and by considering for themselves whether to choose abstinence. We believe it is a spiritual issue to address personal drinking habits and so assert our social testimony, even when this is uncomfortable. By giving more thought to the social use of alcohol we can set an example to children to ensure that nobody, child nor adult, feels pressurised or excluded because of the presence of alcohol.

To encourage a truly inclusive and caring attitude to all, we are concerned to reaffirm our meeting house as an alcohol-free environment, including lettings. We also wish to challenge ourselves to consider the impact that our use of intoxicants has on others, supported by sensitive interpretation of *Advices and queries* 40 and *Quaker faith and practice* 20.40 in our ministry, mindful that, 'For those trapped in substance abuse, such advice [on moderating intake] may seem hollow'. (1994, *QFP* 20.41)

Winchmore Hill Preparative Meeting, December 1999

New queries on racism for elders, overseers and outreach
Oversight
- Do you consider the differences that make each person unique? Do you cherish these differences, and support each according to their need?
- How does your meeting welcome people from a minority ethnic group, and how does it seek to hold them and to continue to include them? Particularly, do others ensure that they don't regard minority ethnic people in the meeting as in need of special help? Are you aware of the difficulties which might confront the person from an minority ethnic group in feeling at home in your meeting?
- What are you doing to make yourself aware of what it feels like to be the object of prejudice, rejection and alienation? To what extent are you a cause of this injustice, ignorance and fear? What are you doing to change yourself and the society in which you live?
- How do we respond to racism in ourselves and in our Society? Do we try to understand why we fail in our human relationships in this field, and are we prepared to take the risks involved in going on learning?
- Do you find ways of supporting Friends who encounter racism in their everyday lives, either towards themselves or others? Do you

help these Friends to challenge this?
- Do we strive, as individuals and as a Society, to overcome the narrowness of our cultural inheritance? Do we seek God's forgiveness for the pain we have caused others in the past, in order to go on and change?
- Are you sensitive to unintentional hurts within the meeting? Can you make this a shared learning experience?

Eldership
- Are you aware of different spiritual needs resulting from cultural backgrounds other than your own?
- How do we encourage one another to lead our lives in the light of awareness of racism and to confront its injustice with the courage of the early Quakers?
- How do you encourage the development of spirituality, drawing on multi-cultural gifts? Is your meeting open to the rich diversity of gifts from people of all backgrounds? How does it recognise and use them? Do Elders ensure that the spiritual gifts of all members are drawn out, especially those of Black or Asian people?
- Are you vigilant concerning the language used in your meeting on matters of race? Do you use inclusive language in welcoming people to meeting?
- How do you encourage an atmosphere in the meeting whereby people of all races will feel valued and accepted?
- Does the programme for the children in your meeting increase their awareness and understanding of our multicultural society?
- Have you examined whether any of the practices of your meeting (e.g. nominations) demonstrate prejudice or racism?

Outreach
- Do you have regular contact with a local Black-led church?
- Does your meeting have contact with local congregations of people of other faiths? Are you aware of, and do you encourage, the wealth of cultural diversity within your local community? Do you acquaint yourself with these interests and priorities, so that you can make outreach relevant? Does your outreach material and programme reflect this diversity? Do you offer our Quaker insights and testimonies as a resource to all our neighbouring communities?
- Does the noticeboard reflect our testimony to that of God in all peoples and cultures?
- Does your meeting ask each of its suppliers of goods about their

Equal Opportunities Policy and the number of ethnic minority
people they employ?
Quakers and race, summer 1996

A public statement by the Religious Society of Friends (Quakers) in Britain agreed in session at London Yearly Meeting 22-25 May 1987

Quakers in Britain have felt called to issue this statement in order to
address a matter of urgent national priority to promote debate and
stimulate action.

We are angered by actions which have knowingly led to the polarisation
of our country – into the affluent, who epitomise success according to the
values of a materialistic society, and the 'have-leasts', who by the expectations
of that same society are oppressed, judged, found wanting and punished.

We value that of God in each person, and affirm the right of everyone
to contribute to society and share in life's good things, beyond the basic
necessities.

We commit ourselves to learning again the spiritual value of each other.
We find ourselves utterly at odds with the priorities in our society which
deny the full human potential of millions of people in this country. That
denial diminishes us all. There must be no 'them' and 'us'.

We appreciate the stand taken by other churches and we wish to work
alongside them.

As a Religious Society and as individuals we commit ourselves to
examine again how we use our personal and financial resources. We will
press for change to enable wealth and power to be shared more evenly
within our nation. We make this statement publicly at a time of national
decision [a general election] in the hope that, following the leadings of the
Spirit, each of us in Britain will take appropriate action.

1987, *QFP* 23.21

The meeting community

'The essential purpose of eldership and oversight is to help in the building of
a true Christian community, of a fellowship in which all are united by a
shared spiritual life and from which all in the meeting may draw inspiration
and strength for God's service in the world.' *Church Government* 854

Despite such comments, Friends do not often think of their preparative
meeting as a community. Physically, they may be far more scattered than
the members of most groups that consciously regard themselves as communities

– monasteries, homes, our street, our village – but proximity is not an essential characteristic of community.

The essence of a community is the sharing of a way of life, in common purpose and outlook, in being part of a caring 'family'. Meetings are based on the shared communion of meeting for worship, and members hold in common their Quaker concerns and outlook, their business meetings, and the activities they enjoy together, and so it is evident that meetings are communities, whether we have realised it or not.

Sharing and co-operation, mutual encouragement and support enable members of a community to be more effective together than they could ever be as individuals. This spiritual and practical support by members one of another is especially needed when the objectives of the group, the values it embraces, the methods it seeks to employ, the way of life it wishes to follow are markedly different from the aims and customs of the larger society of which it forms a part.

Friends have always tried to overcome the isolation of Friend from Friend, and to enrich the fellowship of the meeting for worship by fellowship at other levels. The well-tried methods are sound, so long as we are not satisfied that they are enough. Sharing cars, visiting the sick, encouraging the children, pot-luck lunches, weekend retreats, social and study groups meeting at several venues instead of only at the meeting house, sewing sessions for sales of work – are all useful in themselves and valuable in helping the community to develop. As the elders shake hands after meeting *this* Sunday we begin the 'preparation of heart and mind' for next Sunday's meeting by speaking with Friends, learning how we can keep them in our thoughts and prayers during the week. Awareness of each others' needs can lead to the growth of small groups who meet regularly to know each other at a deeper level, so that mutual trust and understanding grows and each can rejoice and weep together in all aspects of life, and the caring extends to the whole meeting – and beyond.

The central activity of any Quaker meeting is the meeting for worship. If Friends really care for the spiritual life of their meeting, their work and play together will become more worthwhile. If Friends work and celebrate together their worship can become a deeper communion and guidance can be found to bring the whole of life into right ordering; into community. Community is never a static state, it is always moving, growing or declining, being and doing, needing constant care, patience, understanding, and love. Shared activities and worship are helping to break down the barriers that normal society puts up between people, the barriers that prevent us from discussing with friends the things that worry us, that say 'don't interfere' when we suspect someone has a problem, that make us believe that we can do nothing about third world poverty, about the arms race, about industrial strife; the barriers that convince us that the individual is helpless in the mass of society.

As we persist in trying, by whatever means we can, to raise the level of caring and sharing in our meetings there will come a point when members no longer feel alone and impotent, but know that they can do something that will make a real difference in the world. There will come a point where our trust and confidence in each other and in the Spirit has made us into a real community, living more often in the life and power that takes away the occasion of all wars, able to witness to the truth not only in ministry, at demonstrations and on petitions but in our lives also. If we don't want to be involved every day in the life of the Community of the Kingdom of God on earth, why did we become Friends?

Audrey Urry, ' The meeting community', *Towards community*, 1980

Part V – Afterwords in several voices

Armley

Gazing up at those
Grim walls
My small son
Shuddered.

OK, we passed it
On a bad day:
Cold, dank mist
Permanent dusk.

Yet I shall not forget
His condemnation;
We let it stand,
Continue our lives.

Paul Henderson, Affirming Flame 1989

Do something

All of us who throw our minds towards a more just and equitable world feel discouraged at times, that we're fighting against a tide, we're hopeless dreamers, we ought just to accept the way the world is. I hold in my mind a proverb that goes something like 'she is a fool who does nothing because she could only do a little' – that and a gritty determination to *make a difference*.

M4 in *Who do we think we are?* 1998

A glimpse of the divine

My awareness of the spiritual, you might call it God, has often come through my work. I spent a year working with children from the poorest areas of Belfast, and in the course of this work I found a deeper spirituality than I had experienced before. One moment in particular stands out in my mind, a 'Wow!' moment, through which I had a glimpse of the divine.

I was on the beach with a group of children. Some hadn't seen the sea before, and they rarely had the chance to experience the true freedom of childhood. Two brothers, Alan and John, were playing football in tracksuits and trainers. They were real hard Belfast lads, although they were both under ten. Where they were playing the sea had left pools of water in the sand. Every so often their ball would fly into one of these pools. At first they would carefully fish it out, but as they became more involved in their game they became less careful. Soon they were running in and out of the pools with a childlike delight that I had never seen in them before. Their faces were shining with joy. As I watched them play I knew I should have told them not to get their shoes and socks so wet, but I felt that something much too important was going on to worry about such trivial things. These boys were experiencing true freedom for the first time, and I felt privileged to witness it. It is through simple things such as the happiness of children that I feel a higher force at work in the world.

N17 in *Who do we think we are?*,1998

... more than we yet realise

Under the international and economic complexes which dominate, I have come to see more clearly that there is also a spider's web of human relationships which either supports or undermines all that happens. It is here that hope appears. As someone said to me recently: 'How on earth can you get these new ideas of peace and co-operation across to the people who matter?' The answer is that we are doing so far more than we yet realise. Our acts which often appear too insignificant to challenge the great machinations of history at this time are culminating in an enormous wave of inner being which is already drastically altering all the culture patterns. The world itself is caught up in a crisis which will result either in its destruction or a break-through.

Damaris Parker-Rhodes, *The way out is the way in*, p.6

Developing our spiritual strength

'How can we walk with a smile into the dark?' There can be no standing still ... The more we live in that still place of silence, the more we find ourselves open to leadings which take us into the fight for peace, for justice. The more we live in that ultimate place of aloneness in God, the more we are led to connect with, to want to understand each other and the world in which we live. The more we live in that place of joy, the more we recognise the evil, darkness, urgent problems which tear our world and each other. And the more we acknowledge and try to address those evils, the more our strength and joy grow. The more we use our muscles of mind and heart, the more the life-blood of the Spirit strengthens them.

The coming years are going to be ones of bitter, chaotic regional conflicts and instability, of growing environmental pressures. A time of refugee movements and terrible human suffering, of siege mentality and racism amongst the privileged. There can be no doubt of that. In this context, I find the potential uses of information technology, genetic engineering and military technology very frightening. We must struggle to understand the roots of these problems and their interconnectedness, to be clear in our thinking and decisive in responding to the evils which we see.

Deborah Padfield, Introduction to Yearly Meeting session 1994;
Quaker monthly, December 1994

Learning from the desert people

I happen to stand in the Judaeo-Christian tradition, and while there is much in this tradition that I criticise and reject, I see also that there have been people in it who have been engaged in the task of trying to move out of a Conventional Script into a Quest Plot, who have dared to follow their passion, their vision of a Promised Land – a New Heaven and a New Earth.

I am not speaking here of *all* people in the Judaeo-Christian tradition. I am not speaking of those who used the tradition and its structure to further their own ends, or as a means to acquire power over others, or as a way of escaping the radical demands of the Quest Plot. I am referring to those who really went out to the edge, who chose the power of simplicity and community, when others around them were choosing the powers of wealth, domination and competition; who chose to live lives at variance with, if not radically opposed to, the values of the society around them. Out of this tradition have come prophets, poets, seers, monks, nuns, preachers, travellers, story-tellers, nurses, shoe-makers, teachers, weavers, singers; a whole line of people, many of whom have enlarged my vision and faith by the light of their own lives. These are the people who, in Audre Lorde's words, 'decided not to settle for the convenient, the shoddy, the conventionally expected nor the merely safe.' (*Sister Outsider*, p.57) I call these people the Desert People, and I acknowledge a great debt to them. I call these people the Desert People because I believe that in order to do this work of coming out, in order to take part in this Exodus, this Quest, one has to be prepared for the Desert experience which the mystics of many religious traditions have described.

I believe that in order to come out of slavery, in order to face the great powers, the alienated political and social regimes which deny dignity and freedom to humanity and to the creation, one has to be willing to enter the desert – to feel deserted by the known, and to face a fearful intimacy with the unknown. Not only does one have to be prepared to enter the desert: I would say that it is a necessary part of what is involved in building the New Creation and of 'speaking Truth to Power'. We have to face the terrors that are within, if we are to find the courage and spiritual authority to confront the tyrannies without.

I would like to mention here some of the things I have learnt from the Desert People, and from my own attempts to follow their example.

I have learnt that the Desert People have to trust each other. We need the support of a community of friends, sisters, brothers, lovers, who will help us to survive the periods of nakedness and vulnerability which we inevitably encounter. We need others to hold us, to keep us from falling into idolatry; guides and companions who will help us remain steadfast in our refusal to worship images of ourselves reflected from the Conventional Script. We need friends and lovers to help us keep balanced and centred, because the alienated/addictive society has the power to keep us unbalanced and off-centre. By promising short-term, superficial solutions to our deepest needs and longings, the Conventional Script has the power to keep our gaze continually turned away from the reality of our own pain and to keep us from striving for a mature way of being in the world in which we take responsibility for our own needs and risk the terrors of true intimacy with God, ourselves and others. We need friends and lovers who will help keep us honest; who will help us shift the focus away from our illusions, from the False Saviours who come along offering Cheap Grace or a Quick Fix. We need friends and lovers who will, instead, help us keep our gaze firmly fixed on the long-term goals of faithfulness and mutuality which alone can satisfy our deepest longings for companionship and love.

I have learnt that the Desert People know themselves to be in a 'mutual' relationship with that which calls them out into the unknown. It is a

Covenant Relationship in which both parties have rights, responsibilities and privileges. The Quest makes demands on us even as we make demands upon it. The Desert People are called out not just for the sake of being called out. We are called out to become lovers of that which calls us; to let this love inform our lives, to let it shape us into the Holy Community. In this Covenant Relationship, we find that we are only truly powerful to the extent that we are abandoned to the embrace of our Quest. Faith is the gradual release of ourselves into the embrace of the Quest. Conversion is the gradual erosion of our resistance to self-abandonment.

Zoe White, *Living faithfully with passion*, pp.10-12

A community for spiritual struggle

An important link between my work [as a social worker in Tower Hamlets] and my inner life is the importance of having other people who will walk alongside: people who will witness to the work that is being done out there in the inner cities, and people who will walk with me as I orienteer my way around my city within.

Quakers over the centuries have been good at identifying and testing out areas of work where they as individuals can make a significant impact – areas where they can shake a few foundations and look for creative alternatives.

For me, these most effective points of intervention occur most often within a concrete and highly specific situation, where personal contacts touch a need that is struggling to express itself. When that need is expressed, it makes connections with elements within our history and memory, which make us want to stand up and shout, 'Over there, that is where the Spirit is quickening and quaking! Bring your young people and let them listen, see, smell and feel the Spirit moving. Quick, before they get a management committee and a budget!'

How important that is for my spiritual life – a sense of spiritual solidarity with others. I need a base community of people who will encourage that seepage inwards of energy and love, in through the cracks. I need a group of people who will help me name my everyday experiences of God's action in my life. People who will occasionally look me in the eye, and say, 'Who are you? What are you experiencing? How is your Inner City at the moment?' not just, 'How is your Gran?' or 'What are you planning to do next?'

I am beginning to be aware that the prayer of my life is ongoing, all the time. It is not an exciting luxury that we can pick up and play with when we have the energy. Therefore, I need people who will struggle with me to help me find my own prayer, and acknowledge with me when one prayer is prayed, and I need to find expression for another. The exciting part is never being able to predict who those people may be, when they will appear, if and how long they may be going to walk alongside you.

We surely need both kinds of witness, out to the world, and towards each other. As we find the witnesses in our own lives, we find that spiritual solidarity that is essential for us in building a prayerful community; a community of people in our lives who will provide a place for the listening that happens in God's presence; a place for embracing our pain, and encouraging the seepage through the cracks; a place for us to recognise God's actions within and around us.

Helen Carmichael, *Working in the city within*, George Gorman Lecture, 1991

Community guided by the spirit

Life is a gift. Science may piece together how living creatures evolve, how they behave, and how our bodies work; but its source and nature remain a mystery. The context in which I view the circumstances of my life can give it meaning and purpose. So I accept life with thanks as the gift of the One who cherishes every creature. Thus the beauty of the world, the richness of experience, and the wonderful acts of which humanity is capable are reminders of the constancy and pervasiveness of the Love that sustains my life.

But the people of my world, all living things, the earth and seas themselves are exploited for profit. In countless acts of betrayal these living gifts are offered for sale and, as Jesus, crucified. Mankind may soon discover that we have done such harm that, perhaps only a few generations ahead, human life will cease. I share in that act, because my way of life demands that price.

Our culture is committed to enabling people to compete for riches and enjoy them securely once gotten. My part in the global economy ensures me, in return for moderate effort, income and possessions denied to the world's poor, at their expense and that of the natural world. Campaigning on behalf of the environment or supporting charities does not redress the balance.

The suffering I see saddens and diminishes me. The prospect for the world appals me. I want to live in the peace of the One who has given me life. I want to do work that is truly serviceable and to possess and consume no more than the Earth could sustain as the share of all her people. In these wants I am not alone – many people I believe feel the same. But on my own I feel helpless, and so remain dependent on the easy life that brings me no peace.

On a recent visit to the Christian community at Taizé, I brought my problem to one of the Brothers. He said that I needed two things – the guidance of the Holy Spirit, and community: without these I would achieve nothing. He said that community was not limited to the monastic life, but could also be found in family and in marriage.

Living simply enough is a challenge. We have to master our addiction to luxury and our laziness. I would like to show that with this help ordinary people can do so and be happy, free and creative; not having to choose between isolated poverty and letting their lives be run by killjoys and bigots.

But how simple is simple enough? How much should be shared? What work should we do? What place should religion have? What should be our relationship with the services of health, education and welfare? These and many other questions will need to be answered before any community life can succeed. There is no one answer to them: many different forms of community are needed.

Nigel Worth, *earthQuaker*, Issue 25, Winter 1998

Violence/non-violence

First, I want to hear about beauty. I want to know what you love. I want to know what words of love have been written on your heart – how you could smile at the bold beauty of a solitary hedgerow campion in December; how your taste buds might find sweet delight in freshly dug early potatoes, the way your flesh glows in the summer sun. I will tell you one of my amazing delights – how I held my wife up, her arms clamped around my neck, and how I felt against my body the bulge in her belly slip downwards as our daughter came into the world. Love creates beauty. I want to know how you taste beauty, about the woods and beaches that you love; I want to know if God-resonant Bach harmonies lift the top off your head. I want to know how you suck life into your being and live it, feel it, like sharp air in the lungs on a frozen, moon-smiling, diamond-clear night, and how your chest opens to compass the Kosmos.

And I want to hear about grief. I want to know how often you weep, for whom and for what you weep. I want to know how you feel in your guts when you wake up every morning to a world always half an hour away from nuclear night. I want to know where you were and how you wept when you heard that Chico Mendes was dead. I want to know how your heart cries out against the poison in the soil, air and water, against the perversion of fire from comforter to killer; I want to know how you mourn for the cancered green lungs of the planet, for the juicy greenness that is being sucked out of your very soul. I want you to look through the eyes of the East Timorese boy who is forced to watch as Indonesian soldiers torture his father to death, and just tell me how your bowels turn over.

I don't want to hear the bone-dead words of testimonies. I don't want to hear entreaties to calmness and civic responsibility. Who will *go gentle into this good night*? I want to know if you have sunk down the black well of despair to meet all the concepts of yourself and humanity, all the self-hating and world-hating violence which is nowhere else but in our own hearts, and yet how you find at the bottom the unborn, ever-bearing Spirit which shouts 'Live!'

For myself, if life is not lived on the evolutionary quest for greater embrace, greater kindness, then it is a life without meaning. As part of this quest, I have found at times of taking non-violent direct action that outrage melts into knowledge that we are all one, and compassion arises, for we suffer together, somehow we rise and fall together. It is not, in my experience, words of violence that come from the lips of protesters to the ears of police, magistrates, juries, press, politicians, and the world at large. Instead I hear fertile, prophetic words of love and grief, words that turn dust into soil, turn rust and hate back into passion.

The world is suffering, and we are suffering, from greed, hatred and ignorance. But action which bears the yoke of love gives birth to beauty, harmony and greater love even if the means of action seem partial, imperfect.

> *My heart is moved by all I cannot save:*
> *so much has been destroyed*
> *I have to cast my lot with those*
> *who age by age, perversely,*
> *with no extraordinary power,*
> *reconstitute the world*
>> (Adrienne Rich)

Adrian Rose, *Making waves*: the newsletter of the Turning the Tide programme, August 1998

Guide to study and further reading

(the publications listed in this first section discuss the testimonies generally and then in the order they appear in Parts III and IV)

Geoffrey Hubbard (1974) Penguin Books
  Quaker by convincement

Phillips Moulton, editor (1971) OUP New York
  The journal and major essays of John Woolman

John Punshon (1990) Swarthmore Lecture QHS
  Testimony and tradition

Rediscovering our Social Testimony Group (1995) QSRE
  Rediscovering our social testimony in Britain Yearly Meeting

Rediscovering our Social Testimony Group (1996) QSRE
  Responses and challenges

Thomas Silcock (1972) Pendle Hill Pamphlet 186
  Words and testimonies

Harvey Gillman and Alastair Heron, editors (1996) QHS
  Searching the depths: essays on being a Quaker today

Mary Lou Leavitt (1993) QPS
  'Testimonies in the Quaker tradition' in *The Quaker peace testimony: a workbook for individuals and groups*

Young Friends General Meeting (1998) Swarthmore Lecture QHS
  Who do we think we are? Young Friends' Commitment and Belonging

(1995) QHS
  Who we are (parts 1 & 2): Questions of Quaker identity

Ben Pink Dandelion, Douglas Gwyn and Timothy Peat (1998) Curlew Productions/Woodbrooke College
  Heaven on earth; Quakers and the second coming

Douglas Gwyn (1989) Friends United Press
  Unmasking the idols

Douglas Gwyn (1997) Kimo Press
  Words in time

Jonathan Dale in *Friends quarterly* April 1996
  Rediscovering our Social Testimony

Jonathan Dale (1996) Swarthmore Lecture QHS
Beyond the spirit of the age

(1986) QHS
The nature and variety of concern

Committee for Truth and Integrity in Public Affairs (1993) London Yearly Meeting
Questions of Integrity

Richard Foster (1980) Hodder & Stoughton
Celebration of discipline: the path to spiritual growth

Lilamani Woolrych (1998) Joseph Rowntree Charitable Trust
Communicating across cultures

Quaker Women's Group (1986) Swarthmore Lecture QHS
Bringing the invisible into the Light: some Quaker feminists speak of their experience

John Banks and Martina Weitsch, editors (1982) Friends Homosexual Fellowship
Meeting gay Friends

Peggy Heeks (1994) Joseph Rowntree Charitable Trust
Reaching to community

Janey O'Shea (1993) Margaret Fell Quaker Booksellers and Publications
Living the Way: Quaker spirituality and community

Parker J. Palmer (1977) Pendle Hill Pamphlet 212
A place called community

(1999) QSRE
Crime and community justice resource pack

(1998) QSRE Housing Group
Home truths

(1998) QSRE Housing Group
'No home, no life'; study pack on housing and homelessness, incorporating also 'Housing: our spiritual concern'

(1998) QSRE Housing Group
'Having a home is important' Materials for use in children and young people's groups in meetings

Adam Curle (1981) Swarthmore Lecture QHS
True justice – Quaker peace makers and peace making

(1993) QPS
The Quaker peace testimony: a workbook for individuals and groups

(1995) QPS
Ways out of war: Twelve personal accounts of Quaker peacemaking since World War II

Anne Adams, compiler (1996) Quaker Green Concern
The Creation was open to me: an anthology of Friends' writings on that of God in all creation

Richard Foster (1985) Hodder & Stoughton
Money, sex and power

Christine Peaker (1991) Communication Services Department of the Religious Society of Friends
A plain Quaker guide to political action

Simon Risley (1996) QHS Outreach
Letting the Light shine: a Quaker guide to political action

Michael Jacobs (1996) The Real World Coalition
Politics of the Real World

Social testimony concerns – periodicals available from BYM or BYM informal groups

Leavenings; Quaker Performing Arts Project newsletter
Ground Floor, 1 The Lodge, 1046 Bristol Road, Birmingham B29 6LJ

Quaker socialist; Quaker Socialist Society newsletter
Barbara Forbes, 141 Heathfield Road, Handsworth, Birmingham B19 1HL

TIPA occasional papers and briefings
Truth and Integrity in Public Affairs Committee, Friends House

Quaker Women's Group newsletter
Eileen Williams, 15 Kent Road, Littlehampton, W. Sussex BN17 6LQ

Quakers and race
Friends House

Quaker Lesbian & Gay Fellowship newsletter
QLGF, Betty Hagglund, 59 Esme Road, Birmingham B11 4NJ

BIA Quaker social action update
Bunhill Fields Meeting House, Quaker Court, Banner St, London EC1M 8QQ

Quaker homeless action newsletter
QHA, c/o 10 Laburnum Grove, Eastleigh, SO50 9DJ

Acorn; newsletter for friends concerned with housing
BYM

Home thoughts; Quaker-run accommodation schemes for elderly people
Friends House

Quakers in criminal justice newsletter
Adrian Smith, 153 Chignall Road, Chelmsford, Essex CM1 2JD

Opportunities for action; ideas and tools for peace and international service
Friends House

Education advisory programme: Developing peace work internationally:
incorporating Schools without Violence Project, European Network for Conflict
Resolution in Education, and support for workers on overseas projects
Friends House

Alternatives to Violence Project newsletter
Information, newsletter and training, AVP Britain,
547 Leytonstone High Road, London E11 4PB

Around Europe; news on European issues
Quaker Council for European Affairs British Committee,
c/o Arthur Hughes, Bron-y-Gader, Dolgellau LL40 1TA

Geneva reporter and *Briefing papers*
Quaker United Nations Office, Avenue du Mervelet 13, 1209 Geneva,
Switzerland

earthQuaker; newsletter of the Quaker Green Concern
6 Phoenice Cottages, Dorking Road, Bookham, Surrey KT23 4QG

Quaker network for economic change
QUNEC, Friends House

Making waves; Turning the Tide Programme newsletter, information on
non-violence/social change
Friends House

New agenda for defence
Parliamentary Liaison Secretary, Friends House

Social Testimony Network Newsletter
John Maynard, 11 Belvedere Close, Kidderminster, Worcester DY10 3AT

Additional references for works quoted in this publication

Rex Ambler and David Haslam, editors (1980) The Bowerdean Press
Agenda for prophets: towards a political theology for Britain

Helen Carmichael (1991) George Gorman Lecture
Working in the city within

Sandra Cronk (1991) Pendle Hill Pamphlet 297
Gospel order

Ben Pink Dandelion (1996) The Edwin Mellen Press
A Sociological analysis of the theology of Quakers

Caroline Graveson (1937) Swarthmore Lecture QHS
Religion and culture

Vaclav Havel (1985) M. E. Sharpe
The power of the powerless

R Melvin Keiser (1991) Pendle Hill Pamphlet 295
Inward Light and the new creation: a theological meditation on the center and circumference of Quakerism

Pam Lunn (1993) QPS
Deeds not creeds: insights on Friends' peace testimony at Yearly Meeting 1993

Grigor McClelland (1976) Swarthmore Lecture QHS
And a new earth

Thomas Merton (1953) Harcourt, Brace & Co
The sign of Jonas

Elisabeth O'Connor (1975) Harper and Row
Journey inwards, journey outwards

Paul Oestreicher (1986) Darton Longman and Todd
The double cross: Christianity in a world that's dying to live

Damaris Parker-Rhodes (1985) QHS
The way out is the way in

Cecil W. Sharman, editor (1980) QHS
No more but my love, letters of George Fox, Quaker

Douglas Steere (1986) The Upper Room
Gleanings